Visual Basic®
Programming

for the absolute beginner

Check the Web for Updates

To check for updates or corrections relevant to this book and/or CD-ROM, visit our updates page on the Web at http://www.prima-tech.com/support/.

Send Us Your Comments

To comment on this book or any other PRIMA TECH title, visit our reader response page on the Web at http://www.prima-tech.com/comments.

How to Order

For information on quantity discounts, contact the publisher: Prima Publishing, P.O. Box 1260BK, Rocklin, CA 95677-1260; (916) 787-7000. On your letterhead, include information concerning the intended use of the books and the number of books you want to purchase. For individual orders, turn to the back of this book for more information.

Visual® Basic
Programming

for the absolute beginner

MICHAEL A. VINE

 A Division of Prima Publishing

Prima Publishing and colophon are registered trademarks of Prima Communications, Inc. PRIMA TECH is a registered trademark of Prima Communications, Inc., Roseville, California 95661.

Visual Basic is a registered trademark of Microsoft Corporation.

All other trademarks are the property of their respective owners.

Important: Prima Publishing cannot provide software support. Please contact the appropriate software manufacturer's technical support line or Web site for assistance.

Prima Publishing and the author have attempted throughout this book to distinguish proprietary trademarks from descriptive terms by following the capitalization style used by the manufacturer.

Information contained in this book has been obtained by Prima Publishing from sources believed to be reliable. However, because of the possibility of human or mechanical error by our sources, Prima Publishing, or others, the Publisher does not guarantee the accuracy, adequacy, or completeness of any information and is not responsible for any errors or omissions or the results obtained from use of such information. Readers should be particularly aware of the fact that the Internet is an ever-changing entity. Some facts may have changed since this book went to press.

ISBN: 0-7615-3553-5

Library of Congress Catalog Card Number: 2001091129

Printed in the United States of America

00 01 02 03 04 DD 10 9 8 7 6 5 4 3 2 1

Publisher:
Stacy L. Hiquet

Associate Marketing Manager:
Heather Buzzingham

Managing Editor:
Sandy Doell

Acquisitions Editor:
Melody Layne

Project Editor:
Heather Talbot

Technical Reviewer:
Duane Birnbaum

Copy Editor:
Kris Simmons

Interior Layout:
Marian Hartsough

Cover Design:
Prima Design Team

CD-ROM Producer:
Dan Ransom

Indexer:
Johnna VanHoose Dinse

Proofreader:
Jessica Ford McCarty

This book is dedicated
to my mother, Nancy,
who never ceases to amaze me
with her ability to love, nurture, and inspire.

Acknowledgments

As the author, I would like to acknowledge you, the reader of this book. Thank you for choosing this book over many others.

I would like to thank all the hard-working people at Prima Publishing who made this book possible. A special thanks to Andy Harris, who has been an active mentor in my teaching and writing career, Melody Layne, who helped me transform from writer to author, and Duane Birnbaum for his professional advice and superb technical editing.

Many thanks to my parents, family, and friends for unconditional love and friendship—love you all.

Most importantly, I would like to thank my wife and best friend, Sheila, for putting up with me when I was teaching, going to school, working full-time, and writing this book and for still loving me anyway. You're the best!

About the Author

Michael Vine spent six years working as a network administrator for various companies in and around Florida, New Mexico, California, Indiana, and Tennessee, implementing and supporting enterprise networks and data centers.

Although networks were his bread and butter, he enjoyed programming as a hobbyist and enthusiast for about six years. It wasn't until he wrote a few successful desktop and client/server-based applications that he discovered his passion for programming and software development.

Realizing his new calling, Vine quickly made the transition from hardware to software, and he has been working as a software engineer for the past two years. As a software engineer, he designs, develops, and supports client/server-based systems using technologies such as Visual Basic, C/C++, PowerBuilder, Oracle, Microsoft SQL Server, Microsoft Access, and Seagate Crystal Reports.

After returning to school to complete a few degrees, he found another passion in teaching, and he currently teaches as a part-time instructor of computer science at Indiana University/Purdue University at Indianapolis (IUPUI).

Contents at a Glance

Contents

CHAPTER 3

Making Decisions 57

CHAPTER 4

Iteration 103

CHAPTER 5

Subprocedures, Functions, and Controls Continued   127

CHAPTER 6

Advanced Controls   157

Debugging and Error Handling   189

Data Files and File Access   209

CHAPTER

Standard Code Modules, Multiple Forms, and Encryption

233

CHAPTER

Arrays

257

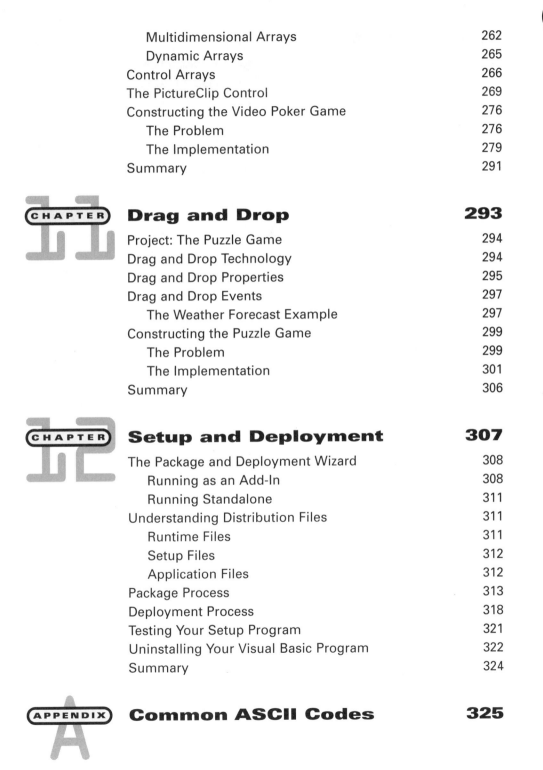

CHAPTER 11 — Drag and Drop — 293

CHAPTER 12 — Setup and Deployment — 307

APPENDIX A — Common ASCII Codes — 325

Introduction

Microsoft Visual Basic is a leader among high-level languages in supporting the event-driven paradigm and Rapid Application Development (RAD). More specifically, Visual Basic's acceptance and popularity can be seen in many facets of application development such as database access, Graphical User Interface (GUI) prototyping, building distributable components, Internet scripting, desktop and client/server design, and even game development.

Because of its common commercial uses and ease of learning, Visual Basic has also become popular with higher education institutions all over the world for teaching people how to program.

While this book's primary objective is to teach you the Visual Basic language, I will also cover some relevant computer science principals in a palatable form suitable for beginning programmers.

What makes this book unique from other programming texts is its ability to replace the sometimes-boring scientific, business, and financial programming examples with games. It is this approach that should make your learning experience engaging and enjoyable.

Although there are no prerequisites for this book (math or otherwise), you will learn concepts, procedures, and techniques that are rooted in math. This book does, however, assume that you are familiar with at least one Microsoft operating system, such as Windows 95, 98, NT, or 2000.

How to Use This Book

To learn how to program a computer, you must acquire a complex progression of skills. If you have never programmed at all, you will probably find it easiest to go through the chapters in order. Of course, if you are already an experienced programmer, it might not be necessary to do any more than skim the earliest chapters. In either case, programming is not a skill you can learn by reading. You'll have to write programs to learn. This book has been designed to make the process reasonably painless.

Each chapter begins with a complete program that demonstrates some key ideas for the chapter. Then, you'll look at a series of smaller programs that illustrate each of the major points of the chapter. Finally, you'll put these concepts together to build the larger program that you saw at the opening of the chapter. You'll be able to see important ideas in simple, straightforward code, and you'll also see more involved programs that put multiple ideas together. All the programs are short enough that you can type them in yourself (which is a great way to look closely at code), but they are also available on the CD-ROM.

Throughout the book, I'll throw in a few other tidbits, notably the following:

 These are good ideas that experienced programmers like to pass on.

 There are a few areas where it's easy to make a mistake. I'll point them out to you as we go.

 These will suggest techniques and shortcuts that will make your life as a programmer easier.

IN THE REAL WORLD

As you examine the games in this book, I'll show you how the concepts are used for purposes beyond game development.

Definition

Providing useful references, *definitions* reiterate a concept or key term that was discussed in the text.

CHALLENGES

At the end of each chapter, I'll suggest some programs that you can write with the skills you've learned so far. This should help you start writing your own programs.

Introduction to Problem Solving and Visual Basic

elcome. I'm excited that you've chosen this book as your first introduction to programming using Visual Basic. I know first-hand what an exciting and challenging opportunity this is for you. My first IT (information technology) job was as a technical help desk representative, so I took phone calls from confused and sometimes aggravated clients wanting to understand exactly what their software was or wasn't doing. In this job, I learned how to use and support the software my company sold and supported. But the one thing I didn't know was how the application was built or what it took to build something like it. On rare occasions, I could escalate a problem directly to one of the programmers, at which time, I was afforded the so-called privilege of dealing directly with one of the application developers. I used to sit there in envy, wishing one of these programmers would share some of his magic programming knowledge with me. But that never happened. For some time, the whole programming thing remained a mystery to me until I mustered up enough courage to learn it on my own.

During this time, learning how to program meant attending the computer science school in my area. I was able to study such intriguing languages as COBOL, BASIC, FORTRAN, or, if I was lucky, C or C++. I found these languages, well, let's say less than exciting. I wanted to learn how to reach into an empty bag and pull out something interesting, something tangible, or something that someone would say, "Hey, that's pretty cool," and "Where did you learn how to do that?"

It wasn't until years later that I came across a new language called Visual Basic and began to study it on my own. It wasn't until then that I realized what I had been missing during all those computer science courses. Anyone can learn how to program, but not everyone can find enjoyment in it. Visual Basic transcends the programming world by offering something that other languages taught at universities during that time could not offer. And what is this, you ask? The answer, simply put, is instant gratification. Yes, I said it! Instant gratification—the enjoyment of building something quickly and seeing your results immediately. This is what makes Visual Basic so popular as a teaching tool and a very common platform for rapidly building application prototypes in the business world.

Customers want a visual perspective of what it is you as a programmer are building for them. Visual Basic provides the facilities to do this and do it quickly, cheaply, and efficiently. This type of rapid prototyping, known as *RAD* (Rapid Application Development), has proven to be a pot of gold for not only the companies that use it, but also the developers who possess the knowledge to exploit it.

So the question now is "How do I become one of these Visual Basic and RAD experts?" Well, the first step is understanding how to solve problems. Solving

IN THE REAL WORLD

RAD development tools such as Visual Basic provide the facilities for creating graphical interfaces that can depict the functionality and flow of an application before you start any major programming. Prior to RAD tools, customers often waited many months, if not years, to see what their applications would look like. During an extended development period, customers could and did change their requirements for an application. For the programmers, this meant going back to the drawing board and modifying tedious, complicated, and expensive code to accommodate the customers' changing needs. Visual Basic provides the necessary RAD tools for quickly creating graphical interfaces and the ability to change them in a moment's notice without the legacy problems of major code changes. RAD development environments such as Visual Basic have proven to be a solid and popular mechanism for saving companies money and time.

problems is the core of programming. Learning how to solve problems is an important and often overlooked concept when learning how to program. In this chapter, I show you a few basic techniques that programmers use for decomposing a problem, sifting through the rubble, and finding a solution. In addition to learning how to solve problems, it is crucial to fully understand the tools you are working with. Visual Basic provides a multitude of new tools for solution design, development, implementation, and deployment. I show you how to exploit some of these new tools so that by the end of this chapter, you will be able to build a simple program and call yourself a Visual Basic programmer. Specifically, this chapter covers the following topics:

- Problem solving
- Visual Basic projects
- The Visual Basic landscape
- Constructing the light bulb program

Project: How Many Programmers Does It Take to Turn on a Light Bulb?

By the end of this chapter, you will become familiar with the Visual Basic facilities for building simple programs. I also walk you through how to build a simple graphical program that turns on a graphical depiction of a light bulb using the Visual Basic *IDE* (Integrated Development Environment).

Figure 1.1 depicts the light bulb program that you will learn to build at the end of this chapter.

> ### Definition
>
> Most enterprise languages such as Visual Basic, Java, C++, and so on) are packaged into an *IDE*, Integrated Development Environment.
>
> IDEs combine multiple components, such as debugging features, compilers, text editors, help systems, and many other features, into one graphical environment. Though common with many programming languages, IDEs are not necessary to build programs. In fact, many programmers today use basic text editors, such as UNIX's vi, pico, or emacs; a mainframe time-sharing option (TSO) editor; or something resembling Microsoft's Notepad.

Don't worry about the programming specifics or any Visual Basic nomenclature when you build the light bulb program. My intention is to give you a feel for how easy it is to build programs in Visual Basic. In subsequent chapters, you will learn the underlying meaning of what you did in the light bulb program.

FIGURE 1.1

The light bulb
program.

How to Solve Problems

Problem solving is something you have been doing all your life. Whether you know it or not, the way you already solve everyday problems is similar to how programmers solve their programming problems. For example, as an adult, you face all types of problems ranging from easily solvable to seemingly impossible. Here are just a few:

- How do I get my employer to give me a promotion or more money?
- How do I change the toner in my printer?
- How do I pay my bills?
- How do I study for a test?
- How do I bake a cake?
- How do I fix a broken water heater?

Each of these problems, whether simple or complicated, requires some process for obtaining and implementing a solution. It is this process that I want to focus on.

I'll use the broken water heater as an example. To solve this problem, I first make sure that I understand the problem correctly. This might involve going to my water heater and looking for leaks, frozen pipes, loss of electrical power, or faulty hardware. I might also document the make and model (gas or electric) and the conditions surrounding the last time it was working (which will be useful later).

Next I identify all the tools necessary to solve the problem. After that, I come up with a plan of action, or an *algorithm*. In real life, you probably would not bother documenting all these steps on paper. But it's the process that I'm going through, either consciously or subconsciously, that's important.

> **Definition**
>
> An *algorithm* is a well-defined, finite, step-by-step process for solving a problem.

After identifying the problem and finding all necessary tools, I choose the best course of action or algorithm to implement. I might try to fix the problem myself, or if I'm smart, I call a service-repair person. Either way, I take the time to state and understand the problem and identify the tools I need so that if I go to a hardware store for replacement parts, I know what to get. Or if I decide to call a service-repair person, I know whom to call and what to tell her if she asks me questions about my broken water heater.

Although the broken water heater problem is simple to solve, you know as an adult that if you don't understand the problems you are trying to fix, they can cost you unnecessary time, money, and frustration. Programmers face the same issues and consequences when developing their programs, with one major exception. Most professional programmers or developers take the time to formally document their thought processes in some form of analysis and design. Without a process for analyzing a problem and coming up with the design, you will find yourself in trouble time and time again. This I promise you.

There are literally sciences and engineering practices behind software analysis and design, also known as *software engineering*. As a beginning programmer, you do not need to concern yourself with the intricacies of software engineering, but I would be doing you a disservice if I didn't share some foundations for how programmers solve problems.

> ### Definition
>
> *Software engineering* is the act of constructing software programs through specifications derived through a form of analysis and design. Often considered to be the Wild West of the engineering world, software engineering is a new and constantly changing practice. Some engineers do not even consider software engineering a real engineering practice because there are few standards, guidelines, and industry-approved certifications. Just think: What would happen to the engineers building skyscrapers or airplanes if their products were allowed to have as many faults or bugs as the software running on your computer? Would you still want to fly?

STAIR

Made popular at Indiana University Purdue University Indianapolis (IUPUI) by instructor Andy Harris, STAIR is one of many processes for solving problems in the scientific, engineering, and information technology worlds. I use parts of the STAIR problem-solving process in each chapter to give you a feel for how you can solve problems with it. Specifically, STAIR is an acronym for the following:

- State the problem.
- Identify the tools available for solving the problem.
- Write an algorithm.
- Implement the solution.
- Refine the solution.

Stating the Problem

Stating the problem is the first and most important part of solving any programming problem. It begins by stating the problem, defining the problem, and understanding the problem. Although seemingly an easy task, stating and understanding a problem is where most beginning and even seasoned programmers sometimes get into trouble. If you don't fully understand a problem, you might find yourself creating unnecessary work or implementing an incorrect solution. Take your time when presented with a problem to fully understand its nature and origin before writing a single line of code. Once you have this knowledge, everything else falls into place.

Identifying Your Tools

The next process is identifying any tools you have or might have available for solving a problem. Defining tools can be as simple as listing the major components that you will use for solving a problem. Or it can be a more detailed description of specific component subsets.

Tools specific to this book include the Visual Basic programming environment and its many facilities.

Writing an Algorithm

The algorithm is the process by which you sequentially list the steps needed to solve a problem. Algorithms can start out as a simple paragraph, but you should carry it further to a finite list of well-defined steps.

Implementing the Solution

Implementation is the process by which you use your tools and algorithms to build a solution. For this book's purpose, implementation is the process by which you add controls to forms, modify their properties, and write Visual Basic code to respond to events.

Refining the Solution

The refinement process involves various aspects of testing the solution, fixing bugs, and making enhancements. For the most part, I do not use the refinement part of the STAIR

Definition

The word *bug* in a technical sense most often means an unintentional software or hardware problem or glitch. Its origins date back to Admiral Grace Hopper (a computer pioneer best known for inventing the COBOL programming language), who told a story of a technician removing an insect from between the relays of a computer.

process in this book. Why, you ask? Because we programmers don't make mistakes! Well, uh, okay; I'm just joking.

I can guarantee you that most programs I wrote for this book went through some form of refinement, modification, and debugging to better them in some way. Even though you might not see the refinement step in this book, I can promise you it was done. So don't worry; I'm sure you will find yourself conducting the refinement process on your own programs because it is a natural process when developing applications and writing code. It's a rare if not impossible feat for any programmer to write even the simplest program without returning to the program design or code to make enhancements or fix bugs.

Here's how I would use the STAIR process to solve the water heater problem:

- **State the problem.** My water heater does not work. Cold water comes out of all faucets in the house, but no hot water. I had hot water last night, but none this morning. The temperature outside has been below freezing for the past week. The water heater is located in the garage, and all exposed pipes are insulated but are cold to the touch. I've determined that pipes are frozen. The product is made by XYZ Company and uses gas.

- **Identify your tools.** I have a portable heater that I could use to assist in thawing the exposed pipes if they are frozen. I have identified a couple of service-repair companies in the Yellow Pages.

- **Write an algorithm.** I choose to fix the problem myself by following these steps:

  1. Make sure the portable heater has gas.
  2. Plug in the portable heater.
  3. Place the portable heater next to the water heater, and turn it on.
  4. Leave the heater running, and check for hot water every hour or two.

- **Implement the solution.** Implement the preceding algorithm.

- **Refine the solution.** Does the hot water ever come on? If so, did it take a long time? Was this a good solution, and should I use it in the future? Is there a better long-term solution?

In this book, I mostly concentrate on the S (state the problem), T (tools), A (algorithm), and I (implementation) parts of STAIR to build a program at the end of each chapter.

Visual Basic Projects

A Visual Basic project consists of many files that directly correlate with the types of Visual Basic *components* you are working with.

Project Files

Here is a list of Visual Basic project files that you will work with throughout this book:

- The group project file (.vbg) contains a list of all Visual Basic projects in one group.

- Project files (.vbp) list all project files and components in the project. The project file also contains information on the project's environmental settings.

- The form modules (.frm) file contains textual descriptions of forms, controls, and their properties. The form module file can also contain form-level declarations of variables, constants, and procedures.

- The form data file (.frx) is created for each form. It contains binary information for graphics such as pictures and icons.

- Standard modules (.bas) can contain global declarations and public and external procedures.

> **Definition**
>
> *Components* are simply modularized pieces of code in a Visual Basic application. Components allow you to modularize your program because you create and use separate pieces that work together to build an entire program.

Project Templates

Visual Basic provides project templates to assist you with program development for a specific type of project. When building a new Visual Basic program, you have the opportunity to select from a number of project templates, as shown in Figure 1.2.

Before you start coding, you should give some thought to what type of project you will be working with.

 HINT Deciding what type of Visual Basic project to use falls under the tools step of the STAIR process.

You can choose from a number of project templates in Visual Basic; however, this book concentrates on the standard EXE project.

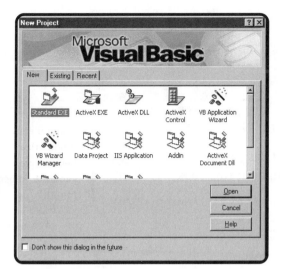

FIGURE 1.2

New project window showing available project templates.

Standard EXE is the default project template and is used to build standalone desktop applications. When you create a standard EXE project, Visual Basic provides you with one Form object by default. The standard EXE is the project you will use throughout this book.

The Visual Basic Landscape

Definition

The term *object* has many definitions and applications in the world of computer science and information technology. To narrow the scope of the word "object," I define it for use in this book in the following manner: Visual Basic programs use windows called Forms that act as containers for controls, such as images, buttons, and labels, to name just a few. These controls and the forms they reside on are called objects.

The Visual Basic landscape consists of many windows and tools that you will use throughout this book. You will not only become familiar with these tools and windows, but you will also learn how to exploit all that they have to offer you as a programmer.

Figure 1.3 shows the most common windows and toolbars you will use throughout this book.

The menu bar contains menu commands that you have probably seen in other Windows-based applications—such as File, Edit, View, Tools, Window, Help, and

Toolbox   Menu bar   Toolbar   Project Explorer window

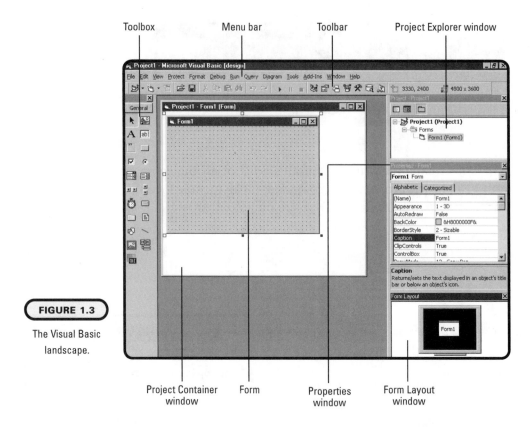

FIGURE 1.3

The Visual Basic
landscape.

Project Container   Form   Properties   Form Layout
window   window   window

others. The menu bar also has many other commands specific to Visual Basic—such as Project, Format, Debug, Run, Query, Diagram, Add-Ins, and many others.

The toolbar includes a number of clickable icons that represent various program functions. To find out what a specific icon represents on the menu bar, simply move your mouse cursor over the icon and pause for a moment to see a small balloon containing a description.

Toolbox is a popular facility for aiding you in designing graphical programs. It contains clickable icons that represent objects you can place on your form. Some of the toolbox's objects that you will use in the light bulb program are the image, label, frame, option button, and command button control.

The Project Container window is what its name implies, a container. Its function is to house other windows such as form and code windows.

A form is technically a container for other objects, but I like to equate it to a canvas for painting a picture. You can use the toolbox to add objects to a form by clicking an object icon on the toolbox and using your mouse to draw the control. Or you can simply double-click the object icon in the toolbox to instantly place the object on your form.

 Once a control has been added to a form, you can resize it by using the mouse's pointer to click and drag the edges of the control.

The Project Explorer window contains a list of all the components included in your Visual Basic project. Such components can include forms and code modules, which I discuss in Chapter 9.

The Properties window contains the properties or attributes of one object. To view an object's properties, simply click on an object such as a form, text box, label, image, or command button to have its properties displayed in the Properties window. The Properties window not only displays an object's properties, but allows you to modify the object's properties as well.

The Form Layout window allows you to position forms relative to your screen's size.

The Form Code window is a container that you use to write your Visual Basic code. Essentially, the Form Code window is a high-powered text editor that aids you in programming and debugging.

 The preceding components can be accessed from the View menu item.

Constructing the Light Bulb Program

How many programmers does it take to turn on a light bulb? The answer is one. I walk you through how a programmer might go about solving this program using the STAIR process.

The Problem

How do I build a program using Visual Basic that graphically depicts a light bulb turning off and on?

The tools you have on hand are easy to identify: the Visual Basic IDE and one standard EXE project. Table 1.1 is a list of the controls and their properties for the light bulb program.

TABLE 1.1 CONTROLS AND PROPERTIES FOR THE LIGHT BULB PROGRAM

Object	Property	Setting
Label1	Caption	The light is off.
	Font	MS Sans Serif, regular font, size = 18
	Alignment	2- center
Frame1	Caption	Light Switch:
Option1	Caption	On
Option2	Caption	Off
Image1	Picture	(None)
	Stretch	True
Image2	Picture	Lighton.ico
	Stretch	False
	Visible	False
Image3	Picture	Lightoff.ico
	Stretch	False
	Visible	False
Command1	Caption	Exit

HINT The icons Lighton.ico and Lightoff.ico (and many other graphics) appear in the common directory of Visual Studio (for example, C:\Program Files\Microsoft Visual Studio\Common\Graphics). Visual Studio is Microsoft's suite of development tools, which include Visual Basic and many others. If you do not have access to these graphics, you can find a multitude of free clip art in Microsoft's Clip Gallery at http://cgl.microsoft.com/clipgallerylive/default.asp.

Write your algorithm in the form of a list:

1. Launch Visual Basic, and select a standard EXE as project template.

2. Build the user interface using the default form that comes with the standard EXE project and the controls located in the toolbox.

3. Write code to respond to user events.

4. Test the program.

The Implementation

Figure 1.4 depicts one of many possible graphical implementations for the light bulb program. You can see that I have two image controls, each with a picture of a light bulb, one with the light bulb turned on and one with it turned off. A third image control contains no picture. I will use this empty image control to perform a simple image swap.

To turn the light bulb on and off, I've decided to use two option buttons. You generally place option buttons in a container such as a frame control. (I discuss controls in more detail in Chapter 2.)

In addition to the graphical representation of the light bulb's condition, I've placed a label control on the form to give the user a textual description of the light bulb's status. Last but not least, I've included a command button on the form to allow the user a friendly way of exiting the program.

Remember, to add these controls to a form, simply click on the control that you want (located in the toolbox), and use your mouse pointer to draw it on the form. You can also double-click the control in the toolbox, and Visual Basic will automatically add the control to your form.

Once you have all the necessary controls on your form, you can modify their properties accordingly, or you can modify individual control properties as you add them.

Once you've completed building the graphical interface, it's time to write code that responds to events triggered by the user. To begin writing your program code, you must first open the Visual Basic code window. To do so, simply double-click one of your controls on the form.

FIGURE 1.4

A possible form design for the light bulb program.

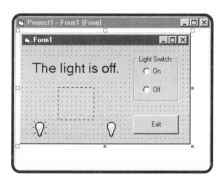

HINT There's more than one way to navigate the code window and the graphical form window. You may also use the function keys on your keyboard. Pressing the F7 key opens the code window for the current form. To navigate back to your form window, press Shift+F7.

Another way to navigate between code and form windows is to use your Project Explorer window. Simply right-click your form in the Project Explorer window and choose either View Code or View Object.

Events make up the core component for a new programming paradigm called event-driven programming. Event-driven programming is still a relatively new way of thinking about how programs are written. The old way to program was to write code in a step-by-step procedural way, which gives the user little or no control over when program actions occur. Using events allows a programmer to write code that gives the user more control over when programming actions occur in an application. Each control that you will use in Visual Basic, such as a text box, command button, option button, or image control, has a number of events associated with it.

When a user triggers an event, such as by clicking on a command button, an event procedure—statements of code—is executed within a program block. An event procedure for a command button's click event looks like the following:

```
Private Sub Command1_Click()
    'Visual Basic code goes here
End Sub
```

When the light bulb program is first loaded, I want the light bulb set to the off setting and the label control to describe its state. This is my default state for the program. You can set default settings at design time (when you are creating your program) or through code in the Form Load event. Here's the Form Load event for the light bulb program:

```
Private Sub Form_Load()
  Image1.Picture = Image3.Picture
  Option2.Value = True
End Sub
```

When the form loads, I set the picture property of the Image1 image control to the picture property of Image3 (lights off). In addition, I set the value property of the Option2 control to True. Setting the value property of an option button control to True makes it appear selected.

When the user clicks an option button, in this case either "on" or "off," you can write code in the click event to handle some action. I want the light bulb to turn on when the user clicks the Option1 option button and turn off when she clicks the Option2 option button. Here's the code for each option button's click event:

```
Private Sub Option1_Click()
    Image1.Picture = Image2.Picture
    Label1.Caption = "The light is on."
End Sub


Private Sub Option2_Click()
    Image1.Picture = Image3.Picture
    Label1.Caption = "The light is off."
End Sub
```

When the user clicks the command button, I want the program to end. I can accomplish this by using the keyword End, which terminates the program. Here's the code for the Command1 control:

```
Private Sub Command1_Click()
    End
End Sub
```

Here is all of the code for the light bulb program as shown in the form's code window:

```
Private Sub Command1_Click()
    End
End Sub


Private Sub Form_Load()
    Image1.Picture = Image3.Picture
    Option2.Value = True
End Sub


Private Sub Option1_Click()
    Image1.Picture = Image2.Picture
    Label1.Caption = "The light is on."
End Sub


Private Sub Option2_Click()
    Image1.Picture = Image3.Picture
    Label1.Caption = "The light is off."
End Sub
```

This is all that is required to build a light bulb program. Hey, that wasn't too bad, was it?

Running Your Visual Basic Program

The Visual Basic IDE contains three modes for building, running, and testing your programs:

- Design time is the mode in which you add controls to containers (such as forms) and write code to respond to events.

- The runtime environment allows you to see your program running the same way a user would. During runtime, you can see all your Visual Basic code, but you cannot modify it.

- Break mode allows you to pause the execution of your Visual Basic program (during runtime) to view, edit, and debug your program code.

There are three main ways to access each of these modes. You can use Visual Basic's Run menu as seen in Figure 1.5, function keys, or icons located on the toolbar as depicted in Figure 1.6.

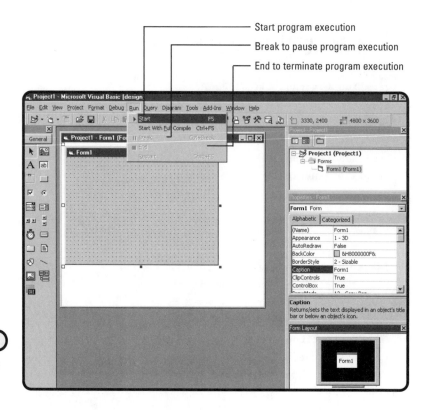

Start program execution

Break to pause program execution

End to terminate program execution

FIGURE 1.5

The Visual Basic Run menu item.

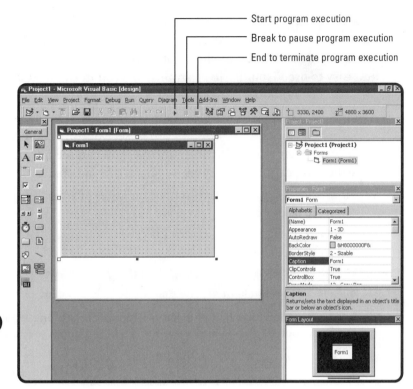

Start program execution

Break to pause program execution

End to terminate program execution

FIGURE 1.6

Visual Basic mode
access via the
toolbar.

Summary

Congratulations: You have made it through the first chapter, and you are well on your way to becoming a Visual Basic programmer. I hope that you see how easy it is to use Visual Basic as a programming platform for rapidly building programs.

In the first part of the chapter, you learned about solving problems the programmer's way. You learned how to use design tools such as the STAIR process for breaking down a problem and implementing a solution. Later, you learned about the files and projects associated with Visual Basic, what components compose the Visual Basic landscape, and how to use them to your advantage. With this introduction to problem solving and Visual Basic you should now feel confident that you have the right background to start solving problems using the Visual Basic IDE.

In the next chapter, you will dive deeper into the Visual Basic GUI (graphical user interface) world to further investigate controls, objects, and events and the tools needed to manipulate them. I show you these techniques through a number of fun and easy-to-use Visual Basic programs. See you in the next chapter.

CHALLENGES

1. Write the S, T, and A parts of the STAIR process for the following problems:

   - How to bake a cake
   - How to drive a car
   - How to type a letter

2. Modify the light bulb program to use command buttons instead of option buttons to turn the light off and on.

3. Build a program that has one command button and one label. Make the command button show your name in the label's caption property when it is clicked.

CHAPTER 2

Visual Basic Fundamentals and GUI Basics

Welcome back. Chapter 1 provided you with an overview of how to solve problems the programmer's way with an introduction to the Visual Basic landscape. You will now peel back the Visual Basic landscape layers to expose various *GUI* (graphical user interface) techniques and Visual Basic programming fundamentals. To accomplish this, I show you how to build a number of small programs throughout this chapter, leading up to a larger program and its design at the end of the chapter.

This chapter specifically covers the following:

- Controls and their associated properties

- Variables, numbers, and strings

- Programming events

- Compiling a Visual Basic program

Project: Word Art

As seen in Figure 2.1, the Word Art program takes text entered by you as input and allows text manipulation in various fashions. It is a fun and easy way for you to better understand the many powerful capabilities of Visual Basic controls, variables, numbers, strings, and programming events. You might find that the Word Art program closely resembles word processors or text editors that you

> ### Definition
>
> The term *GUI* represents a graphical user interface that acts as a front end to various programming functions and procedures. Most high-level languages (such as Visual Basic) include the facilities to create GUIs. Most GUIs consist of windows containing buttons, labels, text boxes, images, menus, and other controls.

have used before. This is because the Word Art program offers many features that today's high-end word processors use, such as the ability to change fonts, colors, and alignment.

After completing this chapter, you will see how easy it is to build seemingly complicated graphical programs using the Visual Basic IDE. I hope you're as excited as I am about the possibilities, so let's get started.

Controls and Properties

As mentioned in Chapter 1, controls are objects you can place on forms and in other containers such as frames and picture boxes. Controls can take the form of images, pictures, command buttons, labels, frames, and text boxes. The form you put your controls on is also considered a control. In addition to their graphically

FIGURE 2.1

The Word Art program.

appealing presence, controls serve other functions as well. Visual Basic controls have events, properties, and methods associated with them.

Properties of controls are considered their attributes. For example, some properties of a word processor might include font size, fore color, back color, and alignment. You can change the properties of controls when you're designing your program (also known as design-time changes) by clicking on the control or by selecting it from the drop-down list box. You can also modify a control's properties through program code during runtime (when your program is running). You can start to see that the properties describe a control or object.

IN THE REAL WORLD

Properties, methods, and events are really one in the same. In the truest sense of programming and its relation to mathematics, properties, methods, events, and even procedures are really just a function or part of a function in some way.

In the object-oriented world, properties are controlled by functions for reading and writing information; methods are no more than functions that perform some action; events are functions that respond to some intrinsic or user-controlled events; procedures are simply void functions (functions that return no value); and, well, functions are just functions (give something as input and get something as output).

Naming Conventions

You should use some standards when naming your controls as you add them to forms or other containers. Naming your controls something meaningful becomes an invaluable part of programming when you are dealing with program code. If you are looking at someone else's program code, you can easily identify the type of control by looking at the control name. This can save you from navigating between code and form windows to verify what control you are working with.

As a general rule of thumb, you should prefix your control name with three letters that signify what type of control you have and follow that with a name that denotes the control's purpose. For more information on naming conventions, see "Naming Conventions Continued" later in this chapter. Table 2.1 contains some sample control names.

TABLE 2.1 SAMPLE CONTROL NAMES

Control Name	Control Type
frmMain	Form used as a main interface
cmdExit	Command button that exits an application
lblEmployeeName	Label control that describes an employee name
txtTelephoneNum	Text box control used for entering a phone number
imgPlane	Image control that contains a picture of a plane
picOutput	Picture box that prints some output
fraColorOptions	Frame control that contains color options
optRed	Option button control for the color red
chkSunday	Check box control for the day Sunday

Form

Sometimes called windows or dialog boxes, forms act as an interface to programs' functionality. Forms also serve as containers for other controls. Figure 2.2 depicts a form.

Table 2.2 represents a few common properties of the form control.

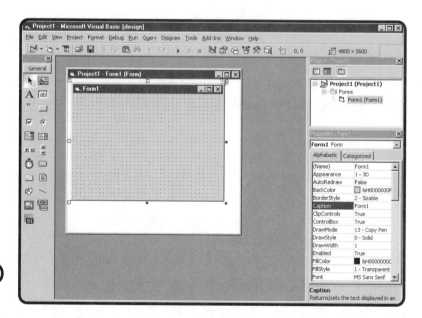

FIGURE 2.2

A form.

TABLE 2.2 A FEW COMMON FORM PROPERTIES

Property	Description
Name	Control name; used to identify the control through code
BackColor	Changes the back color of the form
BorderStyle	Changes the border style of the form (design time only)
Caption	Text that appears on the control during design time and runtime
ControlBox	Determines whether or not the control menu box is visible (TRUE or FALSE)
Enabled	Enables the form; can be set to TRUE or FALSE
Font	Sets the font type of the caption property
ForeColor	Changes the fore color of the form
Height	Used to set the height dimensions of a form (measured in twips)
Icon	Displays a selected icon in the upper-left corner of the window (also seen when the form is minimized)
Picture	Assigns a picture to the form's background
StartUpPosition	Determines the position of the form when it first appears
Visible	Makes the form visible or not during runtime
Width	Used to set the width dimensions of a form (measured in twips)
WindowState	Used to determine the state of a window (such as normal, minimized, or maximized)

Definition

Twips are a unit of measurement equal to 1/20 of a printer's point.

Command Buttons

Command buttons are some of the most common controls found in any graphically driven language. Because of their raised, three-dimensional appearance, they have a distinct and intrinsic graphical presence. It is almost as if they are saying, "Click me, please." Figure 2.3 depicts a typical command button as seen on a Visual Basic form.

Command buttons are most commonly used for starting or triggering *procedures* through an event.

Definition

Procedures are simply blocks of code that perform a certain task. In Visual Basic, procedures are broken down into subprocedures and functions. The key difference between the two is that subprocedures do not return a value and functions do. Remember from math class that functions simply take an input and return an output. You will learn more about functions and subprocedures in Chapter 5.

Table 2.3 represents a few common properties of the command button control.

FIGURE 2.3

The command button.

TABLE 2.3 A FEW COMMON COMMAND BUTTON PROPERTIES

Property	Description
Name	Control name; used to identify the control through code
Caption	Text that appears on the control during design time and runtime
Enabled	Enables the command button; can be set to TRUE or FALSE
Font	Sets the font type of the caption property
Picture	Assigns a picture to the button face
Style	Used in conjunction with the picture property to assign a picture to the button face instead of a caption
Visible	Makes the command button visible or not during runtime

HINT

If you add the ampersand (&) symbol to any control's Caption property, it underlines the character to its immediate right. This is a useful tool for creating shortcut keys. Shortcut keys let a user hold down the Alt key and press the letter underlined to invoke the click event of that control.

Labels

Label controls are often used as descriptive text for other controls that do not have their own caption properties. A good example is the text box control, which has no self-describing property viewable to a user in runtime. Often, a programmer will put a label control to the left of a text box to describe what the user should enter into the text box. Figure 2.4 depicts the label control as seen on a form.

Table 2.4 represents a few common properties of the label control.

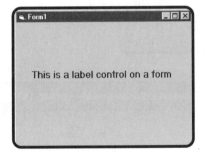

This is a label control on a form

FIGURE 2.4

A label control
on a form.

TABLE 2.4 A FEW COMMON LABEL PROPERTIES	
Property	**Description**
Name	Control name; used to identify the control through code
Alignment	Aligns the label's text in the caption property
BackColor	Changes the back color of the label
BackStyle	Sets the control to transparent or opaque
BorderStyle	Changes the border from nothing or fixed-single (sunken)
Caption	Text that appears on the control during design time and runtime
Enabled	Enables the label; can be set to TRUE or FALSE
Font	Sets the font type of the caption property
ForeColor	Changes the fore color of the label
Visible	Makes the label visible or not during runtime

Text Boxes

The text box control is popular for acquiring user input and displaying various outputs. You might find it useful when expecting a user to enter either numbers or text or a combination of both. The text box control has no caption property, so a label generally signifies to the user what it is you want him or her to enter as input. Figure 2.5 depicts a text box as seen on a form.

Table 2.5 shows a few common properties of the text box control.

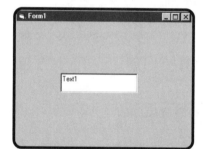

FIGURE 2.5

A text box control on a form.

TABLE 2.5 A FEW COMMON TEXT BOX PROPERTIES

Property	Description
Name	Control name; used to identify the control through code
Alignment	Aligns the label's text in the caption property
Appearance	Selects from 1-3D (default) or 0-Flat
BackColor	Changes the back color of the text box
BorderStyle	Changes the border from nothing or fixed-single (sunken)
Enabled	Enables the text box for data entry; can be set to TRUE or FALSE
Font	Sets the font type of the text property
ForeColor	Changes the fore color of the text displayed or entered
Locked	Determines whether or not the control can be edited
Multiline	Allows multiple lines (carriage returns) to be entered
PasswordChar	Used for entering passwords; displays characters entered as asterisks (*)
ScrollBars	Allows a user to scroll through text vertically, horizontally, or both
Text	Text entered or displayed in the text box

Image Controls and Picture Boxes

You can use both the image control and the picture box to display various graphics (such as .bmp, .gif, .jpg, or .ico files). However, applying a number of graphics to your program can consume a lot of memory and create excessive overhead. If you plan to develop games or other graphically intensive programs with Visual Basic, it is important for you to understand each of these control's benefits and disadvantages. See Figure 2.6 for an image control and picture box located on a form.

Some benefits to the image control are that it uses much less memory and overhead than the picture box does and that it can re-paint itself much faster than the picture box. An advantage of the picture box is that it is actually a window or container that can contain other controls, unlike the image control.

Table 2.6 depicts a few common properties of the image control.

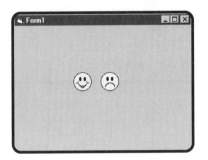

FIGURE 2.6

An image control
on the left and
a picture box on
the right.

TABLE 2.6 A FEW COMMON IMAGE CONTROL PROPERTIES

Property	Description
Name	Control name; used to identify the control through code
Appearance	Selects from 1-3D (default) or 0-Flat
BorderStyle	Changes the border from nothing or fixed-single (sunken)
Enabled	Enables the picture (can be useful for clickable events); can be set to TRUE or FALSE
Picture	Assigns a picture to the image control
Stretch	Stretches the original picture size to that of the image control size (unique to image control)
Visible	Makes the image visible or not during runtime

Table 2.7 depicts a few common properties of the picture box.

TABLE 2.7 A FEW PICTURE BOX PROPERTIES

Property	Description
Name	Control name; used to identify the control through code
Appearance	Selects from 1-3D (default) or 0-Flat
Autosize	Automatically resizes the control to fit the size of the assigned graphic
BackColor	Used to change the back color of the picture box
BorderStyle	Changes the border from nothing or fixed-single (sunken)
Enabled	Enables the picture box; can be set to TRUE or FALSE
Font	Sets the font type
ForeColor	Changes the fore color of any text displayed in the picture box
Picture	Assigns a picture to the picture box
Visible	Makes the picture box visible or not during runtime

Frame Controls

Like a form or a picture box, the frame control is considered a container for other controls. Frames are often used to isolate various functionalities on a form. For example, I might use frames if I were developing a loan application that had a section for the applicant and a section for the co-applicant on the same form. I would put all the applicant's labels, text boxes, and other controls in one frame control and the co-applicant's controls in another frame. This way, I graphically isolate groups of items or tasks.

Frames also serve an important role when you use option buttons (sometimes called radio buttons) or check boxes, as you will see shortly. Figure 2.7 depicts a frame control located on a form.

Table 2.8 depicts some common properties of the frame control.

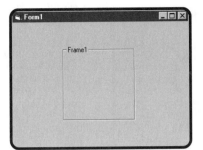

FIGURE 2.7

A frame control.

TABLE 2.8 A FEW COMMON FRAME PROPERTIES

Property	Description
Name	Control name; used to identify the control through code
Appearance	Select from 1-3D (default) or 0-Flat
BackColor	Used to change the back color of the frame
BorderStyle	Changes the border from nothing or fixed-single (sunken)
Caption	The frame's caption
Enabled	Enables the frame; can be set to TRUE or FALSE
Font	Sets the font type of the frame's caption
ForeColor	Changes the fore color of the frame's caption
Visible	Makes the frame visible or not during runtime

Check Boxes

You use check boxes when you want to give the user the ability to select one or more choices. You should place check boxes in a container such as a frame control to denote a related grouping. As with the command button, you can visually enhance check boxes using graphics in the DownPicture and DisabledPicture properties. Check boxes are often managed in a control array, which you will learn about in Chapter 10. Figure 2.8 shows check boxes located in a frame control.

Table 2.9 lists a few common check box properties.

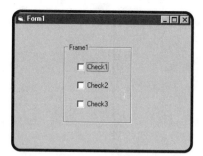

TABLE 2.9 A FEW COMMON CHECK BOX PROPERTIES

Property	Description
Name	Control name; used to identify the control through code
Alignment	Aligns the check box's caption property
BackColor	Used to change the back color of the check box
Caption	The check box's caption
DisabledPicture	Changes the check box's picture property when disabled
DownPicture	Changes the check box's picture property when clicked
Enabled	Enables the check box; can be set to TRUE or FALSE
Font	Sets the font type of the check box's caption
ForeColor	Changes the fore color of the check box's caption
Picture	The default graphic for the check box (used in conjunction with the style property)
Style	Used to change the look of a check box, either 0-Standard or 1-Graphical
Value	Used to identify the check box as checked, unchecked, or grayed
Visible	Makes the check box visible or not during runtime

Option Buttons

Option buttons are often referred to as radio buttons. The term *radio button* refers to old car stereos that used push-in buttons. You could push in only one button at a time. This still holds true with the concept behind the graphical option button. Option buttons are similar to check boxes with one main exception. As with the old car radio buttons, you can click only one button at a time. They are useful when you want to give a user a selection of various items but let her select only one out of many. As soon as a user selects one option button out of many, the rest of the option buttons in a group become unavailable. Like check boxes, option buttons are generally placed in a container such as a frame control. Figure 2.9 depicts option buttons located in a frame control.

A few common properties of the option button control are displayed in Table 2.10.

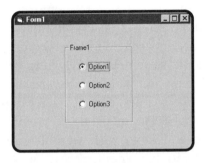

FIGURE 2.9

Three option buttons located in a frame control.

TABLE 2.10 A FEW COMMON OPTION BUTTON PROPERTIES

Property	Description
Name	Control name; used to identify the control through code
Alignment	Aligns the option button's caption property
BackColor	Used to change the back color of the option button
Caption	The option button's caption
DisabledPicture	Changes the option button's picture property when disabled
DownPicture	Changes the option button's picture property when clicked
Enabled	Enables the option button; can be set to TRUE or FALSE
Font	Sets the font type of the option button's caption
ForeColor	Changes the fore color of the option button's caption
Picture	The default graphic for the option button (used in conjunction with the style property)
Style	Used to change the look of an option button, either 0-Standard or 1-Graphical
Value	Used to identify the option button as clicked or unclicked (value is either TRUE or FALSE)
Visible	Makes the option button visible or not during runtime

Variables, Numbers, and Strings

In this section, you will roll up your sleeves and get your hands a little dirty by learning some basic (forgive the pun) Visual Basic programming. You will get experience through building two small programs.

Variables

Variables can temporarily store the value of data in memory during the execution of your program. They are often referred to as containers for various types of data. But in reality, they are address placeholders to a memory location in your computer. In addition, variables act as templates, defining what type of data should be kept in a memory location and its allowable size. The programming world has many different types of variables, and not every programming language treats them the same. Visual Basic (in my opinion) must be one of the friendliest languages to use when dealing with variables and data because Microsoft built in a multitude of variable types for creating, storing, and using data in Visual Basic.

Table 2.11 outlines some common Visual Basic variable types that you might use throughout this book.

IN THE REAL WORLD

At the core level of computer architecture, data is represented in electrical currents that pass through digital circuits. Electrical currents are represented in binary form (1s and 0s), which in turn are translated into various numbering systems that make up memory addresses of a location where data might be stored. Languages such as C and C++ use a facility called pointers to directly access memory locations of variables. Although pointers provide powerful capabilities to deal directly with the operating system and memory modules, they require a thorough knowledge of C or C++ and a basic understanding of the science behind computer architecture. For the most part, Visual Basic takes care of pointers and memory management for you.

TABLE 2.11 COMMON VISUAL BASIC VARIABLE TYPES

Variable Type	Description	Size
Boolean	True or false	2 bytes
Byte	0 to 255	1 byte
Date	Date data type, December 25, 2000	8 bytes
Double	Number data type, -1.79769313486232E308 to -4.94065645841247E-324 for negative values; 4.94065645841247E-324 to 1.79769313486232E308 for positive values	8 bytes
Integer	Number data type, -32,768 to 32,767	2 bytes
Long	Number data type, -2,147,483,648 to 2,147,483,647	4 bytes
Single	Number data type, -3.402823E38 to -1.401298E-45 for negative values; 1.401298E-45 to 3.402823E38 for positive values	4 bytes
String	String data type (holds numbers, characters, or a combination of both)	10 bytes plus length of string

The syntax for assigning a variable type to a variable name is as follows:

```
[declaration type] variableName As variableType
```

Here is an example of a variable called myInteger declared as an integer variable type:

```
Dim myInteger As Integer
```

Declaring Variables and Scope

As mentioned earlier, variables are stored temporarily in your computer's memory. Therefore, it is important for you to know when your variable goes out of scope or, in other words, when you can lose the value of your variable. Variables derive their scope from either their location in the program code or their declaration type.

Variables declared in a procedure (for example, the form load event or a button click event) with the keyword Dim have what's known as procedure-level scope; they are called local variables. That is, the variable maintains its value only throughout the execution of that procedure.

You can also declare variables in a procedure with the keyword Static. Variables declared with the keyword Static retain their value the entire time your program is executing.

Here is an example of a variable called myString declared with the keyword Static and the variable myDate declared with the keyword Dim:

```
Static myString as String
Dim myDate as Date
```

 Note that when you declare a variable, Visual Basic provides you with a list of all available variable types. You see this list in a pop-up window as soon as you finish typing the keyword As in a variable declaration statement.

Variables declared with the keyword Dim in a form's code window, but outside of any subprocedures or functions, are considered form-level variables. These code areas outside procedures are known as the General area.

Form-level variables are accessible to any procedures or functions located in that form's code window. You can use them when you want a variable to retain its value or scope when moving from one procedure to another.

You can also declare variables in standard code modules. (I discuss standard code modules in detail in Chapter 8.) Variables declared in a standard code module generally have one or two types of scope. If you declare a variable inside the standard code module with the keyword Dim or Private, then it is available to only that standard code module. However, if you declare the variable with the keyword Public, then it is available to all modules and procedures in your application (and it is also known as a global variable).

 You should use procedure-level variables as much as possible to avoid variable naming conflicts and unknown variable assignments.

Figure 2.10 demonstrates variables with procedure- and form-level scope.

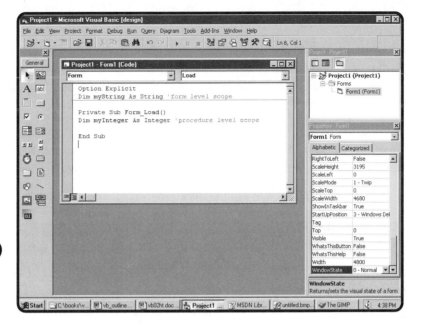

Option Explicit

A nice feature of Visual Basic is its ability to warn you or prevent you from typing a variable name without explicitly declaring it as a variable. You should always use this built-in safety feature. To implement it, simply type the statement Option Explicit in the first line of a form's code window (outside any procedures). You only need one Option Explicit statement for any Visual Basic project. You can also turn on Option Explicit for your standard EXE projects by clicking on the Tools menu, choosing Options, clicking the Editor tab, and selecting Require Variable Declaration.

Naming Conventions Continued

When creating variables, controls, or procedures, you face certain limitations on what you can use in a name. Here are some Microsoft Visual Basic guidelines that you should follow:

- All names must begin with a letter.
- Do not use periods or spaces in names.
- Variable names can be up to 255 characters in length.
- Control and module names can be up to 40 characters in length.
- Do not use any Visual Basic keywords.

In addition to naming limitations, you should follow a certain naming convention just as you learned in the control section of this chapter. As a programmer, you want to set these standards or conventions and follow them religiously throughout your Visual Basic project.

Naming conventions in variable names are especially important to you as a programmer or any other programmer who might have to read or edit your code. You should use variable naming conventions that denote the type and scope. Table 2.12 has some examples.

TABLE 2.12 SAMPLE VARIABLE NAMES

Variable Name	Variable Type	Scope
liEmployeeCount	Integer	Local (procedure level)
fiNumberofWins	Integer	Form level
giEmployeeNumber	Integer	Global
lsName	String	Local
fsAccountNumber	String	Form level
lbHasWon	Boolean	Local
gdRadius	Double	Global

Constants

Constants directly contrast variables by retaining their values throughout your program's execution, whereas variables can lose or change their values during program execution. Once you declare a constant, its value cannot change during program execution. Constants generally denote numbers or strings that do not need to change throughout the life of a program's execution. For example, you might want to put the version number of your program or a number such as pi into a constant.

When naming a constant, make its name as meaningful as possible. I recommend capitalizing the entire constant name so that it sticks out from other names (such as variables). The syntax for declaring a constant is as follows:

```
[Public or Private] Const constantName As [type] = expression
```

Here are some examples:

```
Public Const VERSION_NUMBER as String = "Version 1.2.3"
Public Const PI as Double = 3.14
```

Arithmetic Operations

You will find that performing basic mathematical operations on numbers is common in programming (especially if you are developing games). Visual Basic follows the basic math rules when dealing with arithmetic operations. Adding, subtracting, multiplying, dividing, and the associated order of operations will look very familiar to you. Table 2.13 depicts common Visual Basic arithmetic notations.

Visual Basic provides you with many different ways of performing operations on numbers. One such way that you might find strange or new is the way you can use variables in place of numbers. To give you an idea of how this works, let me show you a small program that I wrote to add two numbers. It's called the simple adder, as depicted in Figure 2.11.

TABLE 2.13 COMMON VISUAL BASIC ARITHMETIC NOTATION

Arithmetic Operation	Visual Basic Notation
Addition	a + b
Subtraction	a – b
Multiplication	a * b
Division	a / b
Exponentiation	a ^ r

FIGURE 2.11

The simple adder program.

The simple adder takes two numbers and adds them together. Well, that certainly sounds simple, but take a look at the code that performs this task to see whether you can follow what is happening:

```
Option Explicit

Private Sub cmdAdd_Click()

Dim lsOperand1 As Single
Dim lsOperand2 As Single
Dim lsResult As Single

lsOperand1 = Val(txtOperand1.Text)
lsOperand2 = Val(txtOperand2.Text)
lsResult = lsOperand1 + lsOperand2

lblResult.Caption = lsResult

End Sub
```

The Option Explicit statement ensures that I explicitly declare variables before I use them. The Private Sub cmdAdd_Click() statement begins the command button's click event. (I discuss events in more detail later in this chapter.)

Next, I declare three variables as type Single. I used the Single type so that someone can enter not only a number such as 12, but also a number such as 674.0954.

Something very interesting happens in the next two lines, so take your time in reviewing them:

```
lsOperand1 = Val(txtOperand1.Text)
lsOperand2 = Val(txtOperand2.Text)
```

Note that I have the variables lsOperand1 and lsOperand2 on the left side of an equals (=) sign. The interesting thing here is that programmers don't refer to this type of operation using the word "equals." What is occurring is that each variable is being assigned something (known as variable assignment). So when you see a variable assignment such as this, you want to say variable lsOperand1 is taking on the text value of txtOperand1.Text.

Another interesting note in this variable assignment is the use of the Val function. The Val function converts a string to a number. This step is necessary because any text (including numbers) inputted or outputted to a text box is saved as a string. Conversely, you can use the Str function to convert a number into a string. For example, if liMyNumber is declared as type integer, I can convert it to a string with the following syntax:

```
Str(liMyNumber)
```

The next assignment operation, lsResult = lsOperand1 + lsOperand2, adds lsOperand1 to lsOperand2 and assigns the result to lsResult. The last assignment, lblResult.Caption = lsResult, takes the value of lsResult and assigns it to the caption property of a label control.

 HINT The equals sign (=) in the preceding examples is used in an assignment context. However, you can also use the equals sign in comparisons. For example, you can write the question "Does x equal y?" as x = y. This type of comparison appears in conditions discussed in Chapter 3 and in loops or iteration discussed in Chapter 4.

The last piece of program code End Sub denotes that this is the end of a program block or the end of a subprocedure or event. Figure 2.12 shows what the output of the simple adder looks like.

Table 2.14 describes the controls and properties of the simple adder program.

String Constants, Functions, and Concatenation

I remember an occasion during a computer science class when the professor was energetically discussing how we could use various functions for dealing with text. The professor was so proud of text and the functions available for manipulating it that I couldn't help but wonder why. I asked him, "So what's so great about text?" He looked perplexed as if I should already know why text is so great. The professor simply answered, "Well, text is text. You can do almost anything with text." Needless to say, I didn't understand his excitement over text, nor did I learn to appreciate what he was talking about until I started programming for a living.

 FIGURE 2.12

Sample output of the simple adder program.

TABLE 2.14 CONTROLS AND PROPERTIES FOR THE SIMPLE ADDER PROGRAM

Control	Property	Setting
frmMain	Caption	Simple Adder
txtOperand1	Alignment	0 – Left Justify
	Font	MS Sans Serif, bold, size 10
txtOperand2	Alignment	0 – Left Justify
	Font	MS Sans Serif, bold, size 10
Label1	Caption	+
	Font	MS Sans Serif, bold, size 10
cmdAdd	Caption	=
	Font	MS Sans Serif, bold, size 10
lblResult	Caption	Leave blank
	Font	MS Sans Serif, bold, size 10

After a year or two of programming, I realized that the professor was and is still right. Text is great, and you can do almost anything with it! How so, you ask? Understand that almost everything in the computing world revolves around data or information. Data can be stored in temporary locations such as variables, or it can be persistent, living in such locations as files or databases. Learning how to access information and manipulate it is the key to success as a programmer. I show you some tricks for manipulating text in string variables through another program called the name game, which is shown in Figure 2.13.

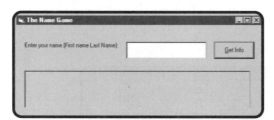

FIGURE 2.13

The name game.

The name game takes a string as input (your name) and searches through it for various tidbits of information. It can tell you your first name and last name and how many characters your name has. It is a good example of how Visual Basic string functions can derive almost any information you want from data.

Before I show you the name game program, take a look at some of the following common Visual Basic string functions in Table 2.15.

TABLE 2.15 COMMON STRING AND STRING-RELATED NUMERIC FUNCTIONS

Function	Example
Left	Left("Visual Basic", 4) results in "Visu"
Right	Right("Visual Basic", 3) results in "sic"
Mid	Mid("2/24/72", 3, 2) results in "24"
UCase	UCase("Number 7") results in "NUMBER 7"
Trim	Trim(" Bob Jones ") results in "Bob Jones"
Len	Len("February") results in 8
InStr	InStr("Visual Basic", "Bas") results in 8

Notice that I use double quotes when directly inserting a string into one of these functions. They are required unless you are using string variables. Also note that these functions do not take the same number of parameters or arguments. Some of the functions require only one argument, and others require two or three. Here's what each of these functions is doing and what is required for their operation to be successful:

- The Left function pulls out a string from an input string starting from the left side of the input string. It takes two parameters: One is the input string that you want to search through, and the other is how far you want the function to go or stop when deriving an output string.

- The Right function is similar to the Left function, except it starts searching through the input string starting from the right side. It also takes two parameters as input.

- The Mid function can pull out a string from anywhere in an input string. It takes three parameters as input. The first parameter is the string you want to search through. The second parameter is the starting position of where you want to search. And the last parameter is how far you want to go from the starting position.

- UCase is commonly used in validating user input. It makes any lowercase letters uppercase. It takes only one string as a parameter.

- The Trim function cuts off any spaces that precede or trail a string. But it does not remove spaces within a string. It takes one string as a parameter.

- The Len function is a string-related numeric function. It can tell you how many characters are contained in any given string (including spaces). It takes only one string as its parameter and returns an integer (the number of characters found in the string).

- InStr is another string-related numeric function. It searches through a string and finds the starting position of what you are looking for. It takes two parameters as input. The first parameter is the string you want to search through, and the second parameter is what you want to search for. The InStr function returns an integer as output (the starting position of the string being searched for). If a match is not found, InStr returns a zero (0).

Using one or more of these string functions, you can pull out almost anything you want from a string or text file. This capability is what makes text and strings and their associated functions so valuable and useful.

Now let me show you the complete code for the name game so you can see how I used some of these functions:

```
Option Explicit

Private Sub cmdGetName_Click()

Dim lsFirstName As String
Dim lsLastName As String
Dim lsFullName As String
Dim liSpace As Integer
Dim liFullNameLength As Integer

lsFullName = txtName.Text
liFullNameLength = Len(txtName.Text)
```

```
liSpace = InStr(lsFullName, " ")
lsFirstName = Left(lsFullName, liSpace - 1)
lsLastName = Right(lsFullName, liFullNameLength - liSpace)

picOutput.Print "Your first name is " & lsFirstName
picOutput.Print "Your last name is " & lsLastName
picOutput.Print "There are " & liFullNameLength - 1 & _
" characters in your name"

End Sub
```

I have put all the necessary code for the name game in the click event of one command button. First, I declare three string variables and two integer variables. My goal is to derive the first name, last name, and length of the name from what the user has entered into one text box. Of course, I can give the user two separate text boxes to enter first and last names, but hey, that takes away from the fun of strings and their functions.

Next, I assign the text property of the txtName text box to the variable lsFullName. Now that I have this string, I want to find out how long the user's name is. I can use the Len function and assign its output to an integer variable (in this case, liFullNameLength).

Now, I want to pull out the first and last name separately. To accomplish this, I rely on the assumption that the user entered his first name first and last name last and used a space, and not something like a comma, to separate the names. I use the InStr function to search for the space in the name. Once I have the starting position of the space in the name, I can use the Left and Right functions to assign output to string variables:

```
lsFirstName = Left(lsFullName, liSpace - 1)
```

When searching for the user's first name, I use the starting position of the space subtracted by 1 (otherwise, I end up with the space in the first name) as the stopping point for the string I want:

```
lsLastName = Right(lsFullName, liFullNameLength - liSpace)
```

To get the last name, I use the length of the name (rightmost position in the name) subtracted by the space. These two numbers represent the section in which the last name lives.

To output this information, I use a picture box. That's right; picture boxes aren't just for pictures. You can use them for outputting text as well. Take another look at the code that completes this program:

```
picOutput.Print "Your first name is " & lsFirstName
picOutput.Print "Your last name is " & lsLastName
picOutput.Print "There are " & liFullNameLength - 1 & _
" characters in your name"
```

I'm using a method of the picture box called Print to print a string in the picture box. Each time you call the Print method of a picture box, it adds a new line. The Print method takes a string as its argument. Here, I pass it two strings concatenated, or glued together. You can accomplish concatenation in Visual Basic using the special symbol & or the + sign. Notice that I include double quotes around a string but that I do not need them around a variable name. Another interesting note here is that I subtract 1 from the name length. If I didn't do this, the name length would represent the space between the two names. Figure 2.14 shows the output of the name game.

Table 2.16 describes the controls and properties of the name game.

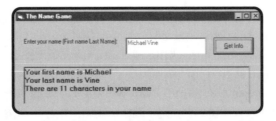

FIGURE 2.14

Manipulating strings with the name game.

TABLE 2.16 CONTROLS AS PROPERTIES OF THE NAME GAME

Control	Property	Setting
frmMain	Caption	The Name Game
lblName	Caption	Enter your name (First Name Last Name):
txtName	Text	Blank
cmdGetInfo	Caption	Get Info
picOutput	Picture	(None)

Programming Events

Events make up a substantial part of the Visual Basic world. They are a key component of what makes Visual Basic so popular and powerful. As mentioned in Chapter 1, event-driven programming is a new way of thinking; it takes the responsibility of designing the flow or control of a program away from the programmer and puts it in the hands of a user through the means of events. A user triggers an event through a keyboard or mouse, and you as a programmer write code to respond to it.

Hey, what else can I say: It's an event-driven world, it works, and users love it whether they know it or not. Anyone who used a program 10 or 20 years ago knows that she had little or no say over program control. The event-driven world has changed that. Users are now able to control program execution through programmable events.

Virtually every object or control in Visual Basic has events associated with it. It is your job as a Visual Basic programmer to write code that responds to these events. Now, it's not necessary to write code for every event that a given control may have, but you should be aware of what events a user (or a portion of code) can trigger in your program.

You can find a list of programmable events for an object or control in the Visual Basic code window. In Figure 2.15, I use the list boxes in the code window to view the programmable events of a command button in the name game program.

Figure 2.16 shows another small program that exhibits the usefulness of events. The program is called Around the World. It uses mouse events to trigger the changing of a label's caption property.

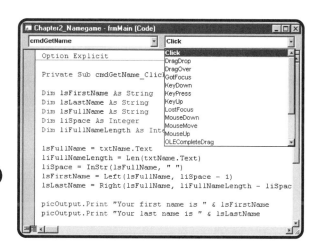

FIGURE 2.15

Programmable
events in the
code window.

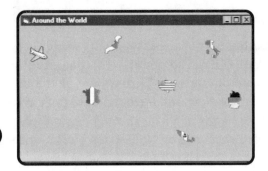

FIGURE 2.16

Around the World.

In previous programs, I placed most if not all code into one event procedure. In the Around the World program, I use multiple intrinsic mouse events called DragOver (I discuss in detail DragOver and DragDrop events in Chapter 11). The program setup is pretty simple; I use seven image controls and one label. I want someone to be able to drag the airplane image around the window, and when the airplane image is over an image of a country, I want the label's caption property to display the country name.

Here's all the code for the Around the World program:

```
Option Explicit


Private Sub Form_DragOver(Source As Control, X As Single, _
Y As Single, State As Integer)
    lblLocation.Caption = ""
End Sub
```

In this code segment, I want the label's caption property to display nothing when the plane is dragged over the form, but not over an image. I can accomplish this by writing code for the form's DragOver event. The DragOver event happens when a user clicks on a control and drags it over something. The DragOver event takes parameters that Visual Basic automatically creates for you when you access a DragOver event from the code window. Do not concern yourself with these parameters for now:

```
Private Sub imgFrance_DragOver(Source As Control, X As Single,_
    Y As Single, State As Integer)
    lblLocation.Caption = " You're now over France"
```

```
End Sub

Private Sub imgGermany_DragOver(Source As Control, X As Single,_
    Y As Single, State As Integer)
    lblLocation.Caption = " You're now over Germany"
End Sub

Private Sub imgMexico_DragOver(Source As Control, X As Single,_
    Y As Single, State As Integer)
     lblLocation.Caption = " You're now over Mexico"
End Sub

Private Sub imgUSA_DragOver(Source As Control, X As Single,_
    Y As Single, State As Integer)
    lblLocation.Caption = " You're now over the USA"
End Sub

Private Sub imgItaly_DragOver(Source As Control, X As Single,_
    Y As Single, State As Integer)
    lblLocation.Caption = " You're now over Italy"
End Sub

Private Sub imgJapan_DragOver(Source As Control, X As Single,_
    Y As Single, State As Integer)
    lblLocation.Caption = " You're now over Japan"
End Sub
```

When the plane is dragged over any of the country images, I want the label's caption property to change to that of the country name. To make an image (in this case, the airplane) drag-able, you have to set the DragIcon and DragMode Image properties.

The controls and properties of the Around the World program are described in Table 2.17.

Note that these icons can be found in the common directory of Visual Studio (that is, C:\Program Files\Microsoft Visual Studio\Common\Graphics).

TABLE 2.17 CONTROL AND PROPERTY SETTINGS FOR THE AROUND THE WORLD PROGRAM

Control	Property	Setting
frmMain	Caption	Around the World
imgPlane	DragIcon	(Icon)
	DragMode	1 – Automatic
	Picture	(Icon)
imgJapan	Picture	(Icon)
imgItaly	Picture	(Icon)
imgFrance	Picture	(Icon)
imgUSA	Picture	(Icon)
imgGermany	Picture	(Icon)
imgMexico	Picture	(Icon)
lblLocation	Caption	Blank

Compiling and Running Your Visual Basic Program

So far, so good; I hope by now you have created a few fun and easy-to-use programs. You would probably like to show off some of your work. How can you share your Visual Basic programs with others? Well, you can always bring someone over to your computer, open your Visual Basic project, and press F5 or click the right-arrow button on the toolbar to run your program. But, hey, that's not cool. What you probably want to do is to give your friend, spouse, or client a floppy disk with one file that she could run to view and use your program. Or maybe you can send him your program over a network, maybe through email, or, better yet, post it on your Web site. Hey, that would be really cool!

Most of the programs that you will learn to build in this book can be distributed in one file. However, sometimes one file is not enough. Microsoft does provide a Packaging and Deployment Wizard for these types of situations, which you will learn how to use in Chapter 12.

To run your Visual Basic program outside of the design-time IDE, you need to compile your project into an executable file. This process takes your project's files and turns their information into machine code that is contained in one executable file (exe). Once you create an executable file, it can be distributed and accessed by double-clicking it or opening it in a Microsoft environment such as Windows 95, Windows NT, Windows 98, Windows Millennium, or Windows 2000.

To compile your project, simply click the File menu and select Make *.exe, where the asterisk (*) represents the name of your project. Begin the compiling process as seen in Figure 2.17.

This process opens a new window where you can specify the location and name of your executable file. You can also click the Options button to change the version numbers of your program. Create an executable in Visual Basic as seen in Figure 2.18.

FIGURE 2.17

Selecting to make an exe file from the File menu.

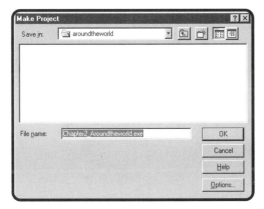

FIGURE 2.18

Creating an executable file.

Constructing the Word Art Program

It's time to build a program that allows a user to modify text entered into a text box control.

The Problem

How should the user be able to modify the text? I want users to be able to change the text's alignment, font, font size, and color. I also want to keep track of how many characters the user has entered into the text box through the use of events.

The tools you can use are controls and properties as seen in Table 2.18.

TABLE 2.18 CONTROLS AND PROPERTIES OF THE WORD ART PROGRAM

Control	Property	Setting
frmMain	Caption	Word Art
lblFont	Caption	Font:
txtFont	Text	Empty
	Enabled	False
txtDocument	Multiline	True
	Scrollbars	3 – Both
fraFont	Caption	Font Type:
cmdArial	Caption	&Arial
	Font	Arial
cmdTimesNewRoman	Caption	&Times New Roman
	Font	Times New Roman
cmdMsSansSerif	Caption	&MS Sans Serif
	Font	MS Sans Serif
fraFontStyle	Caption	Font Style:
cmdRegular	Caption	&Regular
cmdBold	Caption	&Bold
	Font	Bold
cmdItalic	Caption	&Italic
	Font	Italic
fraSize	Caption	Size:
optFont8	Caption	8

TABLE 2.18 CONTROLS AND PROPERTIES OF THE WORD ART PROGRAM (continued)

Control	Property	Setting
optFont10	Caption	10
optFont18	Caption	18
optFont24	Caption	24
fraAlignment	Caption	Alignment:
cmdLeft	Caption	&Left
cmdCenter	Caption	&Center
cmdRight	Caption	&Right
fraForeColor	Caption	Fore Color:
picForeBlack	BackColor	Black
	Picture	(None)
picForeWhite	BackColor	White
	Picture	(None)
picForeBlue	BackColor	Blue
	Picture	(None)
picForeYellow	BackColor	Yellow
	Picture	(None)
picForeGreen	BackColor	Green
	Picture	(None)
picForeRed	BackColor	Red
	Picture	(None)
fraBackColor	Caption	Back Color:
picBackBlack	BackColor	Black
	Picture	(None)
picBackWhite	BackColor	White
	Picture	(None)
picBackBlue	BackColor	Blue
	Picture	(None)
picBackYellow	BackColor	Yellow
	Picture	(None)
picBackGreen	BackColor	Green
	Picture	(None)
picBackRed	BackColor	Red
	Picture	(None)

HINT You can make a text box control appear to be something similar to the text editor you use every day in a program like Microsoft Word, Notepad, or WordPad by setting its Multiline and Scrollbars properties.

The process of building algorithms can be simplified by starting with a broad approach to identifying your steps. As you can see below, I only used four steps in my algorithm for the Word Art program.

1. Open a new Visual Basic standard EXE project.
2. Place all necessary controls on the default form.
3. Set applicable properties for each control.
4. Write code to respond to events.

The Implementation

All program code for the Word Art program can be seen below.

```
Option Explicit
'form level variables
Dim fiNumberOfCharacters As Integer
```

Here I declare one form-level variable that I will use in various procedures. Also note that I have a single quote in front of the phrase "form level variables." The single quote (')—or, as it is sometimes called, tick mark—denotes the start of a comment. As a programmer, you should get in the habit of commenting sections of your code. You will find comments useful when you return to a section of code that you haven't seen for some time. Comments are also useful to other programmers who might have to maintain or update your code. They help other people know what and why you are doing something.

The three command-button click events change the text box's FontName property. The FontName property takes a string as its argument. I also display the current font name in the smaller text box (txtFont) so the user will know what the current font is:

```
Private Sub cmdArial_Click()
    txtDocument.FontName = "Arial"
    txtFont.Text = txtDocument.FontName
End Sub

Private Sub cmdMsSansSerif_Click()
    txtDocument.FontName = "MS Sans Serif"
```

```
    txtFont.Text = txtDocument.FontName
End Sub


Private Sub cmdTimesNewRoman_Click()
    txtDocument.FontName = "Times New Roman"
    txtFont.Text = txtDocument.FontName
End Sub
```

To set the text in a text box to either italic or bold, you can call the Font.Bold or Font.Italic properties and set them to True:

```
Private Sub cmdBold_Click()
    txtDocument.Font.Bold = True
End Sub


Private Sub cmdItalic_Click()
    txtDocument.Font.Italic = True
End Sub
```

To un-bold or un-italicize text, you simply set the Font.Bold and Font.Italic properties to False:

```
Private Sub cmdRegular_Click()
    txtDocument.Font.Bold = False
    txtDocument.Font.Italic = False
End Sub
```

Next I change the alignment of the text with the alignment property of the text box. You can assign the alignment property the integers 0 for left (the default), 1 for right, or 2 for center:

```
Private Sub cmdCenter_Click()
    txtDocument.Alignment = 2
End Sub


Private Sub cmdLeft_Click()
    txtDocument.Alignment = 0
End Sub


Private Sub cmdRight_Click()
    txtDocument.Alignment = 1
End Sub
```

In the form load event, I do a little housekeeping by setting the txtFont text property to that of the txtDocument's FontName property. I also set the default font size to 8 and set the label's caption (lblNumCharacters) property:

```
Private Sub Form_Load()
    txtFont.Text = txtDocument.FontName
optFont8.Value = True
End Sub
```

I can change the font size by simply assigning a valid integer to the text box's FontSize property:

```
Private Sub optFont10_Click()
    txtDocument.FontSize = 10
End Sub


Private Sub optFont18_Click()
    txtDocument.FontSize = 18
End Sub


Private Sub optFont24_Click()
    txtDocument.FontSize = 24
End Sub


Private Sub optFont8_Click()
    txtDocument.FontSize = 8
End Sub
```

The following events are triggered when a user clicks on one of the picture boxes. In these events, I change either the foreground color with the text box's ForeColor property or the background color with the BackColor property. Either way, I assign the property to that of a Visual Basic intrinsic color constant such as vbYellow or vbBlack:

```
Private Sub picBackBlack_Click()
    txtDocument.BackColor = vbBlack
End Sub


Private Sub picBackBlue_Click()
    txtDocument.BackColor = vbBlue
End Sub
```

```vb
Private Sub picBackGreen_Click()
    txtDocument.BackColor = vbGreen
End Sub

Private Sub picBackRed_Click()
    txtDocument.BackColor = vbRed
End Sub

Private Sub picBackWhite_Click()
    txtDocument.BackColor = vbWhite
End Sub

Private Sub picBackYellow_Click()
    txtDocument.BackColor = vbYellow
End Sub

Private Sub picForeBlack_Click()
    txtDocument.ForeColor = vbBlack
End Sub

Private Sub picForeBlue_Click()
    txtDocument.ForeColor = vbBlue
End Sub

Private Sub picForeGreen_Click()
    txtDocument.ForeColor = vbGreen
End Sub

Private Sub picForeRed_Click()
    txtDocument.ForeColor = vbRed
End Sub

Private Sub picForeWhite_Click()
    txtDocument.ForeColor = vbWhite
End Sub

Private Sub picForeYellow_Click()
    txtDocument.ForeColor = vbYellow
End Sub
```

Summary

Whew! You have covered a lot of ground in this chapter, and you deserve a pat on the back.

In this chapter, you were able to dive deeper into the Visual Basic landscape to learn more about the controls you saw in the first chapter and new controls presented in this chapter. Along with the controls, you uncovered their associated properties and events and how to use and manipulate them. You also took your first step into the world of programming to unearth programming fundamentals associated with Visual Basic variables, constants, arithmetic, strings, basic functions, and naming conventions.

In addition, you learned how to exploit new events such as DragOver and learned what events are capable of and what they should mean to you as a programmer. Last but not least, you now know how to compile your Visual Basic programs so you can run them from other locations or distribute them to friends, family, co-workers, or even clients.

You did all this work by looking at various programs associated with specific topics in this chapter. I hope that you had a chance to build these programs yourself. If so, you know how far you have come since the first chapter and what a great future you and Visual Basic can have.

See you in Chapter 3, where I cover conditions and making decisions.

CHALLENGES

1. Create a program that adds, subtracts, multiplies, and divides two numbers.

2. Build a Mad Lib game. A Mad Lib game takes various inputs from a user and builds a story around it. You can use controls that you have learned in this chapter to provide a user with choices or options and maybe a text box that allows her to enter a phrase. You could then take this information to build a funny story using strings and string concatenation displayable in either a text box or picture box.

3. Create a whack-a-mole game with image controls and click events.

4. Design a child's educational game that allows him to drag an icon or image around a window to visit various places in your neighborhood, state, country, or even the solar system. Each time a place is visited, a brief textual description should appear. Also, see whether you can figure out how to not only drag one image over another, but also drop the image being dragged onto the other image. Sounds like drag and drop to me.

CHAPTER 3

Making Decisions

Welcome back, fellow programmer. You will now move into an interesting programming territory that computer scientists like to call conditional expressions. Conditional expressions are really a way to include decision-making.

In this chapter, I specifically cover the following topics:

- Boolean logic

- If conditions

- Select case conditions

- Timer control

- Intelligent programs

You will learn in this chapter how to make decisions the programmers' way or, more specifically, the Visual Basic way. You will find that once you learn conditional expressions, the programming and Visual Basic world becomes even more exciting than what you have seen so far.

How so, you ask? Well, decisions are not only a staple in programming, but they also let you build some interesting programs—programs I like to call games! That's right: It's all about decisions, and games are loaded with them. In fact, you might have heard of an area in computer science called artificial intelligence. Artificial intelligence (AI) is a relatively new science with math, engineering, and theoretical foundations. Sitting on top of these mathematical, engineering, and theoretical foundations are decisions that a software program must make to seem intelligent.

To teach the art of decision-making in Visual Basic, I show you some history behind conditional expressions and various programming techniques for implementing decision-making through various programs. At the end of this chapter, you will build the time-honored game of tic-tac-toe with simulated intelligence for the chapter's capstone experience. This is going to be an exciting and challenging chapter, so put your seat belt on and get your mouse and keyboard ready. I know you are up for it, so let's get started.

Project: Tic-Tac-Toe

This ain't your sister's tic-tac-toe game; this is tic-tac-toe with an attitude. You don't play this tic-tac-toe game against another person; instead, you and the computer play. You will build the necessary intelligence to make the computer think about defensive moves to keep you from winning.

As depicted in Figure 3.1, the tic-tac-toe game uses various forms of conditions to simulate intelligence.

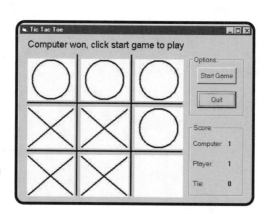

FIGURE 3.1

Tic-tac-toe game.

Before you learn how to build conditional expressions, I share with you the history and science behind programmable conditions.

Boolean Logic

Programmable conditions in Visual Basic, and any other language, for that matter, are based on a branch of mathematics called Boolean algebra, or *Boolean logic*. Boolean logic lets you represent and manipulate two values called true and false. Remember from Chapter 2 that computers store data in a binary form such as 0s and 1s. It is easy to compare Boolean logic to computer architecture if you equate true to the binary value 1 and false to the binary value 0. If you can see that anything stored in your computer is represented by 1s and 0s, you can also see that data stored in your computer can also be represented by the Boolean terms true and false.

> ### Definition
>
> *Boolean logic* is named after its father, George Boole, who was a mathematician in the 19th century. He had little formal schooling but was still able to teach himself mathematics. Though interested in other areas of mathematics, George went on to develop his own branch of logic containing the values true and false and the operators AND, OR, and NOT that manipulate them. It's ironic that the importance of George Boole's research and development into this new branch of logic was not realized until the invention on today's computer architecture.

The expressions AND, OR, and NOT represent the basic Boolean expressions for manipulating the Boolean values true and false. Each of these expressions evaluates to either a true or false value. To see how these expressions can produce Boolean values, take a look at the following *truth tables*.

> ### Definition
>
> *Truth tables* present the graphical representation of Boolean expressions and their associated inputs and outputs.

Figure 3.2 represents the truth table for the AND expression. The AND expression takes two inputs, a and b. Each input can be either true or false, and two inputs produce a total of four combinations or possibilities for output.

The only occasion when the Boolean expression AND results in a true expression is when each input is true. Any time either or both inputs are false, the whole expression is false.

Inputs		Output a AND b
a	b	
True	True	True
True	False	False
False	True	False
False	False	False

FIGURE 3.2

Truth table for the
AND expression.

Take a real-world example of the Boolean expression AND. "I can go to the grocery store if I have money and transportation." I have two inputs for my AND expression, money and transportation. The only time that I can go to the grocery store is when I have money (when true) and transportation (when true). If either of these inputs is false, then the whole expression is false.

The OR expression is similar to the AND expression in that it takes two inputs (a and b). However, the resulting outputs are quite different, as you can see in Figure 3.3.

The OR expression can result in a true output as long as one of the inputs is true. The only circumstance where an output is false in an OR expression is when both inputs are false.

For example, "My spouse will be happy with me if I cook dinner or clean the dishes." Here, I have "cook dinner" and "clean the dishes" as two inputs for an OR expression. As long as I perform one of the inputs (or both of them), my spouse will be happy. However, if I perform none of the inputs (both are false), then the whole expression is false, and I'll be sleeping on the sofa (but that's another story).

As seen in Figure 3.4, the NOT expression takes one input. Because it takes only one input, there are only two possible scenarios for the output. You can think of

Inputs		Output a OR b
a	b	
True	True	True
True	False	True
False	True	True
False	False	False

FIGURE 3.3

Truth table for the
OR expression.

Input a	Output NOT a
True	False
False	True

FIGURE 3.4

Truth table for the
NOT expression.

the NOT expression as the opposite of whatever the input is. For example, the NOT of false is true, and the NOT of true is false.

Let me show you a mathematical approach to solving Boolean expressions through the following Boolean problems. Assume that x = 1 and y = 5:

- (y = 4) AND (x = 1) results in the value false.
- (x = 5) OR (x = 1) results in the value true.
- (x = 1) AND (y = 5) results in the value true.
- (y = x) OR (x = 5) results in the value false.
- NOT [(x = 1) OR (x = y)] results in the value false.

If Then Else

One way Visual Basic uses the Boolean values true and false is with the If Then Else keywords. Here are some basic syntax examples:

```
If (condition1 = condition2) Then
    'Do this
End If
```

 HINT Notice that I used parentheses to surround the condition. Although they're not required, you should get in the habit of using them to eliminate any confusion or incorrect results. The benefits of parentheses will be more apparent when you learn and use compound conditions.

For the 'Do this to happen, condition1 has to equal condition2; otherwise, the 'Do this part will not happen.

Here's another example of an if condition:

```
If (condition1 = condition2) Then
  'Do this
Else
   'Do that
End If
```

This condition is similar to the previous one with one exception. This condition is using the Else keyword to say "Well, okay, if condition1 does not equal condition2, then do something else (in this case, 'Do that).

You can use the Else keyword when you want something to still happen if the condition is not met. But what if you have many scenarios you want to check in one condition? The answer is to use the Elseif keyword. You can use the Elseif keyword to check one condition for many possibilities. Here's how I would use Elseif to find out who is the current player:

```
If (currentPlayer = Player1) Then
   'Assign high score to Player1
ElseIf (currentPlayer = Player2) Then
   'Assign high score to Player2
ElseIf (currentPlayer = Player3) Then
   'Assign high score to Player3
Else
   'There is no current player
End if
```

I'm checking the currentPlayer variable against three scenarios to see whether the current player is Player1, Player2, or Player3. If none of these scenarios is true, then my Else clause applies.

The statement End If is used to end an If condition. Though generally required at the end of each logical block of conditions, you can create a one-line If condition that requires no End If.

```
If (x  = y ) Then   x = 5
```

The above statement serves no real purpose other than demonstrating a one-line If condition that requires no End If.

TRAP

As a computer science instructor, I can tell you that the most common problem I see in people learning how to use conditions is not with the logic, but with their style. What do I mean by style? With conditions, I'm referring to style as indenting and using parentheses. I promise that if you do not get in the habit of indenting your conditions early, it will come back to haunt you later. Conditions that are not indented properly can be difficult and frustrating to read. A general rule of thumb is to indent two spaces or one tab when using conditions. You can come up with your own standard as long as it's easy to read and you stay consistent.

Take a look at the following two If conditions. They are both the same, but one is indented correctly and uses parentheses accordingly. Can you see a difference?

Here's the correct way:

```
If (condition1 = condition2) Then
    If (conditionX >= conditionY) And (Temp1 = Temp2) Then
        'Go here
    Else
        'Go there
    End If
Else
    'Do that
End If
```

This is the incorrect way:

```
If condition1 = condition2 Then
If conditionX >= conditionY And Temp1 = Temp2 Then
'Go here
Else
'Go there
End If
Else
'Do that
End If
```

Compound Conditions

Compound conditions are based on Boolean logic. They take the same form as the If Then Else statements you learned earlier with one exception. Compound conditions use Boolean expressions to evaluate a condition. Here's an example:

```
If (condition1 = condition2) And (conditionX = conditionY) Then
    'Do this
End If
```

For the 'Do this code to run, condition1 must equal condition2 and conditionX must equal conditionY. There are no exceptions to the And expression; both sides of the And expression must be true for the whole expression to evaluate as true.

If we take the same condition and replace the And expression with an Or expression, we get different possibilities:

```
If (condition1 = condition2) Or (conditionX = conditionY) Then
    'Do this
End If
```

Unlike the And expression, the Or expression needs only one side of the expression to evaluate to true for the whole expression to be true.

When necessary, compound conditions need not stop at two conditions. You can combine multiple conditions of various types to make one compound condition. Here's an example that uses two And conditions and one Or condition to make a compound condition.

```
If ((condition1 = condition2) And (conditionX = conditionY)) Or (condi-
tion1 = conditionX) Then
    'Do this
End If
```

Notice that I've embedded my parentheses to make clear the order of operations in the above compound condition.

Using the following values, what do you think the compound condition would evaluate to? In other words, would the 'Do this part of the code execute?

```
condition1 = 5
condition2 = 10
conditionX = 5
conditionY = 10
```

If you answered either True or Yes, you are correct. I'll place the preceding values into the condition so that you can get a better look at what is happening.

```
If ((5 = 10) And (5 = 10)) Or (5 = 5) Then
  'Do this
End If
```

Each condition above evaluates to an equivalent Boolean expression below that results in an overall True value.

```
(False And False) Or True
False Or True
True
```

Nested If Statements

Sometimes you need to embed conditions using If statements. For example, let's say you are adding an enhancement to a game that not only checks for a direct hit but also checks for a high score. To accomplish this, you could use the following nested conditions:

```
If (directHit = target) Then
    If (currentScore > highScore) Then
        'Display new high score
    End If
    'Increment current score
End If
```

The first part of this condition checks for a direct hit. If this condition is True, a new nested condition is checked for a high score. If there is a new high score, then it is displayed. If there is no new high score, then nothing else happens in the nested If condition. After the nested If condition is complete, the current score is incremented, but only if the parent condition (first condition) evaluated to True.

Interestingly, if the first condition is not met, then the nested If statement is never processed. It is important to understand that nested conditions belong to their parent (if you will) conditions. If I want to ensure that a high score is always checked, regardless of a direct hit; then I pull the high-score condition check out of its parent condition.

The best way to understand conditions is to see them in action or, in other words, to program. Here's a more advanced adder program that I built using If conditions and the KeyPress event.

Figure 3.5 depicts a more advanced adder program that uses conditions.

HINT

The KeyPress event is similar to the KeyDown event that you have already seen. Remember, the KeyDown event captures all keyboard responses, such as numbers, letters, function keys, arrow keys, Shift, Alt, Ctrl, and many others.

In contrast, the KeyPress event only tracks alphabetic and numeric keyboard responses. Another difference is that the KeyDown event takes the KeyCode as a parameter, and the KeyPress event takes the KeyAscii as a parameter.

Both KeyAscii and KeyCode parameters are integers and take an ASCII value. However, be careful: Not every ASCII value will be translated correctly from the KeyDown to the KeyPress event. For a list of character codes and character sets, refer to Appendix A, "Common ASCII Codes."

The advanced adder program is a continuation of the adder program that I did in Chapter 2. However, it has more features than its predecessor, such as a better graphical interface and the ability to use keyboard and mouse for input. Here's the code that runs the advanced adder program. First I declare three form-level variables:

```
Option Explicit
'Form-level variables
Dim fsOperand1 As Single
Dim fsOperand2 As Single
Dim fbPeriodUsed As Boolean
```

Two of the variables house the values of the first and second operand. The third form-level variable fbPeriodUsed tells me whether the user has already used a period in one of the operands. What this really does is prevent the user from entering more than one decimal in a number for a given operand.

The advanced
adder program.

In all of the following click events, I add the appropriate number to the Text property of the text box. You can also see that I do more than add a number to the text box; I concatenate it to the existing text:

```
Private Sub cmd0_Click()
    txtDisplay.Text = txtDisplay.Text + "0"
End Sub


Private Sub cmd1_Click()
    txtDisplay.Text = txtDisplay.Text + "1"
End Sub


Private Sub cmd2_Click()
    txtDisplay.Text = txtDisplay.Text + "2"
End Sub


Private Sub cmd3_Click()
    txtDisplay.Text = txtDisplay.Text + "3"
End Sub


Private Sub cmd4_Click()
    txtDisplay.Text = txtDisplay.Text + "4"
End Sub


Private Sub cmd5_Click()
    txtDisplay.Text = txtDisplay.Text + "5"
End Sub


Private Sub cmd6_Click()
    txtDisplay.Text = txtDisplay.Text + "6"
End Sub


Private Sub cmd7_Click()
    txtDisplay.Text = txtDisplay.Text + "7"
End Sub


Private Sub cmd8_Click()
    txtDisplay.Text = txtDisplay.Text + "8"
End Sub
```

```
Private Sub cmd9_Click()
    txtDisplay.Text = txtDisplay.Text + "9"
End Sub
```

In the cmdAdd_Click() event, I assign the value of the text box's Text property (only if there's something in it) to that of a variable. Note that I also use the Val function to convert the string (which contains numbers) to a number. In addition, I perform some other cleanup to prepare for the next operand, such as setting the fbPeriodUsed to False (so another operand can use it), clearing the text box, disabling the add command button, and setting the equals command button to true:

```
Private Sub cmdAdd_Click()


If txtDisplay.Text <> "" Then
    fsOperand1 = Val(txtDisplay.Text)
    fbPeriodUsed = False
    txtDisplay.Text = ""
    cmdAdd.Enabled = False
    cmdEquals.Enabled = True
End If


End Sub
```

I perform the same check in the cmdEquals_Click() event to look for an empty text box so that if the text box is empty and the user presses the equals command button, nothing happens. However, if the user enters a number, I assign that number to a variable; take it and the first operand's result (via addition); and assign it back to the Text property of the text box. After that, I perform some more cleanup by setting the operand variables to 0 and disabling the add and equals command buttons:

```
Private Sub cmdEquals_Click()


If txtDisplay.Text <> "" Then
    fsOperand2 = Val(txtDisplay.Text)
    txtDisplay.Text = fsOperand1 + fsOperand2
    fsOperand1 = 0
    fsOperand2 = 0
    cmdAdd.Enabled = False
    cmdEquals.Enabled = False
```

```
End If


End Sub
```

The cmdClear_Click() event is strictly a housekeeping event. Just like the clear button in any given calculator, it clears everything for a new start:

```
Private Sub cmdClear_Click()
    txtDisplay.Text = ""
    fbPeriodUsed = False
    cmdAdd.Enabled = True
    cmdEquals.Enabled = False
    fsOperand1 = 0
    fsOperand2 = 0
End Sub
```

The Click() event of the cmdPeriod command button is quite interesting. Here I declare a new local variable lbPeriodFound for use only in this procedure: (Do not confuse this local variable with fbPeriodUsed.)

```
Private Sub cmdPeriod_Click()

Dim lbPeriodFound As Boolean

'Make sure period has not been deleted
If InStr(1, txtDisplay.Text, ".") = 0 Then
    fbPeriodUsed = False
End If

If fbPeriodUsed = False Then
    txtDisplay.Text = txtDisplay.Text + "."
    fbPeriodUsed = True
Else
    Beep
End If


End Sub
```

I perform this additional check to look for one case in particular. What happens if a user successfully enters the period in a number? The fbPeriodUsed variable is then set to True. But what happens if the user deletes the period using the delete key and tries to re-enter a period? This is what the new condition looks for. To successfully look for this condition, I can use the string function InStr, which searches for a pattern in a string. (In my case, I'm looking for a period.) If I do not find the period in the string, I then set the fbPeriodUsed variable to False so the period can be used in the condition below it.

The Sub Form_Load() event sets the fbPeriodUsed to False and disables the equals command:

```
Private Sub Form_Load()
    fbPeriodUsed = False
    cmdEquals.Enabled = False
End Sub
```

The KeyPress event of the text box contains some interesting code. The first thing you probably notice is that I perform the same check as I did in the period command button. I have to perform this check twice so if the incoming keystroke is a period (not a mouse event on the period command button), I can see whether it really is already in use by the current operand:

```
Private Sub txtDisplay_KeyPress(KeyAscii As Integer)

Dim lbPeriodFound As Boolean
'Make sure period has not been deleted
If InStr(1, txtDisplay.Text, ".") = 0 Then
    fbPeriodUsed = False
End If


If KeyAscii = 46 Then
    If fbPeriodUsed = True Then
        KeyAscii = 0
        Beep
    Else
        fbPeriodUsed = True
    End If
    Exit Sub
End If


If (KeyAscii < 48 Or KeyAscii > 57) Then 'Only use numbers 0-9
    KeyAscii = 0
End If


End Sub
```

Notice that I use the same variable lbPeriodFound in two different procedures. As far as the operating system is concerned, these are two separate variables because as soon as the procedure is left, the variable loses its scope.

Next I perform some tricky work with KeyAscii values. The KeyAscii value 46 represents the period (.). If the incoming keystroke is a period, then do one of two following things. If it is a period and the period has already been used, then set the KeyAscii value to something else (0) and use the Beep function to warn the user that he can't do that. However, if the period has not been used, then go ahead and use it and set fbPeriodUsed to True. Either way, if the incoming keystroke is a period, I exit the procedure using the keyword Exit Sub.

The keyword Exit Sub exits the procedure immediately without performing any further processing and returns control to the calling procedure, event, or function. It's most often used for error-handling purposes, but I use it here because there is no need for me to continue with the last conditional check if the incoming keystroke is a period.

The last check in the KeyPress event basically indicates that you allow the user to press only numbers on the keyboard (at least when the cursor is in this particular text box). In other words, if the KeyAscii value is not between 48 and 57 (numbers 0 through 9), then set the KeyAscii value to something else.

Note that some controls such as Forms and Text Boxes have their own KeyPress and KeyDown events. In the case of the adder program, keystrokes can only be captured when the txtDisplay Text Box has focus.

TRICK Focus can be changed with code by setting the TabIndex property to 0.

```
Private Sub Form_Load()
Command1.TabIndex = 0
End Sub
```

Definition

Focus indicates that a control is ready to receive input either from the mouse or keyboard.

Using the SetFocus method can also change focus. The SetFocus method is only available with controls that can receive focus.

```
Private Sub Command1_Click()
Option1.SetFocus
End Sub
```

Table 3.1 shows the controls and properties of the adder program.

TABLE 3.1 CONTROLS AND PROPERTIES FOR THE ADVANCED ADDER PROGRAM

Control	Property	Setting
frmMain	Caption	Advanced Adder
fraCalculator	Caption	Adder:
txtDisplay	Text	Empty
cmdClear	Caption	C
cmdAdd	Caption	+
cmdEquals	Caption	=
cmdPeriod	Caption	.
cmd0	Caption	0
cmd1	Caption	1
cmd2	Caption	2
cmd3	Caption	3
cmd4	Caption	4
cmd5	Caption	5
cmd6	Caption	6
cmd7	Caption	7
cmd8	Caption	8
cmd9	Caption	9

Select Case Conditions

Most languages provide another mechanism for generating conditions and making decisions in addition to the If statement. Visual Basic provides this alternative with the Select Case structure. The Select Case structure is useful when you want to check a variable or an expression against multiple possible values. Any condition generated with the Select Case structure can also be constructed via If statements.

Here's the general syntax for the Select Case structure:

```
Select Case expression or variable
    Case range, constant, or variable
        'Statements
```

```
Case range, constant, or variable
    'Statements
Case range, constant, or variable
    'Statements
Case Else
    'Statements
End Select
```

The first part of the Select Case structure tells Visual Basic what you want to compare, such as properties, variables, or expressions. Each case thereafter contains a specific scenario with values, such as variables, constants, properties, numbers, characters, or a range. The Case Else statement executes if none of the cases is met. There is no limit to how many cases you can have.

Here's another example that looks for the current player of a game:

```
Select Case CurrentPlayer
    Case Player1
        'Statements
    Case Player2
        'Statements
    Case Player3
        'Statements
    Case Else
        'Statements
End Select
```

And here's an example that uses number ranges in each case to check for the current temperature:

```
Select Case CurrentTemp
    Case > 90
        'Statements
    Case 60 To 89
        'Statements
    Case 32 To 59
        'Statements
    Case Else
        'Statements
End Select
```

Timer Control

The timer control is another built-in control available in the Visual Basic standard EXE project. You can find it within the Visual Basic toolbox during design time. As seen in Figure 3.6, you can add the timer control to a Visual Basic form just as you would add any other control.

Once placed on a form, the timer control is only visible during design time and its size and position have no relevance. However, two timer control properties that do have relevance are Enabled and Interval:

- The Enabled property is what triggers the timer control to start or stop. Its values are Boolean (true and false).

- Interval is the number of milliseconds between the timer events. Generally speaking, 1,000 milliseconds equals 1 second, which it does mathematically, but there can be some error in the interval's precision.

TRAP Be aware that using multiple timer controls can consume substantial CPU resources, in turn slowing the overall performance of your computer.

Timer controls can serve many purposes, such as automating the triggering of events, functions, and subprocedures on an automatic or semi-automatic basis. As illustrated in Figure 3.7, I've built a small digital clock program with the timer control.

FIGURE 3.6

The timer control.

FIGURE 3.7

The clock program.

I think you will be surprised about how easy it is to build the clock program. Looking at the program code, you can see that it requires only one small procedure to generate the time:

```
Option Explicit


Private Sub Timer1_Timer()
    lblDisplay.Caption = Time
End Sub
```

I set the Interval property of the timer control to 1,000 milliseconds, or 1 second. So once per second, the program triggers the Timer event, which assigns the time function to the caption property of the label control.

HINT The time function is a built-in Visual Basic function that returns the current system time. In addition to the time function, Visual Basic provides the date function, which returns the current date of the system.

Unlike other functions such as Val, the date and time functions do not require any parameters. See Chapter 5 for more information on functions.

Table 3.2 depicts the controls and properties on the clock program.

Timer controls can serve another useful purpose through animation. Using a timer control, you can swap various images to give the appearance of movement, such as flying, walking, running, exploding, and shooting.

The trickiest part of animation is finding the right sequence of graphics to animate. Lucky for us, I found a great Visual Basic site on the Internet (http://www.vbexplorer.com), which lets us use its great character pictures created by professional artist Hermann Hillmann.

Figure 3.8 shows a simple program that animates a figure to walk and run.

TABLE 3.2 CONTROLS AND PROPERTIES OF THE CLOCK PROGRAM

Control	Property	Setting
frmMain	Caption	Clock
lblDisplay	Caption	None
Timer1	Enabled	True
	Interval	1000

FIGURE 3.8

Simple animation using the timer control.

This simple animation program appears to show only one image that is walking or running. But you see during the design-time view of the program in Figure 3.9 that it actually uses nine images. Eight of the images are still figures depicting a particular movement (in this case walking forward), and the ninth image is just an empty container.

Note that the images used for this program can be found on the CD-ROM accompanying this book.

Let's take a look at how this works. Here I declare one form-level variable that I use in the Form Load event and in the Timer event:

```
Option Explicit
Dim x As Integer
```

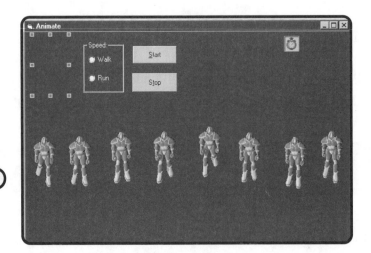

FIGURE 3.9

Simple animation program during design time.

In the Form Load event, I set the variable x to 1 (you will see why in a moment), the walk option button to True, and the empty image control to one of the eight images that contain a picture:

```
Private Sub Form_Load()
    x = 1
    optWalk.Value = True
    imgAnimate.Picture = Image3.Picture
End Sub
```

For the start command button, I set the timer control's Enabled property to True. This starts the automatic triggering of the Timer event based on the Interval property:

```
Private Sub cmdStart_Click()
    Timer1.Enabled = True
End Sub
```

If the user wants to stop the animation, he can simply click the stop command button, which sets the Timer's Enabled property to False:

```
Private Sub cmdStop_Click()
    Timer1.Enabled = False
End Sub
```

When the run option button is clicked, the timer's Interval property is set to 50.

```
Private Sub optRun_Click()
    Timer1.Interval = 50
End Sub
```

To slow down the character to a walking speed, I simply increase the Interval property to 200:

```
Private Sub optWalk_Click()
    Timer1.Interval = 200
End Sub
```

The actual animation occurs in the timer's Timer event. Here you see that I use the Select Case structure you saw earlier in this chapter:

```
Private Sub Timer1_Timer()
Select Case x
    Case 1
        imgAnimate.Picture = Image1.Picture
```

```
    Case 2
        imgAnimate.Picture = Image2.Picture
    Case 3
        imgAnimate.Picture = Image3.Picture
    Case 4
        imgAnimate.Picture = Image4.Picture
    Case 5
        imgAnimate.Picture = Image5.Picture
    Case 6
        imgAnimate.Picture = Image6.Picture
    Case 7
        imgAnimate.Picture = Image7.Picture
    Case 8
        imgAnimate.Picture = Image8.Picture
    Case Else
        x = 0
End Select

'Increment x by 1
x = x + 1

End Sub
```

You should also be able to see that I test the select case structure with the variable x. The first time the timer event is triggered, the Select Case detects that the variable x is equal to 1 (remember the form load event). After that, x is incremented by 1. This continues to happen, and a new image is displayed each time, until x is not equal to some number between 1 and 8. The Case Else clause detects this, and sets x back to 1. The cycle repeats itself until someone sets the timer's Enabled property to False (or clicks the stop button).

Table 3.3 depicts the controls and properties used in the animation program.

If you like this type of program development, you should really enjoy Chapter 10, where you will go much further into the world of animation.

TABLE 3.3 CONTROLS AND PROPERTIES OF THE ANIMATION PROGRAM

Control	Property	Setting
frmMain	Caption	Animation
Timer1	Enabled	False
fraSpeed	Caption	Speed:
optWalk	Caption	Walk
optRun	Caption	Run
cmdStart	Caption	&Start
cmdStop	Caption	S&top
imgAnimate	Picture	None
	Visible	True
Image1	Picture	Bitmap
	Visible	False
Image2	Picture	Bitmap
	Visible	False
Image3	Picture	Bitmap
	Visible	False
Image4	Picture	Bitmap
	Visible	False
Image5	Picture	Bitmap
	Visible	False
Image6	Picture	Bitmap
	Visible	False
Image7	Picture	Bitmap
	Visible	False
Image8	Picture	Bitmap
	Visible	False

Building Intelligent Programs

To build the tic-tac-toe game, you need to learn a little bit more about algorithms and decision-making. A common tool in the development of algorithms is the decision tree. Decision trees consist of nodes and branches, where nodes act as decisions or ending points and branches are the direction taken based on a decision or outcome. Computer scientists use decision trees to search through a list of possible choices until they find a target.

In the case of the tic-tac-toe game, I want to build computer intelligence that plays a defensive role by looking for a number of possible winning scenarios by the opponent.

As seen in Figure 3.10, the game of tic-tac-toe has eight possible combinations for a win.

Knowing that there are eight possibilities for a win in tic-tac-toe is not enough to build a searchable decision tree. To build a defensive decision tree, I need to know the circumstances that appear prior to an opponent reaching one of the eight possible wins.

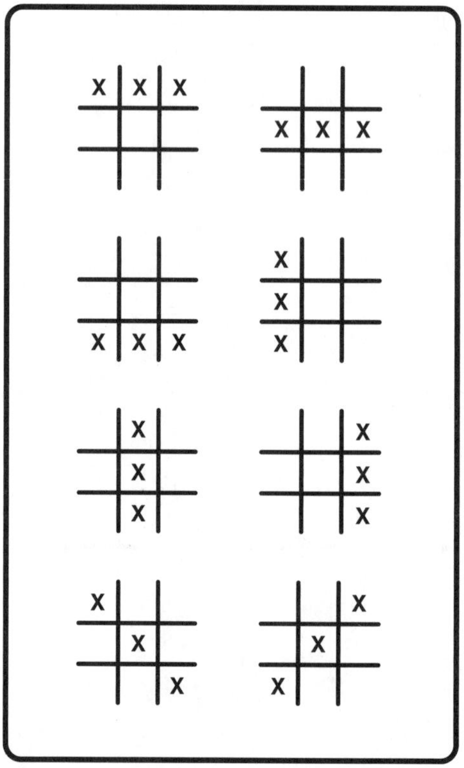

FIGURE 3.10

Eight possibilities for a win in tic-tac-toe.

These circumstances constitute 24 possible scenarios that occur prior to a win. To understand these scenarios, I number each possible tic-tac-toe square from 1 to 9.

Based on the numbered squares in Figure 3.11, I can start to build the 24 possible scenarios that occur prior to a win:

(1,3)	(1,2)	(2,3)	(4,6)
(4,5)	(5,6)	(7,9)	(7,8)
(8,9)	(1,7)	(1,4)	(4,7)
(2,8)	(2,5)	(5,8)	(3,9)
(3,6)	(6,9)	(1,5)	(3,5)
(1,9)	(3,7)	(5,9)	(5,7)

If you are unsure about how I came up with these scenarios, take the numbers in any scenario and place them in their corresponding areas in Figure 3.11. You should see that any of these scenarios represents a potential win in tic-tac-toe.

Now that I have the scenarios, I can start to build my decision tree.

Decision trees should start with a question or statement, in Figure 3.12, where I start with "Checking for a Winning Scenario." I first check for scenario 1 (each scenario contains an X in each corresponding square). If there is a match in scenario 1, then I stop searching, or in other words, the computer puts an O in the necessary square to prevent a win. If no match is found in scenario 1, I then look for a match in scenario 2. If no match is found, I keep searching for a match until the 24th possible scenario is examined. If no matches were found after the 24th scenario, the computer then places an O in the first available square.

My decision tree in Figure 3.12 is what computer scientists call a "brute-force" approach to solving a search scenario. In the game of tic-tac-toe, this is fine

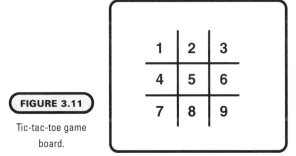

FIGURE 3.11

Tic-tac-toe game board.

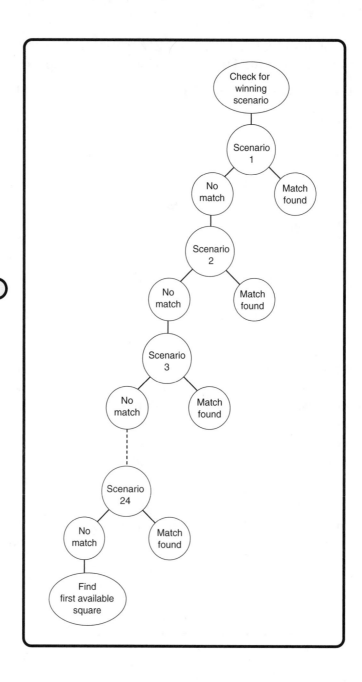

FIGURE 3.12

A decision tree.

because I have a small number of scenarios to search through. But what about other, more complicated games, such as chess? A brute-force approach to building a winning strategy game such as chess (via a decision tree) would take on the proportions of exponential growth. Or in other words, I would have a lot of tree branches in the decision tree.

Understanding that time (your time) and computing resources can be limited, you should make intelligent decision trees by keeping two things in mind:

- Pick a good starting point for your search by thinking about where you are (beginning point) and where you want to be (ending point).
- Make good decisions about where to go from any given node in the decision tree.

These steps should help you to limit the number of tree branches, thus eliminating the possibility of exponential growth in your searches.

Constructing the Tic-Tac-Toe Game

The tic-tac-toe game will challenge everything you have learned so far. You should now have the right knowledge base to follow most of the game's concepts.

The Problem

Build a graphical tic-tac-toe game where you play the computer. The computer should have logic to play defensively so that it counters potentially winning strategies. The game should keep track of the computer's, player's, and tie scores.

Figure 3.13 depicts the tic-tac-toe game in design time. Its controls and properties can be seen in Table 3.4.

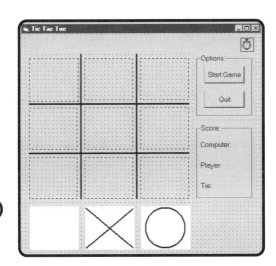

FIGURE 3.13

Tic-tac-toe game
in design time.

TABLE 3.4 CONTROLS AND PROPERTIES OF THE TIC-TAC-TOE GAME

Control	Property	Setting
frmMain	Caption	Tic Tac Toe
lblStatus	Caption	None
	Font	Arial, Size 14
fraOptions	Caption	Options:
cmdStart	Caption	Start
cmdQuit	Caption	Quit
fraScore	Caption	Score:
Label1	Caption	Computer:
Label2	Caption	Player:
Label3	Caption	Tie:
lblComputer	Caption	None
lblPlayer	Caption	None
lblTie	Caption	None
Timer1	Enabled	False
	Interval	2000
Image1	Picture	None
Image2	Picture	None
Image3	Picture	None
Image4	Picture	None
Image5	Picture	None
Image6	Picture	None
Image7	Picture	None
Image8	Picture	None
Image9	Picture	None
imgEmptySquare	Picture	Bitmap
	Visible	False
imgX	Picture	Bitmap
	Visible	False
imgO	Picture	Bitmap
	Visible	False

In the real world, programmers and software engineers take a simple algorithm such as the one that follows and break it down even further into subalgorithms. For instance, the algorithm that implements the artificial intelligence can have a subalgorithm all its own. Most experienced programmers go through a type of algorithm development to pinpoint the exact procedures and logic that they need to follow.

Some programmers even go so far as to take their algorithms down to pseudocode. Pseudocode is basically shorthand for programmers. It allows developers to quickly express the programming logic in English-like language without having to worry about the intricacies of language-specific syntax. Here's an example of pseudocode for checking whether the game is over:

```
If computer won or opponent won or tie, then
      end game
      increment score
else
      put an X or O in the square
end if
```

You can see that I'm using English-like language for pseudocode, but I'm not using procedure names, variable names, or other Visual Basic syntax.

You might notice that my algorithms are starting to get bigger. Well, that is because my games are becoming bigger or, better yet, more complicated:

1. Create a new standard EXE project.

2. Create necessary graphics, and place all controls on the form.

3. Create applicable form-level variables.

4. Write code in the form load event to initialize any variables or control settings.

5. Write code that responds to a user clicking on an image. This code should check for the following situations:

   • Is it the player's turn or the computer's turn?

   • Is there already an X or O in the square?

   • Has someone already won, or is there a tie?

   Depending on these answers, an X can be placed in the square, or the game will end and the score will be incremented appropriately.

6. Write code for the start game command button. This code should start the game by enabling the timer control.

7. Write code in the timer's Timer event that houses the artificial intelligence. The artificial intelligence should play a defensive role in searching the tic-tac-toe board for a potential win by the opponent. The Timer event should also check for a win or tie and increment the score accordingly.

8. Write code to quit the game.

9. Test the program.

The Implementation

All of the following are form-level variables that I use throughout various procedures and events:

```
Option Explicit
'Form-level variables
Dim fbSquare1X As Boolean
Dim fbSquare2X As Boolean
Dim fbSquare3X As Boolean
Dim fbSquare4X As Boolean
Dim fbSquare5X As Boolean
Dim fbSquare6X As Boolean
Dim fbSquare7X As Boolean
Dim fbSquare8X As Boolean
Dim fbSquare9X As Boolean

Dim fbSquare1O As Boolean
Dim fbSquare2O As Boolean
Dim fbSquare3O As Boolean
Dim fbSquare4O As Boolean
Dim fbSquare5O As Boolean
Dim fbSquare6O As Boolean
Dim fbSquare7O As Boolean
Dim fbSquare8O As Boolean
Dim fbSquare9O As Boolean

Dim fbTie As Boolean
Dim fbPlayerWon As Boolean
Dim fbComputerWon As Boolean
```

```
Dim fiTieScore As Integer
Dim fiComputerScore As Integer
Dim fiPlayerScore As Integer
Dim fsWhoseTurnIsIt  As String
```

The quit command button calls the End keyword, which terminates the application:

```
Private Sub cmdQuit_Click()
    End
End Sub
```

When the user clicks the start command button, it first disables itself (to prevent the user from causing funny results during the game if she clicks it again). It then sets a label caption property and calls a procedure Enable_Squares. Note that I created this procedure just for the purpose of enabling the squares, which you will see in a few moments. (I talk more about creating procedures in Chapter 5.) Next it sets the picture property of each image control to that of the empty picture image. And last, but not least, the Timer control is enabled:

```
Private Sub cmdStart_Click()


cmdStart.Enabled = False
lblStatus.Caption = "Your turn"


Enable_Squares


Image1.Picture = imgEmptySquare.Picture
Image2.Picture = imgEmptySquare.Picture
Image3.Picture = imgEmptySquare.Picture
Image4.Picture = imgEmptySquare.Picture
Image5.Picture = imgEmptySquare.Picture
Image6.Picture = imgEmptySquare.Picture
Image7.Picture = imgEmptySquare.Picture
Image8.Picture = imgEmptySquare.Picture
Image9.Picture = imgEmptySquare.Picture


Timer1.Enabled = True


End Sub
```

The form load event sets the timer control to False and performs a number of housekeeping chores, such as initializing form-level variables, setting various label captions, and calling a procedure that disables all squares. Disabling squares is important because you wouldn't want a user clicking out of turn, would you?

```
Private Sub Form_Load()

'Set program defaults and initialize variables
Timer1.Enabled = False
fbTie = False
fbPlayerWon = False
fbComputerWon = False

fbSquare1X = False
fbSquare2X = False
fbSquare3X = False
fbSquare4X = False
fbSquare5X = False
fbSquare6X = False
fbSquare7X = False
fbSquare8X = False
fbSquare9X = False

fbSquare10 = False
fbSquare20 = False
fbSquare30 = False
fbSquare40 = False
fbSquare50 = False
fbSquare60 = False
fbSquare70 = False
fbSquare80 = False
fbSquare90 = False


lblPlayer.Caption = "0"
lblComputer.Caption = "0"
lblTie.Caption = "0"
lblStatus.Caption = "Click start game to play"
```

```
Image1.Picture = imgEmptySquare.Picture
Image2.Picture = imgEmptySquare.Picture
Image3.Picture = imgEmptySquare.Picture
Image4.Picture = imgEmptySquare.Picture
Image5.Picture = imgEmptySquare.Picture
Image6.Picture = imgEmptySquare.Picture
Image7.Picture = imgEmptySquare.Picture
Image8.Picture = imgEmptySquare.Picture
Image9.Picture = imgEmptySquare.Picture


Disable_Squares


'You can toggle this variable for who starts
'the game off: computer or player
fsWhoseTurnIsIt  = "player"


End Sub
```

Because each square's click event contains the same code for images 1 through 9, I will only show the first three. After that you should get a feel for the rest (all code for the tic-tac-toe game can be found on the accompanying CD).

```
Private Sub Image1_Click()


If fsWhoseTurnIsIt  = "player" Then
    If fbSquare1X = False And fbSquare1O = False Then
       Image1.Picture = imgX.Picture
       fbSquare1X = True
       Disable_Squares
       If Checkforwin = False Then
           fsWhoseTurnIsIt  = "computer"
           lblStatus.Caption = "Computer is thinking..."
       End If
    End If
End If


End Sub


Private Sub Image2_Click()
```

```
If fsWhoseTurnIsIt  = "player" Then
    If fbSquare2X = False And fbSquare2O = False Then
        Image2.Picture = imgX.Picture
        fbSquare2X = True
        Disable_Squares
        If Checkforwin = False Then
            fsWhoseTurnIsIt  = "computer"
            lblStatus.Caption = "Computer is thinking..."
        End If
    End If
End If


End Sub


Private Sub Image3_Click()


If fsWhoseTurnIsIt  = "player" Then
    If fbSquare3X = False And fbSquare3O = False Then
        Image3.Picture = imgX.Picture
        fbSquare3X = True
        Disable_Squares
        If Checkforwin = False Then
            fsWhoseTurnIsIt  = "computer"
            lblStatus.Caption = "Computer is thinking..."
        End If
    End If
End If


End Sub
```

When this event is triggered (by a user clicking the image control), it first checks to see whose turn it is. If it is the player's turn, then I check whether there is already an X or an O in the square. If not, I can then add an X to the image and in some fashion let the game know that this square is no longer available. I accomplish this by setting the variable fbSquare9X to True.

Next I check whether there is a win by calling a function named Checkforwin, which returns a Boolean value. (You will see this function in just a moment.) If there is no win, then I set the string variable fsWhoseTurnIsIt to computer.

The Timer event of the timer control contains a lot of code and rightfully so. This event contains most of the artificial intelligence that drives the computer's decision-making:

```
Private Sub Timer1_Timer()


'GAME INTELLIGENCE
If fsWhoseTurnIsIt  = "computer" Then


    'Computer is playing a defensive role by looking for potential
    'winning combinations (by the player).
    'There are a total of 8 possible winning combinations, but there
    'are a total of 24 possible combinations prior to a player winning.
    'So a player has a chance to win, I only test for 12 scenarios,
    ' leaving the rest up to chance (the DEFAULT SECTION)
    If (fbSquare1X = True And fbSquare3X = True) And _
    (fbSquare2X = False And fbSquare2O = False) Then
        Image2.Picture = img0.Picture
        fbSquare2O = True
        If Checkforwin = False Then
            fsWhoseTurnIsIt  = "player"
            lblStatus.Caption = "Your turn"
            Enable_Squares
        End If
    ElseIf (fbSquare7X = True And fbSquare9X = True) And _
    (fbSquare8X = False And fbSquare8O = False) Then
        Image8.Picture = img0.Picture
        fbSquare8O = True
        If Checkforwin = False Then
            fsWhoseTurnIsIt  = "player"
            lblStatus.Caption = "Your turn"
            Enable_Squares
        End If
    ElseIf (fbSquare4X = True And fbSquare5X = True) And _
    (fbSquare6X = False And fbSquare6O = False) Then
        Image6.Picture = img0.Picture
        fbSquare6O = True
        If Checkforwin = False Then
            fsWhoseTurnIsIt  = "player"
            lblStatus.Caption = "Your turn"
```

```
            Enable_Squares
        End If
    ElseIf (fbSquare5X = True And fbSquare6X = True) And _
    (fbSquare4X = False And fbSquare4O = False) Then
        Image4.Picture = img0.Picture
        fbSquare4O = True
        If Checkforwin = False Then
            fsWhoseTurnIsIt  = "player"
            lblStatus.Caption = "Your turn"
            Enable_Squares
        End If
    ElseIf (fbSquare8X = True And fbSquare9X = True) And _
    (fbSquare7X = False And fbSquare7O = False) Then
        Image7.Picture = img0.Picture
        fbSquare7O = True
        If Checkforwin = False Then
            fsWhoseTurnIsIt  = "player"
            lblStatus.Caption = "Your turn"
            Enable_Squares
        End If
    ElseIf (fbSquare2X = True And fbSquare8X = True) And _
    (fbSquare5X = False And fbSquare5O = False) Then
        Image5.Picture = img0.Picture
        fbSquare5O = True
        If Checkforwin = False Then
            fsWhoseTurnIsIt  = "player"
            lblStatus.Caption = "Your turn"
            Enable_Squares
        End If
    ElseIf (fbSquare1X = True And fbSquare4X = True) And _
    (fbSquare7X = False And fbSquare7O = False) Then
        Image7.Picture = img0.Picture
        fbSquare7O = True
        If Checkforwin = False Then
            fsWhoseTurnIsIt  = "player"
            lblStatus.Caption = "Your turn"
            Enable_Squares
        End If
    ElseIf (fbSquare3X = True And fbSquare6X = True) And _
    (fbSquare9X = False And fbSquare9O = False) Then
```

```
    Image9.Picture = img0.Picture
    fbSquare90 = True
    If Checkforwin = False Then
        fsWhoseTurnIsIt  = "player"
        lblStatus.Caption = "Your turn"
        Enable_Squares
    End If
ElseIf (fbSquare6X = True And fbSquare9X = True) And _
(fbSquare3X = False And fbSquare30 = False) Then
    Image3.Picture = img0.Picture
    fbSquare30 = True
    If Checkforwin = False Then
        fsWhoseTurnIsIt  = "player"
        lblStatus.Caption = "Your turn"
        Enable_Squares
    End If
ElseIf (fbSquare1X = True And fbSquare5X = True) And _
(fbSquare9X = False And fbSquare90 = False) Then
    Image9.Picture = img0.Picture
    fbSquare90 = True
    If Checkforwin = False Then
        fsWhoseTurnIsIt  = "player"
        lblStatus.Caption = "Your turn"
        Enable_Squares
    End If
ElseIf (fbSquare5X = True And fbSquare9X = True) And _
(fbSquare1X = False And fbSquare10 = False) Then
    Image1.Picture = img0.Picture
    fbSquare10 = True
    If Checkforwin = False Then
        fsWhoseTurnIsIt  = "player"
        lblStatus.Caption = "Your turn"
        Enable_Squares
    End If
ElseIf (fbSquare7X = True And fbSquare5X = True) And _
(fbSquare3X = False And fbSquare30 = False) Then
    Image3.Picture = img0.Picture
    fbSquare30 = True
    If Checkforwin = False Then
        fsWhoseTurnIsIt  = "player"
```

```
            lblStatus.Caption = "Your turn"
            Enable_Squares
        End If
    End If
End If 'End fsWhoseTurnIsIt  check
```

Each of the If and ElseIf conditions is checking for 12 out of the 24 scenarios that I showed you in the decision-tree section in this chapter.

If you really want to challenge your friends, go ahead and add 12 more ElseIf conditions to check for the remaining conditions.

Not only are the ElseIf conditions looking for one of the 12 conditions, but also they are checking to see whether the square that would win is filled using compound conditions.

If a match is found and the square is empty, the computer places an O in the appropriate square, preventing the opponent from winning (at least for that condition). After that, a check for win is done by the procedure Checkforwin.

The default section in the following code is only reached if it is still the computer's turn—or in other words, there was no match found. The default section basically looks for the first open or available square. This move is pretty predictable, as you will see after running the tic-tac-toe game a few times. Nevertheless, you will learn how to solve this problem by generating random numbers in Chapter 4:

```
If fsWhoseTurnIsIt  = "computer" Then

    'DEFAULT SECTION
    'If the computer has made it this far and there were no possible
    'matches, then just select the first empty box it comes across.
    'Even though I use this code for testing the program, I'm going to
    'leave it in because I'm not testing for all defensive scenarios.
    If fbSquare1X = False And fbSquare1O = False Then
        Image1.Picture = img0.Picture
        fbSquare1O = True
        If Checkforwin = False Then
            fsWhoseTurnIsIt  = "player"
            lblStatus.Caption = "Your turn"
            Enable_Squares
        End If
    ElseIf fbSquare2X = False And fbSquare2O = False Then
```

```
        Image2.Picture = img0.Picture
        fbSquare20 = True
        If Checkforwin = False Then
            fsWhoseTurnIsIt  = "player"
            lblStatus.Caption = "Your turn"
            Enable_Squares
        End If
    ElseIf fbSquare3X = False And fbSquare30 = False Then
        Image3.Picture = img0.Picture
        fbSquare30 = True
        If Checkforwin = False Then
            fsWhoseTurnIsIt  = "player"
            lblStatus.Caption = "Your turn"
            Enable_Squares
        End If
    ElseIf fbSquare4X = False And fbSquare40 = False Then
        Image4.Picture = img0.Picture
        fbSquare40 = True
        If Checkforwin = False Then
            fsWhoseTurnIsIt  = "player"
            lblStatus.Caption = "Your turn"
            Enable_Squares
        End If
    ElseIf fbSquare5X = False And fbSquare50 = False Then
        Image5.Picture = img0.Picture
        fbSquare50 = True
        If Checkforwin = False Then
            fsWhoseTurnIsIt  = "player"
            lblStatus.Caption = "Your turn"
            Enable_Squares
        End If
    ElseIf fbSquare6X = False And fbSquare60 = False Then
        Image6.Picture = img0.Picture
        fbSquare60 = True
        If Checkforwin = False Then
            fsWhoseTurnIsIt  = "player"
            lblStatus.Caption = "Your turn"
            Enable_Squares
        End If
```

```
        ElseIf fbSquare7X = False And fbSquare7O = False Then
            Image7.Picture = img0.Picture
            fbSquare7O = True
            If Checkforwin = False Then
                fsWhoseTurnIsIt  = "player"
                lblStatus.Caption = "Your turn"
                Enable_Squares
            End If
        ElseIf fbSquare8X = False And fbSquare8O = False Then
            Image8.Picture = img0.Picture
            fbSquare8O = True
            If Checkforwin = False Then
                fsWhoseTurnIsIt  = "player"
                lblStatus.Caption = "Your turn"
                Enable_Squares
            End If
        ElseIf fbSquare9X = False And fbSquare9O = False Then
            Image9.Picture = img0.Picture
            fbSquare9O = True
            If Checkforwin = False Then
                fsWhoseTurnIsIt  = "player"
                lblStatus.Caption = "Your turn"
                Enable_Squares
            End If
        End If
    End If 'end fsWhoseTurnIsIt  check
```

Each of the following conditions is checking for a win by the player by checking each of the eight possible wins in a game of tic-tac-toe:

```
End Sub

Public Function Checkforwin()
Dim liSquaresOccupied As Integer
'First, check for a win by the player
If fbSquare1X = True And fbSquare2X = True And fbSquare3X = _
True Then 'Across
    fbPlayerWon = True
ElseIf fbSquare4X = True And fbSquare5X = True And fbSquare6X = _
True Then 'Across
    fbPlayerWon = True
```

```
ElseIf fbSquare7X = True And fbSquare8X = True And fbSquare9X = _
True Then 'Across
    fbPlayerWon = True
ElseIf fbSquare1X = True And fbSquare4X = True And fbSquare7X = _
True Then 'Up and down
    fbPlayerWon = True
ElseIf fbSquare2X = True And fbSquare5X = True And fbSquare8X = _
True Then 'Up and down
    fbPlayerWon = True
ElseIf fbSquare3X = True And fbSquare6X = True And fbSquare9X = _
True Then 'Up and down
    fbPlayerWon = True
ElseIf fbSquare1X = True And fbSquare5X = True And fbSquare9X = _
True Then 'Diagonal
    fbPlayerWon = True
ElseIf fbSquare3X = True And fbSquare5X = True And fbSquare7X = _
True Then 'Diagonal
    fbPlayerWon = True
End If
```

I perform the same check for a win by the computer against each of the eight possible scenarios:

```
'Next, check for a win by the computer
If fbSquare10 = True And fbSquare20 = True And fbSquare30 = _
True Then 'Across
    fbComputerWon = True
ElseIf fbSquare40 = True And fbSquare50 = True And fbSquare60 = _
True Then 'Across
    fbComputerWon = True
ElseIf fbSquare70 = True And fbSquare80 = True And fbSquare90 = _
True Then 'Across
    fbComputerWon = True
ElseIf fbSquare10 = True And fbSquare40 = True And fbSquare70 = _
True Then 'Up and down
    fbComputerWon = True
ElseIf fbSquare20 = True And fbSquare50 = True And fbSquare80 = _
True Then 'Up and down
    fbComputerWon = True
```

```
ElseIf fbSquare30 = True And fbSquare60 = True And fbSquare90 = _
True Then 'Up and down
    fbComputerWon = True
ElseIf fbSquare10 = True And fbSquare50 = True And fbSquare90 = _
True Then 'Diagonal
    fbComputerWon = True
ElseIf fbSquare30 = True And fbSquare50 = True And fbSquare70 = _
True Then 'Diagonal
    fbComputerWon = True
End If
```

I handle the tie scenario a little differently. I simply check for the scenario where every square has either an X or an O but there is no win by the computer nor opponent:

```
'And last, check for a tie game
If fbComputerWon = False And fbPlayerWon = False Then
    If fbSquare1X = True Or fbSquare1O = True Then
        liSquaresOccupied = liSquaresOccupied + 1
    End If
    If fbSquare2X = True Or fbSquare2O = True Then
        liSquaresOccupied = liSquaresOccupied + 1
    End If
    If fbSquare3X = True Or fbSquare3O = True Then
        liSquaresOccupied = liSquaresOccupied + 1
    End If
    If fbSquare4X = True Or fbSquare4O = True Then
        liSquaresOccupied = liSquaresOccupied + 1
    End If
    If fbSquare5X = True Or fbSquare5O = True Then
        liSquaresOccupied = liSquaresOccupied + 1
    End If
    If fbSquare6X = True Or fbSquare6O = True Then
        liSquaresOccupied = liSquaresOccupied + 1
    End If
    If fbSquare7X = True Or fbSquare7O = True Then
        liSquaresOccupied = liSquaresOccupied + 1
    End If
    If fbSquare8X = True Or fbSquare8O = True Then
        liSquaresOccupied = liSquaresOccupied + 1
```

```
      End If
      If fbSquare9X = True Or fbSquare9O = True Then
          liSquaresOccupied = liSquaresOccupied + 1
      End If

      'If liSquaresOccupied = 9 (all squares are occupied) and the
      'computer nor the player has won, then we have a tie game
      If liSquaresOccupied = 9 Then
          fbTie = True
      End If
  End If
```

The remaining conditions look for a win or a tie and increment the score where applicable:

```
'If a win or a tie has occurred, then increment a score.
'Turn off the timer and exit this routine
If fbTie = True Or fbPlayerWon = True Or fbComputerWon = True Then
    Checkforwin = True
    If fbTie = True Then
        fiTieScore = fiTieScore + 1
        lblTie.Caption = fiTieScore
        lblStatus.Caption = "Tie Game, click start game to play"
        fsWhoseTurnIsIt  = "player"
    ElseIf fbPlayerWon = True Then
        fiPlayerScore = fiPlayerScore + 1
        lblPlayer.Caption = fiPlayerScore
        lblStatus.Caption = "You won, click start game to play"
        fsWhoseTurnIsIt  = "player"
    ElseIf fbComputerWon = True Then
        fiComputerScore = fiComputerScore + 1
        lblComputer.Caption = fiComputerScore
        lblStatus.Caption = "Computer won, click start game to play"
        fsWhoseTurnIsIt  = "player"
    End If
```

The remaining code performs housekeeping, which sets the game environment to that of a new game:

```
    cmdStart.Enabled = True
```

```
        fbTie = False
        fbPlayerWon = False
        fbComputerWon = False

        fbSquare1X = False
        fbSquare2X = False
        fbSquare3X = False
        fbSquare4X = False
        fbSquare5X = False
        fbSquare6X = False
        fbSquare7X = False
        fbSquare8X = False
        fbSquare9X = False

        fbSquare10 = False
        fbSquare20 = False
        fbSquare30 = False
        fbSquare40 = False
        fbSquare50 = False
        fbSquare60 = False
        fbSquare70 = False
        fbSquare80 = False
        fbSquare90 = False

        Timer1.Enabled = False
        Exit Function
```

If neither win nor tie was found, then return the value false by assigning false to the name of the function:

```
Else
        Checkforwin = False
End If
```

The procedures Disable_Squares and Enable_Squares do exactly what their names imply, either disable or enable the squares:

```
End Function


Public Sub Disable_Squares()
```

```
Image1.Enabled = False
Image2.Enabled = False
Image3.Enabled = False
Image4.Enabled = False
Image5.Enabled = False
Image6.Enabled = False
Image7.Enabled = False
Image8.Enabled = False
Image9.Enabled = False


End Sub


Public Sub Enable_Squares()

Image1.Enabled = True
Image2.Enabled = True
Image3.Enabled = True
Image4.Enabled = True
Image5.Enabled = True
Image6.Enabled = True
Image7.Enabled = True
Image8.Enabled = True
Image9.Enabled = True


End Sub
```

Summary

In this chapter, you covered a subset of mathematics called Boolean logic, which is the foundation not only for programmable conditions but also computer architecture as a whole. With the knowledge of Boolean logic, you learned how to create and use conditions in Visual Basic through If statements and Select Case structures.

Through program examples, you learned more about Visual Basic events and controls using the KeyPress event and the timer control. With a broader knowledge of events and controls, you should now have an appetite for things to come and a sense of possibilities limited only by your imagination.

Finally, you learned how to build intelligent games by developing decision trees, which help programmers create effective and intelligent algorithms.

I hope that this chapter has challenged you in what you have learned thus far and inspired you to learn more about programming with Visual Basic. After a chapter like this, it is important to realize that not only have you been learning how to program in Visual Basic, but also you have acquired knowledge in the area of computer science.

In the next chapter, you will build some fun games while learning about program control through the use of loops.

CHALLENGES

1. Use the animation program from this chapter as a template to build a program that animates a character walking forward, backward, and side-to-side. You can find more character clips for animation on the accompanying CD for this book.

2. Using the timer control, create a digital stopwatch program that allows a user to start and stop a clock. The program should show how much time has elapsed between the starting and stopping times.

3. Add the remaining 12 winning scenarios to the tic-tac-toe game's logic in the Timer event. Give it to your friends to play; sit back and laugh.

4. Change the tic-tac-toe's artificial intelligence in the Timer event to play an offensive role instead of a defensive role. Before writing any code, give some thought to the following questions:

   - What are the differences in the logic between an offensive role and a defensive role?

   - What will the decision tree look like for an offensive role?

   - Should both defensive and offensive strategies be incorporated into the game's intelligence? What would this decision tree look like?

Iteration

After learning about conditions, you are ready to study another important computer science structure called iteration. Commonly referred to as looping, iteration is a structure you can use to loop through programmable statements.

Loops or iterations are controlled by known or unknown values, which can be changed by the looping process itself or by an outside influence.

Like conditions, iteration is best learned through programming, programming, and more programming. You will walk through a few simple programs in this chapter that showcase the basic functionality of the looping process in Visual Basic. After learning looping fundamentals, you will see how you can use iteration to build more sophisticated programs such as the slot machine game at the end of this chapter.

This chapter specifically covers the following:

- **Iteration basics**
- **For loops**
- **Do loops**
- **Random numbers**
- **Constructing the slot machine game**

Project: Slot Machine

In the slot machine game, you will learn how to build a slot machine using Visual Basic iteration structures and random numbers. You will also learn how to create your own timer using conditions and built-in Visual Basic functions.

The game randomizes four images when a user spins the reels. (Well, in this case, he pushes a button.) If the resulting images make up three or four of a kind, points are added to the player's score. Figure 4.1 showcases the slot machine game.

Been There, Done That

So, why loop? Well, iteration or looping is the programmer's fundamental means of repeating something over and over and over again. Let me show you some obvious and not-so-obvious situations where you might want to create a programmable loop. First are the obvious situations for looping:

- Counting numbers
- Reading a file as input until the end-of-file marker is found
- Searching through database records
- Calculating compound interest
- Animating a figure or image

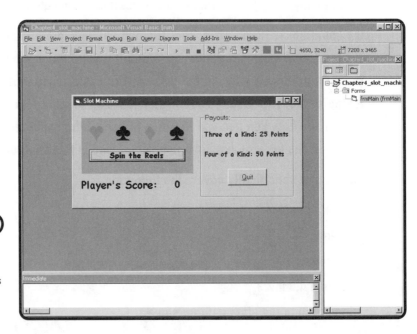

FIGURE 4.1

A slot machine game that randomizes images and tracks the player's score.

Following are not so obvious:

- Displaying a bank's ATM menu
- Building an autopilot system for a plane
- Launching a heat-seeking missile
- Building medical imaging or an MRI system
- Installing an operating system

The point of these looping situations is to realize that programmable iteration is all around us. To make this more obvious, I expand on some of the not-so-obvious situations for looping.

A bank's ATM (automated teller machine) seems to always have a menu displayed. When not in use, ATM menus are not sitting in a state of suspended animation. Rather, they have logic programmed into them that is always looking for a user's response. In other words, the ATM program logic stays in a loop, always ready to serve the customer through displaying a menu.

Something most people never consider when flying in a commercial plane is the autopilot system. One would hope that when the pilot turns on the autopilot, it stays on until the pilot turns it off. Well, that hope rests in the programmer who wrote the autopilot system code. I hope he or she used iteration logic that says, "When autopilot is on, stay on until autopilot is turned off."

For Loops

For loops are often used in Visual Basic to implement iteration. They are a popular choice when you know (or will know through the use of variables) how many times the loop should repeat.

Many languages have their own version of the for loop, and Visual Basic is no exception. In my opinion, Visual Basic provides a friendly means for implementing the for loop as shown in its general form:

```
For variable name = number to number Step number (optional)
    'statements
Next   variable name
```

Here's another example that uses the for loop to repeat five times using the integer variable liCounter:

```
For liCounter = 1 to 5
    'statements
Next liCounter
```

In this example, liCounter is incremented by 1 each time the Next liCounter statement is executed. The statement For liCounter = 1 to 5 tells Visual Basic that you want the for loop to repeat five times incrementing by 1.

This is great, but what if you want to increment by 2s, 5s, or 10s? Well, the Visual Basic for loop implements increments through the use of the Step keyword. Here's an example of a for loop that increments by 10:

```
For liCounter = 1 to 100 Step 10
    'print liCounter
Next liCounter
```

What do you think the output of this for loop would be? You might guess 10, 20, 30, 40, . . . 100. But that is actually incorrect. The output would be 1, 11, 22, 33, 44, and so on. Remember that in the for loop, I tell Visual Basic that I want to count from 1 to 100. Visual Basic accomplishes this by starting at the number 1. When you add 10 to 1, you get 11. To get the output you might have expected, you need to change the for statement to look something like this:

```
For liCounter = 0 to 100 Step 10
```

Also consider that for loops can decrement with negative numbers. Take the following code which decrements by 1.

```
For liCounter = 1 to -10 Step -1
    'print liCounter
Next liCounter
```

 HINT There are times when you may want to exit a looping construct before it has completed all possible iterations. In Visual Basic, this can be accomplished with the Exit Do or Exit For statements. Take the following code segment which exits a for loop when the variable liCounter reaches the number 5.

```
For liCounter = 1 To 10 Step 1
    If liCounter = 5 Then
        Exit For
    Else
        Print liCounter
    End If
Next liCounter
```

I built a small program called The Counter, which implements Visual Basic's for loop structure. It uses a picture box control to output the number of times a for loop has repeated. Figure 4.2 depicts the counter program, which uses for loops to demonstrate iteration.

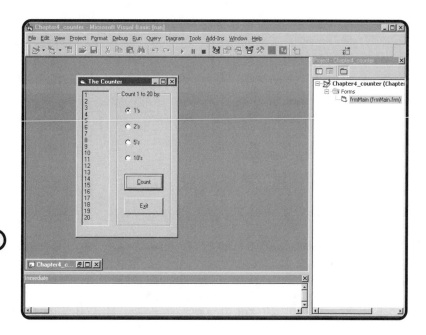

FIGURE 4.2

The Counter
program, which
uses the for loop
structure.

Let's take a look at The Counter program to see how the for loop is implemented:

```
Option Explicit

Private Sub cmdCount_Click()

Dim liCounter As Integer

picOutput.Cls
If opt1.Value = True Then
    For liCounter = 1 To 20
        picOutput.Print liCounter
    Next liCounter
ElseIf opt2.Value = True Then
    For liCounter = 1 To 20 Step 2
        picOutput.Print liCounter
    Next liCounter
ElseIf opt5.Value = True Then
    For liCounter = 1 To 20 Step 5
        picOutput.Print liCounter
    Next liCounter
```

```
ElseIf opt10.Value = True Then
    For liCounter = 1 To 20 Step 10
        picOutput.Print liCounter
    Next liCounter
End If

End Sub

Private Sub cmdExit_Click()
End
End Sub

Private Sub Form_Load()
opt1.Value = True
End Sub
```

Most of the code for the counter program is in the click event of the cmdClick command button. Depending on which option button the user clicks, I use the for loop to repeatedly print the value of liCounter to the picture box. It's really pretty simple!

Table 4.1 describes the controls and properties of the counter program.

TABLE 4.1 CONTROLS AND PROPERTIES FOR THE COUNTER PROGRAM

Control	Property	Setting
frmMain	Caption	The Counter
picOutput	Picture	None
fraOptions	Caption	Count 1 to 20 by:
opt1	Caption	1s
opt2	Caption	2s
opt5	Caption	5s
opt10	Caption	10s
cmdCount	Caption	&Count
cmdExit	Caption	E&xit

Do Loops

Do loops are another popular vehicle for implementing iteration in Visual Basic. They are especially useful when you do not know how many times you want to repeat a process.

 Any for loop you create can use a do loop instead. Although they look quite different syntactically, they produce the same results.

Visual Basic has four ways for implementing a do loop. You can use either the while or until keywords. Each version of the do loop shares the common function of iteration, yet they can produce different results. Take a look at each version of the do loop to better understand their differences and commonalities. The four combinations are as follows:

```
Do   Until(condition)…Loop
Do   While(condition)…Loop
Do…Loop Until(condition)
Do…Loop While(condition)
```

Do While

The do while loop repeats a process while a condition is true. Hey, did you notice that I mentioned the word condition? Both versions of do loops use conditions as their signals to loop or not loop. When I say conditions, I'm not necessarily referring to if conditions, but rather Boolean values and expressions.

Here's the basic syntax for a do while loop:

```
Do While condition
    'statements
Loop
```

You can see that the condition is checked before the statements in a do while loop are executed. This is such an important concept that it is worth mentioning again. If the condition is false in a do while loop, the statements inside it are never executed.

Here's another example of a do while loop that reads a file while it does not detect an end-of-file marker:

```
Do While file1.eof <> true
    'read file contents
Loop
```

The condition in this do while loop should be more apparent to you now that I'm using a real-world condition. Better yet, let's see if we can re-create the for loop in the counter program using a do while loop:

```
Do While liCounter < 20
    picOutput.Print liCounter
    liCounter = liCounter + 1
Loop
```

This do while loop produces the same results as its for loop counterpart. If you want to increment by something other than 1, you can simply change the statement liCounter = liCounter + 1 to liCounter = liCounter + 2 to count by 2s, or liCounter = liCounter + 5 to count by 5s, and so on.

TRAP

Beware of the infinite loop, a common problem that most beginning programmers encounter. Infinite loops are iterative processes that never stop. To demonstrate, let's take a look at a revised do while counter loop:

```
liCounter = 1
Do While liCounter < 20
    picOutput.Print liCounter
Loop
```

In this example, the looping condition Do While liCounter < 20 is always true (resulting in an infinite loop) because I do not change the value of liCounter anywhere in the loop so that it becomes greater than 20.

When creating and using loops, make sure there is a way for the loop to exit. In the event that you find yourself in an infinite loop, don't fret; simply press the keys Ctrl and Break simultaneously to break the loop.

Moreover, you can put the condition (in this case, the condition after the While keyword) at the end of a loop. This change still performs a similar looping process, yet can produce different results. The following do loop construct is similar to the preceding loop, but its condition is at the end of the loop. So, what's the difference? Essentially, the key difference is the loop is guaranteed to iterate at least once. In other words, if the liCounter variable is already set to 5 or greater, the code in the loop will execute at least once before exiting.

```
Do
    picOutput.Print liCounter
Loop While liCounter < 20
```

For a better look at the differences, compare the following do loops.

```
liCounter = 25
Do While liCounter < 20
    picOutput.Print liCounter
Loop

liCounter = 25
Do
    picOutput.Print liCounter
Loop While liCounter < 20
```

You should now be able to see that the second loop's inner statements will execute once, where the first looping construct will not.

Loop Until

Another popular way to implement a do loop is with the loop until structure. Like the do while structure, loop until uses a condition to loop or not loop. However, unlike the do while loop, the loop until structure evaluates its condition after the loop has executed. What this essentially means is that you are guaranteed your loop's statements will execute at least once with the loop until structure.

Here's the basic syntax for the loop until structure:

```
Do
    'statements
Loop Until Condition
```

As mentioned earlier, loop until structures are useful when you know for certain that you want the loop's contents to execute at least once.

 This can also be accomplished with the condition While when placed at the end of a do loop construct.

Here's another example of a loop until structure that displays a menu until the user chooses to quit:

```
Do
    'display menu
    'process menu selection
```

```
Loop Until menu_selection = 'q'
```

With this loop until structure, I'm guaranteed that the menu displays at least once.

Similar to the Do While looping construct, the Until condition can be placed at the beginning of the do loop as seen below.

```
Do Until menu_selection = 'q'
    'display menu
    'process menu selection
Loop
```

Random Numbers

Generating random numbers is an interesting and challenging concept in the mathematical and computer science worlds. The application of random numbers is not limited to scientific and mathematical workings; it is also popular in the gaming industry. For example, here are some scenarios where you might see random numbers used in electronic games:

- Shuffling a deck of cards
- Rolling a die for a board game
- Playing slot machines
- Generating numbers for lotteries
- Spinning a roulette wheel

Each of these games tries to simulate a non-predictable random selection of numbers in a collection. Even though the application might display a hand of cards, or the face of a die, the outcome is derived behind the scenes through random number generation.

Fortunately, Visual Basic provides built-in random number generators.

Rnd Function

The rnd function returns a random number from 0 to 1, but not including 1. For example, the rnd function could return any one of the following numbers:

```
.0000000
.2500000
.5000000
.7500000
```

Because these numbers are real numbers (decimals or fractions) and not integers, you need to perform a little Visual Basic trickery to get whole numbers such as 1, 2, 3, 4, 5, or 6. For example, the following statement generates a random number from 1 to 6 and assigns it to an integer variable:

```
LiRandomNumber = Int(6 * Rnd) + 1
```

I had to add 1 to the equation to get numbers from 1 to 6. This is because the rnd function generates numbers from 0 to 1, but not including 1. So if I did not include the addition of 1 to the equation, I would get random numbers in the range of 0 to 5.

Also, I enclose the rnd function in the int function. Enclosing a non-integer number in the Int() function ensures that you get an integer number.

The rnd function generates a seemingly random pattern the more it is executed. However, you will find that when first executed, the rnd function starts with the same number each time. To solve this problem, Visual Basic provides another function called randomize.

Randomize Function

The randomize function uses your computer's internal clock to assist you in generating random numbers. If your program includes the randomize function, the rnd function generates a more varied number each time it is first executed.

The randomize function requires no parameters and must be called only once in your program. For example, you can put the randomize function in your form's load event:

```
Private Sub Form_Load()
Randomize
End Sub
```

To illustrate the use of random numbers, I show you a small program I wrote called dice in Figure 4.3.

My dice program uses a number of Visual Basic fundamentals that you have already learned so far in this book. Specifically, it uses image swapping, a timer control, select case structures, if conditions, and random numbers.

HINT The dice images used in the dice program were created by *For the Absolute Beginner* series editor Andy Harris and appear in this book's accompanying CD-ROM.

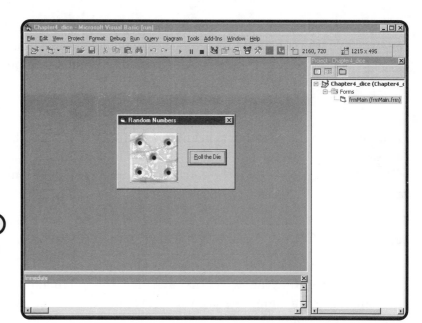

FIGURE 4.3

The dice program simulates the rolling of a die through random numbers.

Here's the entire code for the dice program:

```
Option Explicit
Dim fiRolls As Integer

Private Sub cmdRoll_Click()
cmdRoll.Enabled = False
cmdRoll.Caption = "Rolling..."
fiRolls = 1
Timer1.Enabled = True
End Sub

Private Sub Form_Load()
imgMainDie.Picture = imgDie1.Picture
Randomize
End Sub
```

I'm using the randomize function in the form load event to aid the rnd function in generating a random number:

```
Private Sub Timer1_Timer()

Dim fiRandomNumber As Integer
```

Notice that I use an if condition to check a form-level integer variable called fiRolls. I use this variable and condition to ensure that the Timer event is only kicked off 10 times. To accomplish this, I increment fiRolls by 1 at the end of this procedure:

```
If fiRolls > 10 Then
    Timer1.Enabled = False
    cmdRoll.Enabled = True
    cmdRoll.Caption = "&Roll the Die"
End If


fiRandomNumber = Int(6 * Rnd) + 1
```

Here I use the rnd function to assign a random number to an integer variable. This assignment takes place each time the Timer event is triggered. Next, the select case structure assigns a certain picture of the die to the main picture on the form:

```
Select Case fiRandomNumber
    Case 1
        imgMainDie.Picture = imgDie1.Picture
    Case 2
        imgMainDie.Picture = imgDie2.Picture
    Case 3
        imgMainDie.Picture = imgDie3.Picture
    Case 4
        imgMainDie.Picture = imgDie4.Picture
    Case 5
        imgMainDie.Picture = imgDie5.Picture
    Case 6
        imgMainDie.Picture = imgDie6.Picture
End Select


fiRolls = fiRolls + 1


End Sub
```

 HINT   Changing the Interval property of the Timer control will slow down or speed up the changing of the die's face.

Table 4.2 shows the controls and properties of the dice program.

TABLE 4.2 CONTROLS AND PROPERTIES FOR THE DICE PROGRAM

Control	Property	Setting
frmMain	Caption	Random Numbers
	Border Style	1 – Fixed Single
imgMainDie	Picture	None
imgDie1	Picture	Bitmap
imgDie2	Picture	Bitmap
imgDie3	Picture	Bitmap
imgDie4	Picture	Bitmap
imgDie5	Picture	Bitmap
imgDie6	Picture	Bitmap
cmdRoll	Caption	&Roll the Die
Timer1	Enabled	False
	Interval	500

HINT

The dice program uses the image-swapping technique to animate a die. If a user were to increase the size of the dice program window, she would see the six images I have hidden on the form. I can use the border style property of the form to prevent this.

Setting the border style property of a form prevents a user from changing the window's size through maximizing it or through the clip controls on the edges of the window.

Constructing the Slot Machine Game

Like its more advanced counterparts, the slot machine game generates random images through the use of random numbers. After generating random images, the game's intelligence looks for certain patterns. In this case, it looks for three of a kind and four of a kind.

The Problem

Develop a slot machine that generates random images through the use of random numbers. Once random numbers are assigned to images, look for a predetermined pattern. The patterns should include three and four of a kind. If patterns match, increment the player's score accordingly. Table 4.3 outlines the tools available to you.

Figure 4.4 demonstrates the slot machine game in design mode.

TABLE 4.3 CONTROLS AND PROPERTIES FOR THE SLOT MACHINE PROGRAM

Control	Property	Setting
frmMain	Caption	Slot Machine
	BorderStyle	1 – Fixed Single
fraPayouts	Caption	Payouts:
Label3	Caption	Three of a Kind: 25 Points
Label4	Caption	Four of a Kind: 50 Points
cmdQuit	Caption	&Quit
Frame1	Caption	None
	Appearance	1 – 3D
	BackColor	Blue
	BorderStyle	None
lblSpinning	Caption	Spinning...
	Visible	False
cmdSpin	Caption	Spin
lblScoreCaption	Caption	Player's Score:
lblPlayersScore	Caption	None
imgSpade	Picture	Icon
	Visible	False
imgDiamond	Picture	Icon
	Visible	False
imgHeart	Picture	Icon
	Visible	False
imgClub	Picture	Icon
	Visible	False
imgSlot1	Picture	None
imgSlot2	Picture	None
imgSlot3	Picture	None
imgSlot4	Picture	None

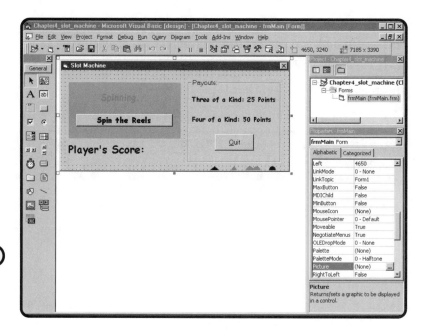

FIGURE 4.4

The slot machine game in design mode.

The following list depicts a possible algorithm for the slot machine game.

1. Create a new standard EXE project.
2. Add all controls to the form.
3. Set all applicable control properties during design time.
4. Write code in the form load event to initialize any variables and images and start the randomize function.
5. Write code for the click event of the command button that spins the reels:
   - Declare variables.
   - Get the current time and determine the number of seconds.
   - Begin an iteration that loops for 5 seconds.
   - While in the loop, generate random numbers and get the latest time in seconds.
   - After the loop is completed (after 5 seconds), assign images based on random numbers generated.
   - Look for four and three of a kind.
   - If a match is found, increment the player's score accordingly.
   - Reset the game for the next round.

The Implementation

I only need one form-level variable to keep track of the player's score:

```
Option Explicit
Dim liPlayersScore As Integer
```

Written in the click event of the quit command button is the Visual Basic end keyword, which stops and exits the game:

```
Private Sub cmdQuit_Click()
End
End Sub
```

In the form load event, I assign pictures to the image controls that eventually display the outputted random images. I also set a few other variables and properties, but most important, I use the randomize function to make better use of the rnd function:

```
Private Sub Form_Load()

lblPlayersScore.Caption = "0"
lblSpinning.Visible = False

imgSlot1.Picture = imgHeart.Picture
imgSlot2.Picture = imgClub.Picture
imgSlot3.Picture = imgDiamond.Picture
imgSlot4.Picture = imgSpade.Picture
liPlayersScore = 0
Randomize

End Sub
```

Most of the code for the slot machine game is located in the click event of the spin command button. I declare a number of variables to hold the random numbers, patterns found (if any), and a number of variant variables to hold time:

```
Private Sub cmdSpin_Click()

Dim liRandomNumber1 As Integer
Dim liRandomNumber2 As Integer
Dim liRandomNumber3 As Integer
Dim liRandomNumber4 As Integer
Dim timeStarted
```

```
Dim hourStarted
Dim minutesStarted
Dim secondsStarted
Dim beginTotalNumberofSeconds
Dim currentTime
Dim currentHour
Dim currentMinutes
Dim currentSeconds
Dim endTotalNumberofSeconds
Dim timeElapsed
Dim lb3ofaKind As Boolean
Dim lb4ofaKind As Boolean
```

Before I enter my loop, I initialize some variables and set the images' visible properties to False. I also get the current system time and determine the number of seconds in it:

```
lb3ofaKind = False
lb4ofaKind = False

timeStarted = Time
hourStarted = Hour(timeStarted)
minutesStarted = Minute(timeStarted)
secondsStarted = Second(timeStarted)
beginTotalNumberofSeconds = ((hourStarted * 60) * 60) + _
(minutesStarted * 60) + secondsStarted

imgSlot1.Visible = False
imgSlot2.Visible = False
imgSlot3.Visible = False
imgSlot4.Visible = False

cmdSpin.Enabled = False
lblSpinning.Visible = True
DoEvents
```

What I essentially do is create my own timer control. To accomplish this, I assign the current system time to a variable using the intrinsic Visual Basic function called time. Once I have this, I can use the hour, minute, and second built-in Visual Basic functions to extract the hours, minutes, and seconds from the current time. With the help of a little math, I can then determine how many seconds the current time has, which is useful when I want to determine how many seconds I want the loop to iterate for.

Notice another new function called DoEvents that I add to the preceding code. DoEvents allows other pending background processes to finish processing. In other words, it allows your system to catch its breath before continuing. For example, if I do not put DoEvents into this code, my loop in the next section might start before I set the visible properties of the images to False.

My next loop is pretty straightforward; I tell Visual Basic that I want to loop for about 5 seconds. During that time, I generate random numbers, get the next current time, and calculate the number of seconds in it:

```
Do While timeElapsed < 5
    liRandomNumber1 = Int((4 * Rnd) + 1)
    liRandomNumber2 = Int((4 * Rnd) + 1)
    liRandomNumber3 = Int((4 * Rnd) + 1)
    liRandomNumber4 = Int((4 * Rnd) + 1)

    currentTime = Time
    currentHour = Hour(currentTime)
    currentMinutes = Minute(currentTime)
    currentSeconds = Second(currentTime)
    endTotalNumberofSeconds = ((currentHour * 60) * 60) + _
(currentMinutes * 60) + currentSeconds
    timeElapsed = endTotalNumberofSeconds - beginTotalNumberofSeconds
Loop
```

The next four comments serve no other purpose than reminding me that I'm associating a unique integer to a certain image. If my random number process generates a 1, I know to assign a heart to it and so on:

```
'heart as 1
'club as 2
'diamond as 3
'spade as 4
```

You can see the assignment process in the following select case statements:

```
'swap imgSlot1
Select Case liRandomNumber1
    Case 1
        imgSlot1.Picture = imgHeart.Picture
    Case 2
        imgSlot1.Picture = imgClub.Picture
```

```
        Case 3
                imgSlot1.Picture = imgDiamond.Picture
        Case 4
                imgSlot1.Picture = imgSpade.Picture
End Select


'swap imgSlot2
Select Case liRandomNumber2
        Case 1
                imgSlot2.Picture = imgHeart.Picture
        Case 2
                imgSlot2.Picture = imgClub.Picture
        Case 3
                imgSlot2.Picture = imgDiamond.Picture
        Case 4
                imgSlot2.Picture = imgSpade.Picture
End Select


'swap imgSlot3
Select Case liRandomNumber3
        Case 1
                imgSlot3.Picture = imgHeart.Picture
        Case 2
                imgSlot3.Picture = imgClub.Picture
        Case 3
                imgSlot3.Picture = imgDiamond.Picture
        Case 4
                imgSlot3.Picture = imgSpade.Picture
End Select


'swap imgSlot4
Select Case liRandomNumber4
        Case 1
                imgSlot4.Picture = imgHeart.Picture
        Case 2
                imgSlot4.Picture = imgClub.Picture
        Case 3
                imgSlot4.Picture = imgDiamond.Picture
        Case 4
                imgSlot4.Picture = imgSpade.Picture
End Select
```

Don't let the number of If/ElseIf conditions in the next code segment worry you. All I do is check for a four of a kind first and a three of a kind second. Notice the method to the madness: If the program finds a four of a kind, then there is really no sense in checking for a three of a kind. Right? Right.

You might be wondering, "How do I know what conditions to look for?" That is a good question because most games that involve random numbers deal with mathematical combinations. Take a look at Figure 4.5 to see a simple matrix that shows the possible combinations for three and four of a kind.

Using the matrix in Figure 4.5, you can see a total of four possible combinations for getting a three of a kind and only one possible combination for getting a four of a kind.

	Slot 1	Slot 2	Slot 3	Slot 4
Hearts = 1, Clubs = 2, Diamonds = 3, Spades = 4				
4 possibilties for 3 of a kind with Hearts (1)	1	1	1	
	1	1		1
	1		1	1
		1	1	1
4 possibilties for 3 of a kind with Clubs (2)	2	2	2	
	2	2		2
	2		2	2
		2	2	2
4 possibilties for 3 of a kind with Diamonds (3)	3	3	3	
	3	3		3
	3		3	3
		3	3	3
4 possibilties for 3 of a kind with Spades (4)	4	4	4	
	4	4		4
	4		4	4
		4	4	4
1 possible combination for 4 of a kind with Hearts	1	1	1	1
1 possible combination for 4 of a kind with Clubs	2	2	2	2
1 possible combination for 4 of a kind with Diamonds	3	3	3	3
1 possible combination for 4 of a kind with Spades	4	4	4	4

FIGURE 4.5

Possible combinations for three and four of a kind in a four-slot game.

After checking for three and four of a kind, I check for a match and increment the player's score accordingly. Finally, I reset the game's environment for the next round:

```
'look for four of a kind and then three of a kind
If liRandomNumber1 = 1 And liRandomNumber2 = 1 And liRandomNumber3 = 1 _
And liRandomNumber4 = 1 Then
    lb4ofaKind = True
ElseIf liRandomNumber1 = 2 And liRandomNumber2 = 2 And _
liRandomNumber3 = 2 And liRandomNumber4 = 2 Then
    lb4ofaKind = True
ElseIf liRandomNumber1 = 3 And liRandomNumber2 = 3 And _
liRandomNumber3 = 3 And liRandomNumber4 = 3 Then
    lb4ofaKind = True
ElseIf liRandomNumber1 = 4 And liRandomNumber2 = 4 And _
liRandomNumber3 = 4 And liRandomNumber4 = 4 Then
    lb4ofaKind = True
ElseIf liRandomNumber1 = 1 And liRandomNumber2 = 1 And _
liRandomNumber3 = 1 And lb4ofaKind = False Then
    lb3ofaKind = True
ElseIf liRandomNumber1 = 1 And liRandomNumber2 = 1 And _
liRandomNumber4 = 1 And lb4ofaKind = False Then
    lb3ofaKind = True
ElseIf liRandomNumber1 = 1 And liRandomNumber3 = 1 And _
liRandomNumber4 = 1 And lb4ofaKind = False Then
    lb3ofaKind = True
ElseIf liRandomNumber2 = 1 And liRandomNumber3 = 1 And _
liRandomNumber4 = 1 And lb4ofaKind = False Then
    lb3ofaKind = True
ElseIf liRandomNumber1 = 2 And liRandomNumber2 = 2 And _
liRandomNumber3 = 2 And lb4ofaKind = False Then
    lb3ofaKind = True'remaining conditions to check for three of a kind
End If
```

To complete the necessary checks for three of a kind, you will need to add the remaining necessary ElseIf conditions (check the CD for the complete code).

```
If lb3ofaKind = True Then
    liPlayersScore = liPlayersScore + 25
ElseIf lb4ofaKind = True Then
    liPlayersScore = liPlayersScore + 50
End If


lblPlayersScore.Caption = liPlayersScore


cmdSpin.Enabled = True
lblSpinning.Visible = False
imgSlot1.Visible = True
imgSlot2.Visible = True
imgSlot3.Visible = True
imgSlot4.Visible = True
lb3ofaKind = False
lb4ofaKind = False


End Sub
```

Summary

In this chapter, you learned how to go round and round with Visual Basic through the use of iteration. You specifically learned how to loop using for, do while, and loop until. You saw some examples of where these loops appear in our daily lives, how to use them in Visual Basic, and how to avoid and break endless loops.

You should also see a correlation between loops and conditions in that loops use conditions to check for the number of iterations. Beyond loops, you now know how to generate random numbers through the use of the rnd and randomize functions.

CHALLENGES

1. Create a simple math quiz game that generates random numbers for addition and subtraction questions. After generating these random numbers, the quiz game should prompt with a question and check whether the user got it right.

2. Create a program that determines the interest paid on a loan over 5 years or on a 30-year mortgage. The program should prompt a user for sale amount, length of loan, and interest rate. It should then use Visual Basic looping techniques to generate the amount of interest paid over the life of the loan.

3. Modify the slot machine game to check for two of a kind and two pairs.

Subprocedures, Functions, and Controls Continued

Visual Basic programming fundamentals such as variables, controls, events, conditions, and iteration are what you have been learning about so far. Hey, these are programming staples, but as my good friend Emeril Lagasse would say, "Let's kick it up a notch!"

Specifically, this chapter covers the following:

- Subprocedures and functions

- Interacting with the user through message boxes and input boxes

- Playing sounds in Visual Basic

- Constructing the shooting gallery game

To become a better-rounded Visual Basic programmer, you should invest some time in learning how to create subprocedures and functions. After learning how to create and use functions and subprocedures, you will be well on your way to studying a more dynamic and, yes, more complicated way of programming called *OOP* (object-oriented programming).

Before you even think about OOP, you should have a firm grip on what functions and modular programming are all about because at the root of OOP are functions and modular programs.

This chapter will help you understand functions and subprocedures and how they are implemented in Visual Basic. In addition to functions and subprocedures, you will learn how to use other Microsoft Visual Basic controls for purposes such as playing sounds.

> ### Definition
>
> *Object-oriented programming* models program code with real-world concepts, such as attributes, nouns, and actions. These real-world concepts translate into properties, methods, classes, and objects (some of which you already know). OOP, as it's known, is a relatively new programming paradigm in the computer-science world and has yet to be thoroughly adopted by most programmers and corporate developers of programming languages.
>
> Visual Basic 6.0 supports most of the OOP concepts but lacks a full implementation of the technology behind OOP science. Full implementations of OOP development environments appear in languages such as C++ and Java.

Project: Shooting Gallery

At the end of this chapter, you will implement most of the topics discussed to create a simple and fun game called the shooting gallery. The game, shown in Figure 5.1, uses sounds, functions, message boxes, input boxes, and additional controls to create an interactive gaming experience.

Subprocedures and Functions

Visual Basic provides a number of facilities for creating modularized and reusable program code. The two you will learn about in this chapter are subprocedures and functions. Both subprocedures (you'll notice the keyword Sub at the beginning and ending of program blocks) and functions are known as procedures, which let you organize large programmable problems into smaller programming pieces.

FIGURE 5.1

The shooting
gallery game.

In Visual Basic, the distinction between subprocedures and functions is minimal:

- Like subprocedures, functions are called with their names; however, they return a value to the calling statement.

- Functions have data types just as variables do. These data types are assigned to the function name and are used to denote the data type of the returning value.

- Assigning a value to the function's name is the resulting returned value. This returning value can be assigned to a variable or used in a larger expression.

In short, procedures are simply void functions. So what's a function, and what's a void function? Whether you know it or not, you have already been using functions in this book. Simply remember the intrinsic Visual Basic functions Left(), Right(), Mid(), UCase(), and InStr(). Each of these functions takes a parameter as input and returns a value as output. Subprocedures, on the other hand, return no output or, in other words, are void of output.

Basically, you will want to use functions when you need a value return to a calling statement and subprocedures when no return value is needed.

Subprocedures

There are two main ways to create a subprocedure in Visual Basic. If you know the syntax by heart, you can simply type in the subprocedure directly, or you can use the Add Procedure menu item depicted in Figure 5.2 to help you out. Personally, I prefer the Add Procedure menu item because it assists you in creating a syntactically correct subprogram or function template each time.

If you choose the Add Procedure menu item, you see a dialog box that prompts you for some information. From the Add Procedure dialog box as seen in Figure 5.3, you simply select the Sub option button (which denotes a subprocedure) and type in the procedure name.

Procedures (subprocedures and functions) denoted as Private can only be called by other procedures in that form. However, procedures denoted as Public become methods or actions of that form and can be called from anywhere within the application.

The Add Procedure dialog box creates your subprocedure template for you, as shown in Figure 5.4. You can add all the necessary code to create reusable procedures.

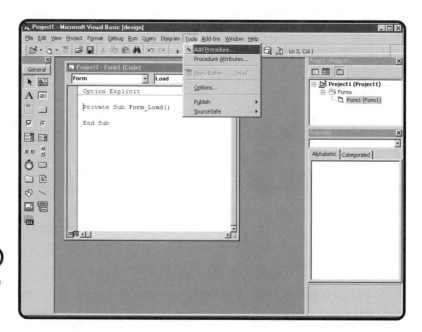

FIGURE 5.2

The Add Procedure
menu item on the
Tools menu.

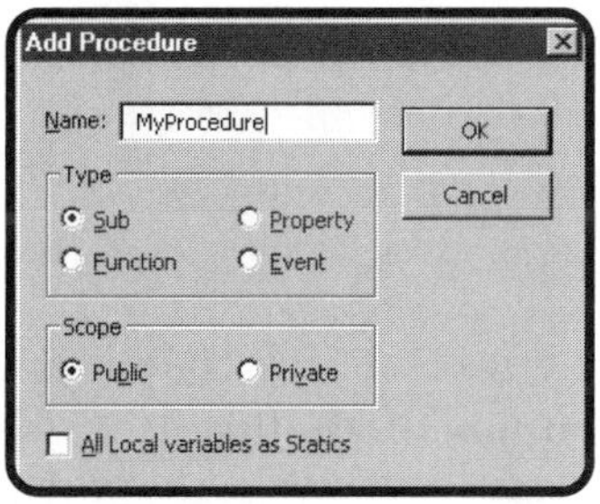

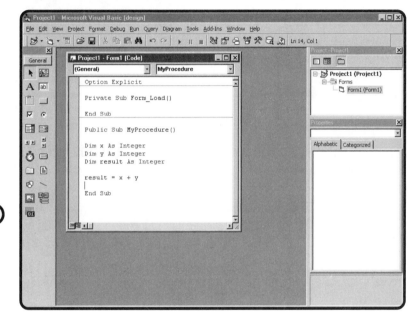

FIGURE 5.3

The Add Procedure dialog box.

FIGURE 5.4

A subprogram template created with the Add Procedure dialog box.

IN THE REAL WORLD

What is reusability as it applies to programming? Reusability in programming is in fact smart programming. When faced with routine programming tasks, smart programmers create reusable code through classes or functions that save them time and their employer's money.

Although often found in the object-oriented paradigm, reusability can and should be implemented in other paradigms, such as the event-driven model of Visual Basic, through functions and subprocedures.

Any time you find yourself in a situation that will or could require repeated code, go ahead and create modularized or reusable code through procedures.

The basic syntax for a subprogram is as follows:

```
Public Sub Procedure_Name()
    'Your code goes in here
End Sub
```

To illustrate a simple subprocedure, I put some silly code into the MyProcedure subprogram of Figure 5.4 to add two numbers together.

Subprocedures can be called with or without the call keyword. Take the following two statements in a form load event as an example.

```
Private Sub Form_Load()
Call MyProcedure
MyProcedure
End Sub
```

Each statement above calls the same subprocedure.

Subprocedures can also take parameters as seen in the Add_Two_Numbers procedure shown next.

```
Public Sub Add_Two_Numbers(x As Integer, y As Integer)
Dim liResult As Integer
liResult = x + y
End Sub
```

To call the Add_Two_Numbers procedure, you can also choose to use the Call keyword, or not.

```
Private Sub Form_Load()
Call Add_Two_Numbers(5, 3)
Add_Two_Numbers 5, 3
End Sub
```

Note that I used parentheses to surround the parameters when I used the Call keyword and no parentheses without the Call keyword.

Within subprocedures there may be times when you want to exit the procedure before executing all remaining statements. This can be accomplished with the Exit Sub command. For example, the following code exits the Add_Two_Numbers procedure before adding the two numbers if either parameter is a negative number.

```
Public Sub Add_Two_Numbers(x As Integer, y As Integer)
Dim liResult As Integer
```

```
If x < 0 Or y < 0 Then
    Exit Sub
End If
liResult = x + y
End Sub
```

So far, you have been writing your Visual Basic code in events such as form load and click events. Writing Visual Basic code in procedures is no different. The only real difference is the code's potential purpose. You can write Visual Basic code in control events to respond to user actions, or you can write code in procedures to modularize code for reusability.

Functions

As you know already, Visual Basic has many built-in or intrinsic functions. Table 5.1 outlines just a few that you have seen in the last few chapters.

The basic format for calling or referencing a function in Visual Basic is the function name followed by zero or more parameters.

In addition to built-in functions, you can also create your own Visual Basic functions know as *user-defined functions*.

Definition

The programmer for reusability purposes creates *user-defined functions* in Visual Basic through the aid of the Add Procedure dialog box. Like built-in functions, user-defined functions return a single value and can be used in expressions.

TABLE 5.1   A FEW COMMON FUNCTIONS

Function Name	Input	Output	Example
Val	String	Number	Val("44") is the number 44
Len	String	Number	Len("Michael") is the number 7
Int	Number	Number	Int(6.3) is the number 6
Str	Number	String	Str(7.75) is the string 7.75
UCase	String	String	UCase("Michael") is MICHAEL

The syntax for creating a Visual Basic function is a little different from that for subprocedures, so let's take a look:

```
Public Function Function_Name(variable1 as DataType, _
variable2 as DataType, ...) As DataType
     'Your code goes here
End Function
```

At first glance, you should see that I do not use the keyword Sub to denote a sub-program; instead, I use the keyword Function. Functions can take many parameters as depicted in the example. What this means is that you can send your function many different values that you want to process. Also note that the function itself is assigned a data type.

Let's take a look at a small function that adds two integer numbers:

```
Public Function Add(operand1 as Integer, operand2 as Integer) _
As Integer
Add = operand1 + operand2
End Function
```

This might look a little strange at first because I assign the output of two integers added together to the name of the function. Don't worry if this seems distressing because this is how functions in Visual Basic work.

After the two integers are added together, they are assigned to the name of the function, in this case Add. After that, the value of the added integers assigned to the name of the function is returned back to the calling procedure. Let's take a look at how I might call this function in the click event of a command button:

```
Private Sub Command1_Click()

Dim result as Integer
result = Add(5, 15)

End Sub
```

The integer variable result is assigned the returning value of the function Add, which in this case is the number 20.

TRAP   When creating functions, it is good programming practice to denote the data type of the return value of your function. Not doing so could lead to incorrect use of your user-defined functions by other programmers and even yourself.

For example, what is the output of the Add function example if I include the two numbers 5.75 and 10.75 as incoming parameters? Instead of the number 16.5, I receive the number 17.

To alleviate any misunderstanding, you can change the Add function name to AddTwoIntegers.

If you have never seen or worked with functions before, they might seem a little intimidating at first. The best way to understand them is to build them and use them.

Let's take another look at a new version of the name game from Chapter 2, shown in Figure 5.5, that uses functions to modularize code for reusability.

At first glance, the name game appears to have much of the same code from its counterpart in Chapter 2, and it does. The difference is in the way the code is arranged and used.

The click event of the GetName command button finds the location of the space in the name (with a little help from the InStr function) and passes it to the Get-FirstName and GetLastName functions. When Visual Basic first reads a function call, it immediately jumps to that function, passing it any parameters included.

```
Option Explicit


Private Sub cmdGetName_Click()


Dim lsFirstName As String
Dim lsLastName As String
Dim lsFullName As String
Dim liSpace As Integer
```

FIGURE 5.5

The name game from Chapter 2 built with functions.

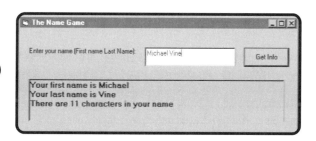

```
liSpace = InStr(txtName.Text, " ")
lsFirstName = GetFirstName(liSpace)
lsLastName = GetLastName(liSpace)

picOutput.Cls
picOutput.Print "Your first name is " & lsFirstName
picOutput.Print "Your last name is " & lsLastName
picOutput.Print "There are " & Len(txtName.Text) - 1 & _
" characters in your name"

End Sub
```

TRAP   If you forget to pass parameters to a function that is expecting parameters, you get a Visual Basic runtime error.

When the function is finished with its processing, it passes back the applicable value to the calling procedure. In my case, I pass the first- and last-name values back to the variables lsFirstName and lsLastName:

```
Public Function GetFirstName(liSpace As Integer) As String
GetFirstName = Left(txtName.Text, liSpace - 1)
End Function

Public Function GetLastName(liSpace As Integer) As String
GetLastName = Right(txtName.Text, Len(txtName.Text) - liSpace)
End Function
```

You can see my two functions in action. Both take the liSpace integer as a parameter and derive a name value using other intrinsic functions. After that, they assign the values to the function name, which is passed back to the calling procedure as a string value.

Like subprocedures, functions can be exited from anywhere in the function before executing all function statements. To accomplish this, use the keywords Exit Function.

HINT   Function procedures created using the Add Procedure menu item do not have an assigned data type or parameter list with data types. It is your job to perform these last steps when creating functions. Before creating functions, you should give some thought to what you want to pass into the function, what data it needs from the outside, and what data type it should pass back (string, integer, double, and so on).

Okay, what's the big deal about these functions in the so-called new name game? Well, adding functions to the name game is not exactly what I call a productive move for such a small program. But what if you were building a much larger program that extracted name information in 50 or more locations in your program code? Would it be productive to write the same code over and over again each time you need to extract name information? Probably not, but if you modularize your code by adding these functions, you can call them from anywhere in your program with a simple one-line function call. Pretty cool, huh?

ByRef and ByVal Keywords

You might remember my mentioning the concept of pointers previously in this book. Essentially, pointers are variables that contain memory addresses as their values. Other variables that you might declare, such as integer or string, contain a specific data-type value. In contrast, pointers contain the memory address that points to the memory address of a variable containing a variable data type such as integer or string. This type of reference is called *indirection*.

> **Definition**
>
> *Indirection* applies to the science behind pointers. Specifically, indirection allows a pointer containing a memory address to reference the memory address of another variable containing a valid data type.

In languages such as C, pointers save memory space and increase program performance. They are often used to pass parameter information to functions by reference. Passing by reference eliminates any duplicate variable data and thus reduces program overhead. Even for experienced C programmers, the concept of pointers and indirection can be difficult to master.

Fortunately for Visual Basic programmers, Microsoft takes care of implementing pointers behind the scenes. When passing parameters to functions in Visual Basic, you can note the concept of pointers with the keywords ByRef and ByVal.

When you use the ByVal keyword in a function parameter, a copy of the original variable is sent to the function. This also means that you cannot directly change the original value of the variable:

```
Public Function Send_By_Value(ByVal studentCount As Integer) _
As Integer
    'Function code
End Function
```

This code block depicts a Visual Basic function where an integer parameter called studentCount expects to receive a copy of an incoming integer variable. Any changes made to the variable studentCount are not seen in the original variable sent by the calling procedure.

If I want to change the original value of the integer variable, I can simply replace the ByVal keyword with ByRef:

```
Public Function Send_By_Value(ByRef studentCount As Integer) _
As Integer
    'Function code
End Function
```

Now, any changes I make to the studentCount variable are directly made to the original variable value. In other words, the ByRef keyword implements the concept of indirection for us.

 If you do not make the specification of ByRef or ByVal, Visual Basic defaults the passing parameter to ByRef.

Interacting with the User

So far, you have been looking at games and programs that sit idle waiting for a user to do something. Well, instead, why don't I get aggressive and force users to do something whether they're ready or not? I think those users need to get in line and shape up anyway. After all, as the programmer, I'm the one who should make the decisions around here. Right?

Well, not quite: The software-development process doesn't work like that anymore. As new-generation programmers, we design program interfaces that meet the needs of the user community, not the other way around. However, programmers can interact a little with the user community, forcing them to respond to something we as programmers or users need to know about right away.

If you have been using Windows-based applications for some time, you have probably seen what I'm talking about. For instance, error messages, dialog boxes, and input boxes are all good examples. In this section, you will learn how to build this interaction with the user through Visual Basic's message boxes and input boxes.

Message Box

Message boxes are perfect when you want to alert the user to something happening in your program. For example, an error has occurred, or a game has just ended. Maybe you want to display a congratulatory note or a question about retrying some action.

Microsoft operating systems such as Windows NT, 95, and 98 all use various sorts of message boxes. For example, have you ever seen the error message box, shown in Figure 5.6, that appears when you reference a disk drive that has no disk?

The error message in Figure 5.6 is a good example of a message box that contains two options for a user response. Another example of a message box is shown in Figure 5.7, which depicts a basic message box with one response option.

You create message boxes with the MsgBox function call. The basic syntax is as follows:

```
MsgBox "Message", Buttons, "Title Bar Caption"
```

The syntax I used to create the message box in Figure 5.7 looks like this:

```
MsgBox "My Message Box", , "Chapter 5"
```

Notice that I did not include any button information in my message box function. If you elect not to include button information, Visual Basic displays the default OK button.

Table 5.2 contains a list of some popular Visual Basic buttons and icons that you can use to create various message box types.

FIGURE 5.6

A Microsoft error message box with two response options.

FIGURE 5.7

A simple message box with one response option.

TABLE 5.2 VISUAL BASIC BUTTON AND ICON TYPES

Button/Icon Constant Name	Value
vbOKOnly	0 (Default)
vbOKCancel	1
vbAbortRetryIgnore	2
vbYesNoCancel	3
vbYesNo	4
vbRetryCancel	5
vbCritical	16
vbQuestion	32
vbExclamation	48
vbInformation	64

Because the first parameter in the message box is a string, you can also insert a string variable name as a parameter. You can accomplish this by first declaring a variable and then assigning a string value to it:

```
Dim lsMessageString as String
lsMessageString = "Visual Basic Programming for the Absolute Beginner" & _

        "by Michael Vine, 2001"
```

Once a string is created, you can then use it in your message box functions as follows:

```
MsgBox lsMessageString, , "Chapter 5"
```

HINT

You may have noticed the ampersand sign (&) and the underscore (_) symbol in the preceding code example. You should already know that the ampersand symbol is used for concatenation, but what about the underscore? In Visual Basic, the underscore symbol is a special character called the line-continuation character. It is most useful when you have a long line of code and want to continue it on the next line.

Give it a try the next time you have a line of code too long for one line. I'm sure you will find it useful.

Input Box

Sometimes message boxes do not provide enough interaction between your program and the user. For example, what if you want to prompt the user for his or her name? Maybe you want to prompt a user to enter a starting level before a game begins. You can implement these types of scenarios with the Visual Basic input box.

You build the input box by referencing a built-in Visual Basic function called InputBox. Its basic syntax is as follows:

```
InputBox(Prompt, [Title], [Default], [XPos], [YPos], _
[HelpFile], [Context])
```

The most commonly used parameters of the input box are prompt, title, and default, which are described in Table 5.3.

Using these parameters, here's how I implement an input box that prompts a user for her name.

```
InputBox "What is your name?", "My Input Box Example", _
"Your name goes here"
```

The output of this InputBox function appears in Figure 5.8.

Because you normally use input boxes for gathering information, it is customary to assign the collected data to a variable or property. For example, I can assign the user's response directly to the caption property of a label control.

```
lblOutput.Caption = "Welcome " & _
InputBox("What is your name?", "My Input Box Example", _
"Your name goes here")
```

TABLE 5.3 A FEW COMMON INPUT BOX PARAMETERS

Parameter Name	Purpose	Example
Prompt	A question	"What is your name?"
Title	The caption of the input box	"My Input Box Example"
Default	Default text property	"Your name goes here"

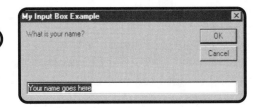

FIGURE 5.8

An example of
Visual Basic's
input box.

TRAP

Remember that all information stored in the text property of text boxes is stored as the string data type. If you want to ask the user for a number and assign it to a number variable type such as an integer, you first have to convert the string representation of the number into a number data type using the val function:

```
Dim liNumber As Integer
liNumber = Val(InputBox("Enter a number between 1 and 10", _
"A number Question"))
```

To better illustrate the applications of input and message boxes, I dissect a small program I wrote called the math quiz. As seen in Figures 5.9 and 5.10, the math quiz program asks the user random math questions through an input box. Depending on the answer, the user sees one of two message boxes.

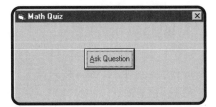

FIGURE 5.9

The math quiz
program.

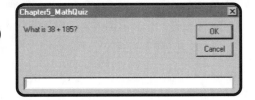

FIGURE 5.10

A demonstration of
the input box in the
math quiz program.

In the following code, you can see that I compare what the user enters into the input box against the correct answer. If the user gets the problem right, I let him know through a message box. Conversely, if the user gets the question wrong, I also let him know through a message box (with the correct answer attached, of course).

```
Option Explicit


Private Sub Form_Load()
Randomize
End Sub


Private Sub cmdAskQuestion_Click()
Ask_Question
End Sub
```

The command button's click event calls the Ask_Question subprocedure.

```
Public Sub Ask_Question()


Dim liOperand1 As Integer
Dim liOperand2 As Integer
Dim liResult As Integer


liOperand1 = Int(200 * Rnd) + 1
liOperand2 = Int(200 * Rnd) + 1


liResult = liOperand1 + liOperand2


If Val(InputBox("What is " & liOperand1 & " + " & _
liOperand2 & "?")) = liResult Then
  MsgBox ("Correct!")
Else
  MsgBox ("Incorrect. " & liOperand1 & " + " & liOperand2 & _
" = " & liResult)
End If


End Sub
```

Playing Sounds in Visual Basic

Only a few versions ago, playing sounds in Visual Basic was a task not for the faint of heart. It took an understanding of the Windows Application Programmer's Interface, also known as the *Windows API*, and a little knowledge of C++ would have been nice, too.

In version 6 of Visual Basic, Microsoft included a new component (along with many others) called the Microsoft multimedia control. The multimedia component is just like any other control that you have seen so far. It contains properties and methods for playing sound and video files.

> **Definition**
>
> The *Windows API* is a collection of Microsoft Windows libraries that contain various procedures for unlocking the power of Microsoft Windows.

The addition of the multimedia control is good news for beginning Visual Basic programmers because it allows you to play sounds and video clips in Visual Basic without having to learn the Windows API.

You can add the multimedia control by right-clicking on the toolbox or by selecting Project and Components from the Visual Basic menu. From the Components window, select the multimedia control as seen in Figure 5.11.

Once you add the multimedia control to your toolbox, you can add it to your Visual Basic application as you do any other control in the toolbox. Figure 5.12 depicts the multimedia control added to a form.

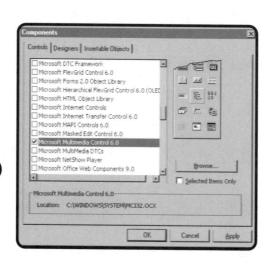

FIGURE 5.11

Adding the Microsoft multimedia control to your toolbox.

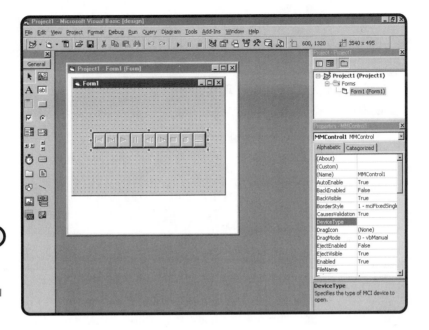

FIGURE 5.12

The Microsoft
multimedia
control on a Visual
Basic form.

Surprisingly, the multimedia control is easy to work with. If you set its visible property to true, the user can see and use the built-in interface for playing, stopping, pausing, ejecting, and searching audio and video. Or you can set the visible property to false and create your own custom interface.

The basic functionality of the multimedia graphical control is as follows:

Previous

Next

Play

Pause

Back

Step

Stop

Record

Eject

Table 5.4 lists the devices supported by the multimedia interface.

TABLE 5.4 POPULAR DEVICES SUPPORTED BY THE MULTIMEDIA CONTROL

Device Type	Description
AVIVideo	Audio/Visual Interlaced video (.avi file type)
CDAudio	CD audio player
DAT	Digital audio tape player
DigitalVideo	Digital video
Sequencer	MIDI devices (.mid or .rmi file types)
VCR	Video cassette recorder
WaveAudio	A Wave device (.wav file type)

Whether you allow the user to use the graphical interface provided by the multimedia control or build your own, you need to set a few other properties during design time to get the multimedia control working.

Depending on when you want sounds or video to play in your application, you can set the multimedia control properties during design time or at runtime through events such as form load. The basic properties that you should set appear in the following code:

```
'Set initial property values
MMControl1.Notify = False
MMControl1.Wait = True
MMControl1.Shareable = False
MMControl1.DeviceType = "WaveAudio"
MMControl1.FileName = _
"C:\book\vb_chapter5\shooting_gallery\Blaster_1.wav"
'Open the media device
MMControl1.Command = "Open"
```

You can see that I assign the string WaveAudio to the DeviceType property. This tells the multimedia control that I want to play .wav files. In the FileName property, I assign the path and filename of the .wav file that I want to play. After that, I open the control by setting the command property to open.

Once these initial properties are set, I can play a sound using the following syntax:

```
MMControl1.Command = "Play"
```

It is also a good idea to close the multimedia control when your program is finished. To do so, you set the command property to close:

```
MMControll.Command = "Close"
```

Constructing the Shooting Gallery Game

As seen in Figure 5.13, the shooting gallery game uses many of the topics that you have learned about in this chapter. All graphics used in the shooting gallery game were produced by professional artist Hermann Hillmann and appear courtesy of http://www.vbexplorer.com.

The Problem

Create a shooting gallery game. The game should place images randomly around a form, allowing a user to hit it with the click of a mouse. When the user presses the left mouse button, a laser sound plays, and if the target is hit, a grunt sound plays. The game should allow the user to pick a level of difficulty and keep track of the number of misses and the number of hits.

Table 5.5 outlines the controls and properties of the shooting gallery game.

FIGURE 5.13

The shooting gallery game.

TABLE 5.5 CONTROLS AND PROPERTIES OF THE SHOOTING GALLERY GAME

Control	Property	Setting
frmMain	Caption	Shooting Gallery
	BorderStyle	1 – Fixed Single
	Picture	Bitmap
lblGameOver	Caption	Game Over
	Visible	False
	Enabled	False
imgTarget	Enabled	True
	Picture	None
	Stretch	False
	Visible	False
imgStanding	Enabled	True
	Picture	Bitmap
	Stretch	False
	Visible	False
imgExplode	Enabled	True
	Picture	Bitmap
	Stretch	False
	Visible	False
Timer1	Enabled	False
MMControl1	Visible	False
MMControl2	Visible	False
fraConsole	Caption	None
	BorderStyle	0 – None
	BackColor	Black
cmdStart	Caption	&Start
cmdStop	Caption	Sto&p
Label1	Caption	Hits:
Label2	Caption	Misses:
lblScore	Caption	None
lblMisses	Caption	None

A draft algorithm for the shooting gallery game is outlined below.

1. Open a new standard EXE Visual Basic project.

2. Build the graphical interface for the game.

3. Set all design-time control properties.

4. Write code in the form load event to set properties and variables. Also in the form load event, call the randomize function.

5. Write a subprocedure to set the properties of the multimedia controls.

6. Write code in the click event for the start command button. This code should prompt a user for a level. Based on that level, it should then set the interval property of the timer control. If a valid level is entered, start a new game.

7. Generate random numbers in the Timer event that will be used for placing images randomly on the form. The Timer event should also check for a win before displaying an image.

8. A click on the form is the same as saying the target was missed. For this event, write program code that takes care of playing a laser sound and incrementing the number of misses.

9. Write code that responds to the player hitting the target. This should cause a new image to appear, a grunt sound to play, and the number of hits to be incremented.

10. Write a function that checks for a win. This function should look for a predetermined number of hits to the target.

11. Write code to respond to stopping and restarting the game. This program code should reset all necessary variables, controls, and properties.

12. Write code to unload the multimedia control when the game is terminated.

The Implementation

The form load event starts the randomize function and sets a few control properties:

```
Option Explicit
Dim fiPlayersScore As Integer
Dim fiNumberofMisses As Integer
Dim fbTargetHit As Boolean
```

```
Private Sub Form_Load()
Randomize
imgTarget.Enabled = False
imgTarget.Visible = False
cmdStop.Enabled = False
lblGameOver.Visible = False
lblGameOver.Enabled = False
End Sub
```

In the click event of the start command button, I prompt the user for a valid level.
Depending on which valid level is entered, I set the timer's interval property:

```
Private Sub cmdStart_Click()
Dim lsUserResponse As String
Dim lbResponse As Boolean

lsUserResponse = InputBox("Enter a level from 1 to 3, 1 being _
the easiest and 3 being the hardest")
lbResponse = False
```

If the response of the user is not valid, I simply send her a message box saying so,
and I set a Boolean variable to false. The following code uses this Boolean variable
to decide whether to start the game:

```
If lsUserResponse = "1" Then
    Timer1.Interval = 1500
    lbResponse = True
ElseIf lsUserResponse = "2" Then
    Timer1.Interval = 1000
    lbResponse = True
ElseIf lsUserResponse = "3" Then
    Timer1.Interval = 750
    lbResponse = True
Else
    MsgBox ("Game not started.")
    lbResponse = False
End If
```

The built-in function LoadPicture might be new to you. It is useful when you want to assign a picture to a picture box manually or to change the icon of your cursor to something else. In this program, I elect to change the mouse cursor to that of a cross-hair when the game is started:

```
If lbResponse = True Then
    cmdStart.Enabled = False
    imgTarget.Picture = imgStanding.Picture
    frmMain.MouseIcon = _
LoadPicture("C:\book\vb_chapter5\shooting_gallery\crosshair.ICO")
```

Setting the MousePointer property to 99 tells Visual Basic that I want to use a custom or user-defined mouse icon. You can find out more on the MousePointer property in Chapter 11.

```
    frmMain.MousePointer = 99
    fbTargetHit = False
    Load_Sounds
    cmdStop.Enabled = True
    fiPlayersScore = 0
    fiNumberofMisses = 0
    lblScore.Caption = fiPlayersScore
    lblMisses.Caption = fiNumberofMisses
    Timer1.Enabled = True
  lblGameOver.Visible = False
  lblGameOver.Enabled = False
End If


End Sub
```

I wrote code in the click event of the stop command button to reset the game in the event the user wants to stop playing before the game has ended:

```
Private Sub cmdStop_Click()
Unload_Sounds
frmMain.MousePointer = vbNormal
Timer1.Enabled = False
imgTarget.Enabled = False
imgTarget.Visible = False
cmdStart.Enabled = True
cmdStop.Enabled = False
cmdStart.SetFocus
```

```
lblGameOver.Visible = True
lblGameOver.Enabled = True
End Sub
```

If the form click event is triggered, I know that the user has missed the target. In this event, I play a laser sound and increment the number of misses:

```
Private Sub Form_Click()
MMControl1.Command = "Play"
MMControl1.Command = "Prev"
fiNumberofMisses = fiNumberofMisses + 1
lblMisses.Caption = fiNumberofMisses
End Sub
```

I created a subprocedure called Load_Sounds that handles the initialization of my multimedia controls. Note that the path assigned to the FileName property is unique to my file and directory system. You will want to change this path to reflect the location of your sound or audio files:

```
Public Sub Load_Sounds()

'Set initial property values for blaster sound
MMControl1.Notify = False
MMControl1.Wait = True
MMControl1.Shareable = False
MMControl1.DeviceType = "WaveAudio"
MMControl1.FileName = _
"C:\book\vb_chapter5\shooting_gallery\Blaster_1.wav"
'Open the media device
MMControl1.Command = "Open"

'Set initial property values for grunt sound
MMControl2.Notify = False
MMControl2.Wait = True
MMControl2.Shareable = False
MMControl2.DeviceType = "WaveAudio"
MMControl2.FileName = _
"C:\book\vb_chapter5\shooting_gallery\Pain_Grunt_4.wav"
'Open the media device
MMControl2.Command = "Open"

End Sub
```

When the target is hit, I play a sound, change the current picture, and increment the player's score. Disabling the Timer control and calling a procedure named pauseProgram aid this process. This procedure also calls the CheckForWin function to see if the player has won the game. If so, the game is stopped by calling the click event of the stop command button.

```
Private Sub imgTarget_Click()


MMControl2.Command = "Play"
MMControl2.Command = "Prev"
Timer1.Enabled = False
imgTarget.Picture = imgExplode.Picture
pauseProgram


fiPlayersScore = fiPlayersScore + 1
Timer1.Enabled = True
If CheckForWin = True Then
    cmdStop_Click
    lblScore.Caption = fiPlayersScore
    Exit Sub
End IflblScore.Caption = fiPlayersScore
fbTargetHit = True
imgStanding.Enabled = False
imgTarget.Visible = False
imgTarget.Enabled = False
Timer1.Enabled = True
End Sub
```

The timer event is triggered based on the level the user selected. Its main purpose is to produce a random place on the form for the image to appear. I can accomplish this by first knowing the Height and Width properties of the form during design time. (Simply look at the form's properties in the Properties window during design time.) Once I have these numbers, I can use the rnd function to generate random numbers that I assign to the top and left properties of the image. Note that for this game, I did not use the exact width and height properties of the form because I do not want the random images to appear in the scoreboard area.

```
Private Sub Timer1_Timer()


Dim liRandomLeft As Integer
```

```
Dim liRandomTop As IntegerImgTarget.Visible=True

If fbTargetHit = True Then
        fbTargetHit = False
     imgTarget.Picture = imgStanding.Picture
End If


liRandomLeft = (6120 * Rnd)
liRandomTop = (4680 * Rnd)
imgTarget.Left = liRandomLeft
imgTarget.Top = liRandomTop
imgTarget.Enabled = True
imgTarget.Visible = True


End Sub
```

The CheckForWin function is pretty straightforward; it simply looks for a prede-termined score of 10. If the user has reached the score of 10, the function returns a true value:

```
Public Function CheckForWin() As Boolean


CheckForWin = False
If fiPlayersScore = 10 Then
    CheckForWin = True
End If


End Function
```

The following event, QueryUnload, is triggered when a user clicks the X icon in the upper-right corner of the form's window:

```
Private Sub Form_QueryUnload(Cancel As Integer, _
UnloadMode As Integer)
Unload_Sounds
End Sub
```

Closing the window through other means also triggers it. This is actually an important event to know because sometimes you might find that your users do not always use your exit or quit command buttons. If you write code for these command buttons to perform some form of program cleanup, and the user closes your program without using the command buttons, your code for program cleanup never runs.

To solve this problem, it is always a good idea to acknowledge the QueryUnload event if you want something to happen when your program terminates.

The Unload_Sounds function's sole purpose is to close the multimedia control:

```
Public Sub Unload_Sounds()
MMControl1.Command = "Close"
MMControl2.Command = "Close"
End Sub
```

As mentioned earlier, the pauseProgram helps to ensure that processes such as image display and sounds occur. Essentially it uses the intrinsic Second and Time functions and a loop to pause for approximately 1 second.

```
Public Sub pauseProgram()
Dim currentTime
Dim newTime
currentTime = Second(Time)
newTime = Second(Time)

Do Until Abs(newTime - currentTime) >= 1
   newTime = Second(Time)
Loop
End Sub
```

Summary

In this chapter, you learned that procedures comprise both functions and sub-procedures. You also have a working knowledge of functions and subprocedures, what they are, and what they can do for you. You know that learning how to build functions is the foundation for learning more complex software engineering tools such as object-oriented programming.

I also discussed the science behind passing parameters to functions through the use of ByVal and ByRef keywords and that these keywords are Visual Basic's hidden implementation of indirection or pointers.

Beyond procedures, you learned how to interact with users through input boxes and message boxes. In addition, you learned how easy it can be to play sounds in Visual Basic using the Microsoft multimedia control.

After this chapter, I encourage you and challenge you to write reusable code through functions and subprograms whenever possible. In the long run, the practice makes you a better programmer; this I promise you.

CHALLENGES

1. Modify the shooting gallery game so that it uses more than one image. Specifically, provide images for good guys and images for bad guys. If the user clicks (hits) a good guy, then her score should be decremented by one.

2. Using the KeyDown event, modify the shooting gallery game to use the arrow keys for cross-hair movement and the spacebar key for the firing mechanism.

Following are the keycodes you need to know for the arrow and space-bar keys:

Keyboard Character	Keycode
Left arrow	37
Up arrow	38
Right arrow	39
Down arrow	40
Spacebar	32

To move an image control, simply use the move method in conjunction with the left and top properties. For example, here is how I move the image control left if the left arrow key is pressed:

```
If KeyCode = 37 Then
    Image1.Move Image1.Left - 50
End If
```

3. Using the Microsoft multimedia control, create a CD jukebox with your own interface. The CD jukebox should allow a user to select multiple songs from a list and play them. If you do not have CD quality music in digital format, search the Internet for free downloadable music. There's a bunch out there.

4. Write your own quiz game that prompts a user with a question using the input box. If the user gets the question correct, respond with a congratulatory message box. And if he gets the question wrong, respond with another message box that gives him the answer.

Advanced Controls

One of Visual Basic's biggest draws is its ability to easily incorporate seemingly complicated and robust controls into a graphical environment. Menus, List Boxes, Combo Boxes, common dialogs, animation, and text-to-speech engines are just a few new controls you learn in this chapter. It is these advanced controls and many others that can aid in the design of a more fluid human-to-computer interaction.

Specifically, this chapter covers the following:

- List Boxes and Combo Boxes
- Common dialog control
- Human/computer interaction
- Microsoft agents
- Constructing the agent program

Project: The Agent Program

As seen in Figure 6.1, the agent program uses some interesting technologies developed by Microsoft to perform various character animations and text-to-speech functions. As you will see, these programmable actions make a more interactive and graphically appealing user experience. The agent program's primary focus is demonstrating Microsoft Visual Basic's easy-to-build yet powerful and appealing object-based controls.

List Boxes and Combo Boxes

Visual Basic provides many graphical ways to display options or choices to users. You have already learned a few such ways through option buttons and check boxes. List Boxes and Combo Boxes also provide the user with a list of choices through items in a selectable box. Although both List and Combo Boxes perform similar functions, each has its own niche in fulfilling different user needs.

List Boxes

The List Box is a popular choice when you want to give the user a list of selectable items. The programmer generally populates List Boxes with items during design time or through program code in runtime.

As with other common Visual Basic controls, you can add the List Box to your form by double-clicking it on the Visual Basic toolbar, shown in Figure 6.2.

You might notice that the List Box control in Figure 6.3 closely resembles a Text Box control. You are right if you made this observation because the List Box shares many of the Text Box's properties. However, what makes the List Box

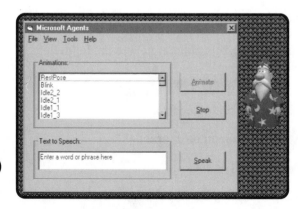

FIGURE 6.1

The agent program.

control unique is its ability to add many selectable items and keep track of them through index properties.

Table 6.1 depicts many of the popular properties and methods of the List Box control.

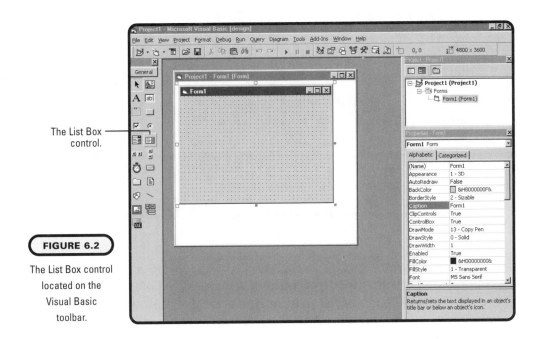

FIGURE 6.2

The List Box control located on the Visual Basic toolbar.

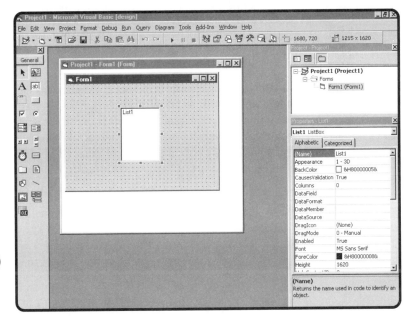

FIGURE 6.3

The List Box control added to a form.

TABLE 6.1 POPULAR LIST BOX PROPERTIES AND METHODS

Name	Purpose
AddItem	Adds an item to the List Box
Clear	Deletes all items from the List Box
Columns	Determines the number of visible columns in the List Box
List(*n*)	Holds the value of an item, where *n* is the index of the item in the List Box
ListCount	The total number of items in a List Box
ListIndex	Index number of the currently highlighted item
Multiselect	Allows a user to select one or more items in a List Box
RemoveItem *n*	Removes an item from the List Box, where *n* is the index of the item
Sorted	Displays items in alphabetical order

The most difficult part of understanding List Boxes (and Combo Boxes) is mastering the ListIndex property. In reality, it is not that complicated; just know that every time you add an item to a List Box, a corresponding index (or ListIndex) is added as well.

TRAP

Note that indexes in List and Combo Boxes start at 0. The first item in a List Box contains the number 0 for its ListIndex property, and the fifth item in a List Box contains the ListIndex property of 4.

This is an important concept to remember because sometimes programmers forget to offset a number by 1 when using the ListIndex property, which ultimately gives them the wrong item or value. This is sometimes referred to as an off-by-1 error, which means that a programmer did not take into an account that an index starts with 0.

Now that you have a feel for what a List Box is, let me show you a program, in Figure 6.4, that uses a List Box to display a list of various states. When a user clicks on one of the states, a message box appears, as in Figure 6.5, showing the user the ListIndex and the value of the item clicked.

FIGURE 6.4

A program that
uses the List Box
control to add the
names of states.

FIGURE 6.5

A message box
displays the
ListIndex and the
value of the item
clicked.

Before adding any items to the List Box, I use the clear method to delete any current items. If I did not do this, the items would be duplicated in the List Box each
time the user clicked the command button:

```
Option Explicit


Private Sub cmdFillListBox_Click()
lstStates.Clear
```

I use the AddItem method to add items to the List Box when the user clicks the
fill List Box command button:

```
lstStates.AddItem "Florida"
lstStates.AddItem "Alabama"
lstStates.AddItem "New York"
lstStates.AddItem "California"
lstStates.AddItem "Tennessee"
lstStates.AddItem "Georgia"
lstStates.AddItem "New Mexico"
lstStates.AddItem "North Carolina"
lstStates.AddItem "Maryland"
```

```
lstStates.AddItem "Oregon"
lstStates.AddItem "Wyoming"
lstStates.AddItem "Nevada"
lstStates.AddItem "Indiana"
lstStates.AddItem "Colorado"
lstStates.AddItem "Ohio"
lstStates.AddItem "Texas"
End Sub
```

 Note that you can also use the List property (found in the Properties window) of the List Box during design time to add items to a List Box.

I use a message box in the click event of the List Box to display information about what the user has chosen. To get the index of the chosen item, I simply call the ListIndex property that contains the index of the currently highlighted selection. I can also get the value of the current item by passing the ListIndex property to the list function:

```
Private Sub lstStates_Click()
MsgBox ("You clicked list index " & lstStates.ListIndex & _
" with the list property of " & lstStates.List(lstStates._
ListIndex) & ".")
End Sub
```

The End keyword in the quit command button's click event ends the program.

```
Private Sub cmdQuit_Click()
End
End Sub
```

 List Boxes are often one part of an overall design strategy for processing information. Sometimes, it is necessary to check whether the user has selected an item in a List Box before an action can occur. You can perform this test through the use of conditions and the ListIndex property:

```
If List1.ListIndex = -1 Then
    'Alert the user
Else
    'Continue processing
End If
```

The ListIndex property is set to -1 if there is no current selection in the List Box.

Combo Boxes

The Combo Box is a more sophisticated cousin of the List Box. Although it shares many of the List Box's main properties and methods, it has one property and graphical appearance that makes it stand apart from its cousin.

The property that determines how the Combo Box looks and works is the style property. Depending on the setting of the style property, the Combo Box can allow a user to enter a value into the top part of its graphical interface. You can almost think of the Combo Box as a Text Box on top of a List Box. In fact, the Combo Box has a Text property that can be used to grab information from the user and input it into the Combo Box as a new item.

The style property has three settings:

0 Drop-down combo

1 Simple combo

2 Drop-down list

To illustrate each of these settings, I use a Combo Box in a program similar to the one in Figure 6.3.

The drop-down combo style shown in Figure 6.6 allows a user to enter an item into the top part of the Combo Box.

The drop-down combo style setting has two useful purposes. First, a user can use the top part to aid in searching for an item. As the user enters characters, the list part of the Combo Box searches for what the user has typed. Second, the user can add an item to the Combo Box.

HINT You cannot expand the height of a Combo Box when its style property is set to drop-down combo or drop-down list.

FIGURE 6.6

A Combo Box with style property set to 0 – drop-down combo.

The simple combo style has the same features and benefits as the drop-down combo style. However, the simple combo style allows you to expand the height of the Combo Box as shown in Figure 6.7.

The last style setting, 2 – drop-down list, shown in Figure 6.8, looks very much like the first setting (0 – drop-down combo), but it does not allow a user to enter anything into the top part of the Combo Box. In fact, when a Combo Box has the style setting of drop-down list, its basic functionality is that of a common List Box.

Drive, Directory, and File List Boxes

The usefulness of List Boxes is evident in Microsoft's Drive, Directory, and File List Boxes. These custom List Boxes allow you as a programmer to display a computer's drive, directory, and file information.

Each of these custom List Boxes is part of Visual Basic's common controls and appears on the toolbar, as shown in Figure 6.9.

Working with the Drive, Directory, and File List Boxes is similar to using the List and Combo Boxes. Visual Basic, however, performs much of the work necessary to view a Microsoft Windows file system.

FIGURE 6.7

A Combo Box with style property set to 1 – simple combo.

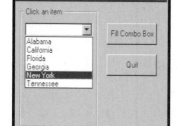

FIGURE 6.8

A Combo Box with style property set to 2 – drop-down list.

The Drive List Box

The File List Box

The Directory List Box

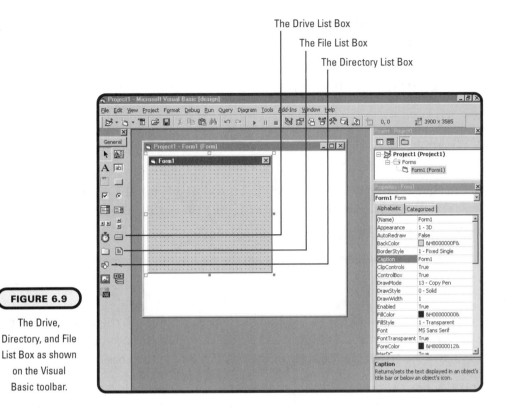

FIGURE 6.9

The Drive, Directory, and File List Box as shown on the Visual Basic toolbar.

Using these List Boxes is easy. To illustrate, the program depicted in Figure 6.10 allows a user to select a picture for preview.

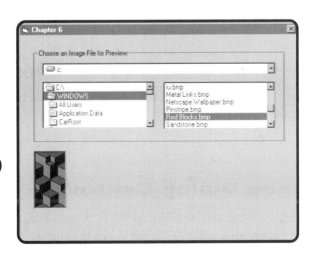

FIGURE 6.10

A picture preview program that uses the Drive, Directory, and File List Boxes.

The Drive List Box automatically loads all available drives as items. You only need to add code in its change event to tell the Directory List Box that it should change its path:

```
Option Explicit

Private Sub Drive1_Change()
Dir1.Path = Drive1.Drive
End Sub
```

In the change event of the Directory List Box, I simply tell the File List Box that it needs to change its path. I do this by assigning the path of the File List Box to the path of the Directory List Box:

```
Private Sub Dir1_Change()
File1.Path = Dir1.Path
End Sub
```

I use the click event of the File List Box to load a picture into the picture property of a Picture Box control. I simply pass the directory path concatenated with a back-slash and the FileName property of the File List Box to the LoadPicture function:

```
Private Sub File1_Click()
picDisplay.Picture = LoadPicture(Dir1.Path & "\" & File1.FileName)
End Sub
```

You can customize what files you want your File List Box to display by using the Pattern property. In the form load event, I tell the File List Box that I want it to display only bitmap files, or files that end with .bmp:

```
Private Sub Form_Load()
File1.Pattern = "*.bmp"
End Sub
```

 HINT You can assign multiple file extensions to the pattern property with semicolons.

```
Private Sub Form_Load()
file1.Pattern = "*.bmp; *.ico; *.gif"
End Sub
```

The Common Dialog Control

The Common Dialog control can be a Visual Basic programmer's best friend. It provides a number of pre-built custom dialog boxes for you to use. These custom dialog boxes are common in Microsoft operating systems, which is a good thing because most users are already familiar with what functions these dialog boxes perform.

The Common Dialog control does not appear on the standard Visual Basic toolbar. To add it to your Visual Basic project, you must add it to the toolbar by finding it in the Components window.

You can access the Components window by right-clicking the toolbar or choosing the Components menu item from the Project menu.

You can select the Common Dialog control from the Components window as seen in Figure 6.11.

Once you add it from the Components window, you have access to the Common Dialog control from the toolbar as seen in Figure 6.12.

The Common Dialog control actually consists of different dialog boxes. Once added to a form, the Common Dialog control itself is not visible during runtime. To launch one of the dialog boxes, use one of the following show methods.

The ShowColor method opens a Color dialog box, shown in Figure 6.13:

```
CommonDialog1.ShowColor
```

The ShowOpen method opens an Open dialog box, shown in Figure 6.14:

```
CommonDialog1.ShowOpen
```

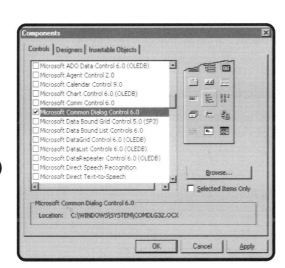

FIGURE 6.11

Selecting the Common Dialog control from within the Components window.

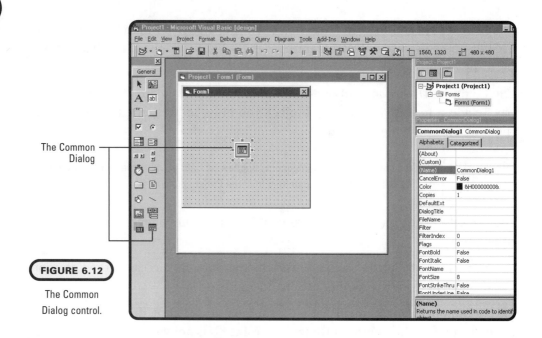

The Common Dialog

FIGURE 6.12

The Common Dialog control.

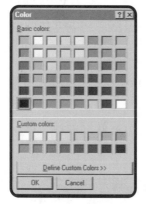

FIGURE 6.13

The Color dialog.

FIGURE 6.14

The Open dialog.

The ShowPrinter method opens a Print dialog box, shown in Figure 6.15:

```
CommonDialog1.ShowPrinter
```

The ShowSave method opens a Save As dialog box, shown in Figure 6.16:

```
CommonDialog1.ShowSave
```

To illustrate the Common Dialog control, I built a fun little paint program, shown in Figure 6.17, that allows you to draw using the mouse and change the background color of the canvas.

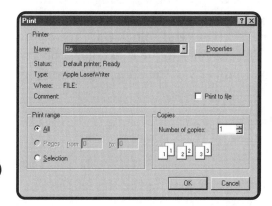

FIGURE 6.15

The Print dialog.

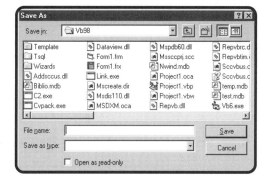

FIGURE 6.16

The Save As dialog.

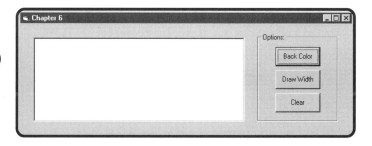

FIGURE 6.17

Demonstrating the Common Dialog control through the Paint program.

In the form load event, I assign the current BackColor property of the Picture Box to a variable (more on this later):

```
Option Explicit
Dim lbDrawing As Boolean
Dim originalBackColor

Private Sub Form_Load()
originalBackColor = picOutput.BackColor
End Sub
```

In the click event, I show the Color dialog box using the Common Dialog control. When the Color dialog box displays, execution of the Visual Basic program pauses until the user makes a choice of colors. Once the color is chosen, execution continues by assigning the color to the BackColor property of a Picture Box. You do this with the Color property of the Common Dialog control:

```
Private Sub cmdBackColor_Click()
CommonDialog1.ShowColor
picOutput.BackColor = CommonDialog1.Color
End Sub
```

The user also has the option of choosing the size of the line being drawn. To accomplish this, I use a Message Box to prompt the user for a number between 1 and 10. If the user enters a valid number, I assign it to the DrawWidth property of the Picture Box:

```
Private Sub cmdChangeLineSize_Click()
Dim lsDrawWidth As String

lsDrawWidth = InputBox("Enter a Draw Width Between 1 and 10: ")

If Val(lsDrawWidth) >= 1 And Val(lsDrawWidth) <= 10 Then
    picOutput.DrawWidth = lsDrawWidth
Else
    MsgBox ("You entered an invalid number for the DrawWidth.")
End If

End Sub
```

If the user wants to start over again, I clear the Picture Box by loading an empty picture and assign the original BackColor (from the form load event) back to the Picture Box:

```
Private Sub cmdClear_Click()
picOutput.Picture = LoadPicture()
picOutput.BackColor = originalBackColor
End Sub
```

Note that I could have used the Picture Boxes Cls method to clear the contents of the picture. Executing the Cls method would, however, only clear any drawings and not bring back the original back color.

Allowing the user to draw with the mouse requires that I use some of the Picture Box's mouse events. In the MouseDown event, all I need to do is tell Visual Basic that the user has started drawing. I do this by assigning the value true to a Boolean variable:

```
Private Sub picOutput_MouseDown(Button As Integer, Shift As _
Integer, X As Single, Y As Single)
lbDrawing = True
End Sub
```

Using the MouseMove event, I draw a single point where the cursor currently is (providing the left mouse button is still down):

```
Private Sub picOutput_MouseMove(Button As Integer, Shift As _
Integer, X As Single, Y As Single)
If lbDrawing = True Then
    picOutput.PSet (X, Y), picOutput.ForeColor
End If
End Sub
```

Drawing a point is easy: You only need to call the PSet method of the Picture Box, which takes x and y coordinates for its parameters. Fortunately for us, we can get the x and y coordinates from the MouseMove event. If you look at the top part of this event, you can see that MouseMove event is passing four values, two of which are the x and y coordinates of the mouse cursor.

Essentially the Pset method draws a point on an object such as a Picture Box or even a Form. As mentioned earlier, you can use the DrawWidth property of the Picture Box to determine the size of the point or points drawn.

The lifting of the left mouse button is captured in the MouseUp event. In this event, I set the Boolean variable to false. This essentially stops the drawing of points in the MouseMove event:

```
Private Sub picOutput_MouseUp(Button As Integer, Shift As _
Integer, X As Single, Y As Single)
lbDrawing = False
End Sub
```

Human/Computer Interaction

Up to now, you've probably been designing and developing Visual Basic programs without much concern for how a user would interact with your programs and how your programs would interact with a user. I hope to change this by showing you a number of Visual Basic and Microsoft-specific techniques for providing a more robust HCI (human/computer interaction) experience.

HCI, or human/computer interaction, has been a part of the computer science and engineering world since the 1960s. Although HCI has been a part of academia and engineering groups for more than three decades, it hasn't been until

> **Definition**
>
> *HCI* is the science behind the interaction of people and computers. It covers a broad spectrum of physical devices, programmable controls, navigational techniques, and human/computer ergonomics.

recently that corporate IT (information technology) departments have started factoring in HCI as part of their overall application-development processes. The recent trend of corporate IT departments understanding HCI can be directly attributed to a number of new technological factors—such as Rapid Application Development (RAD), graphical user interfaces (GUI), the Internet, and application prototyping languages such as Visual Basic.

The application of HCI is evident in keyboard shortcut keys, pointing devices (such as mice, tracking balls, and touch screens), visual interfaces, audio/video programs, fluid navigational links, and programmable events.

To find the right interaction between humans and computers, HCI experts study the science behind computer devices and their programmable events. Although the study of HCI is well beyond the scope of this book, I hope to introduce some of its applications and practices using Visual Basic and Microsoft controls.

ToolTipText

Have you ever been faced with a description-less control on a form or application and wondered what it does? I sure have. ToolTipText is a helpful property that can give your controls a little more meaning to a stumped user. It is especially useful when you're creating toolbars or other controls that do not allow much room for descriptive meanings.

Essentially, the ToolTipText property works when the mouse is moved over an object. A descriptive balloon-like text window appears when your mouse comes to rest over a control that has the ToolTipText property set.

The ToolTipText property appears in the Properties window for most controls.

TabIndex

The TabIndex properties of an application can give the user a more fluid navigational experience through the use of tab keys. Some users prefer to use keyboard events as opposed to mouse events. In other words, a common phrase I hear from users is "I prefer to tab around a window because it's quicker for me to use the keyboard than the mouse."

As you develop your graphical interfaces, you might be unaware of how the tab key on a keyboard will respond during program runtime. This is okay; you should not concern yourself with the TabIndex property of controls during the beginning stages of GUI design—because you will often find yourself removing and adding new controls to your forms. Wait until you feel fairly comfortable that the GUI design is completed before assigning the TabIndex properties of your controls.

 HINT Even though you might not concern yourself with tab index properties during GUI design, Visual Basic does. Visual Basic automatically assigns (in sequential order) a tab index property to each control you add to a form.

You can find the tab index property of a control by clicking the control during design time and looking for the property under the Properties window.

Default Property

The default property applies to all types of applications. It's frequently used with login screens and data entry forms. For example, after you've entered your user name and password, most login screens allow you to simply press the Enter key to log in, whether you actually press the Enter key.

This default process actually performs the equivalent of pressing the Enter key on the screen to log you in. Note that you didn't have to use the mouse, nor did you have to tab over to the Enter key before pressing it. That's the default property! In other words, setting a control's default property to true is like saying that it's the default control or button on your form.

As with the other properties mentioned earlier, you can access the default property in the Properties window.

Building Menus

Like many other graphical controls, menus can provide users with clearly visible navigational links to properties, functions, and other forms. Visual Basic provides an easy-to-use facility for creating menus with its menu editor.

The menu editor allows you to create hierarchical drop-down menus that you've probably seen and used with most Windows-based programs. In fact, if you have been programming in Visual Basic (I assume that you have been by now), you have already been using hierarchical drop-down menus, as shown in Figure 6.18.

You can create your own hierarchical menus using the menu editor, shown in Figure 6.19, which you access from the Tools menu.

A sample hierarchical menu

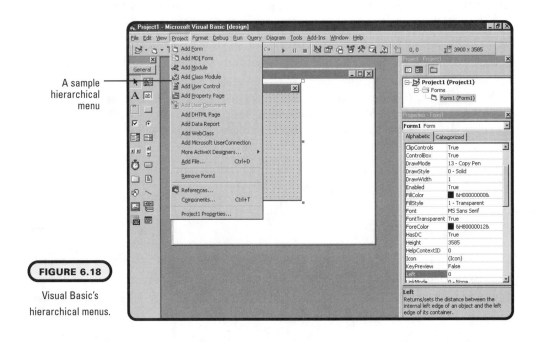

FIGURE 6.18

Visual Basic's hierarchical menus.

FIGURE 6.19

The menu editor allows you to create your own custom hierarchical menus.

To demonstrate the creation of menus using the menu editor, build the menu that you will need for the agent program using the following steps:

1. Open a new standard EXE project in Visual Basic.

2. From the Visual Basic Tools menu, select Menu Editor.

3. Start by adding the text &File to the Caption text box, and give it the name mnuFile in the name text box.

   Remember that the & (ampersand) character creates keyboard shortcuts with the Alt key.

 Note that you will follow the same Microsoft naming conventions that you've used previously in other chapters for your menu names. The first three characters of the menu name are letters mnu, which are followed by the parent menu item name.

4. Click the next command button and then the right arrow button. The right arrow button adds two empty quotes ("") to the bottom List Box under your File menu item. The empty quotes denote that the menu item directly under the File menu item will be a subitem of File. You can use the left arrow button to remove a submenu relationship and the up and down arrows to move the menu item to a desired location.

5. Add the text E&xit to the Caption text box, and give it the name mnuFile-Exit. Notice that I've named the exit menu item mnuFileExit. This naming convention denotes that the menu item Exit is a subitem or child of the File parent menu item.

6. Click the next command button and then the left arrow button to remove the empty quote submenu relationship. This means that the next menu item will be a parent menu item. Enter the text &View to the Caption Text Box, and give it the name mnuView.

7. Click the next command button and then the right arrow button to add a child menu item. Enter the text Hide Agent into the Caption Text Box, and give it the name mnuViewHideAgent.

8. Click the next command button, and leave the child menu item (double quotes) in place. Add a single hyphen (-) to the Caption Text Box, and give it the name mnuViewDash1.

9. Enter a single hyphen into the Caption Text Box of a menu item to graphically display a sunken line in the menu. This is good practice when you want to distinguish logical submenu items that are related to the parent menu item, but not necessarily to other child menu items within the parent menu item.

10. Click the next command button, and leave the empty quotes in place. Enter the text Advanced Character Options into the Caption Text Box, and give it the name mnuViewAdvanced.

11. Click the next command button, and remove the empty quotes (with the left arrow button). Enter the caption &Tools and the name mnuTools.

12. Click Next and leave the empty quotes to denote a child menu item under mnuTools. Leave the caption blank and the name mnuToolsChangeAgent.

13. Click OK to save your work.

After you add all necessary menu items, your graphical user interface should look like Figure 6.20.

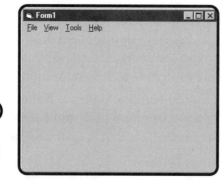

FIGURE 6.20

A hierarchical menu for the agent program.

Pop-Up Menus

Pop-up menus act like floating menus when a user right-clicks on a form. The location of the pop-up menu depends on where the mouse pointer is located on the form.

To create pop-up menus, you simply perform the same steps that you do for creating normal menu items. For example, let's say I want to create a pop-up menu that displays choices a File menu group normally contains, such as Open, Save, and Exit.

First, I create my menu items using the menu editor.

 HINT If I did not want the File menu group to be visible on the menu bar, I would simply set the File menu item's visible property to false. When the parent menu item's visible property is set to false, the menu group can only appear as a pop-up menu. Note that it is not necessary to set the children menu item's visible property to false.

After the File menu group is created, I can use the form's MouseUp event to trigger the pop-up menu using the PopupMenu method:

```
Private Sub Form_MouseUp(Button As Integer, Shift As Integer, _
X As Single, Y As Single)
If Button = 2 Then
    PopupMenu mnuFile
End If
End Sub
```

Because I want the pop-up menu to appear only when the user right-clicks the form, I need to perform a test on what mouse button the user has clicked. I can accomplish this by testing the value of the button variable. If the value is 2, I know that the user has clicked the right mouse button. Note that the variable button is passed into the MouseUp event for you.

Once I'm sure the right mouse button was clicked, I call the PopupMenu method and pass it the name of the File menu item. This displays the child menu items of the File menu group as a pop-up menu. Cool, huh!

Microsoft Agents

If you have been using Microsoft's latest Office products, you may have noticed such characters as the animated paper clip. This animated character appears on your screen to provide help with searching a knowledge base or to provide suggestions when it thinks you need assistance on a particular subject.

The animated paper clip is what's known as a Microsoft agent, which provides animation and text-to-speech capabilities in component form. For a Visual Basic programmer, Microsoft provides these agents free of charge. Although they are free of charge, the Microsoft agent controls are copyrighted by Microsoft and should be treated as such. To find more about Microsoft's licensing and copyright issues, visit Microsoft's Web site at http://www.microsoft.com.

Installing the Agent

As of this writing, you can download Microsoft's agent control, control documentation, program samples, and licensing information for free from http://msdn.microsoft.com/workshop/c-frame.htm#/workshop/imedia/agent/licensing.asp.

To completely design and develop the agent program, you need to download the following software from Microsoft's agent Web site (see above URL):

> MSagent.exe
>
> spchapi.exe
>
> tv_enua.exe
>
> Genie.exe
>
> Merlin.exe

Download these files to a temporary directory on your PC. When you launch each EXE file, it extracts the necessary files to your computer. I recommended that you also download the agent documentation and sample programs for future reference.

FIGURE 6.21

The Microsoft Agent Control 2.0 in the Components window.

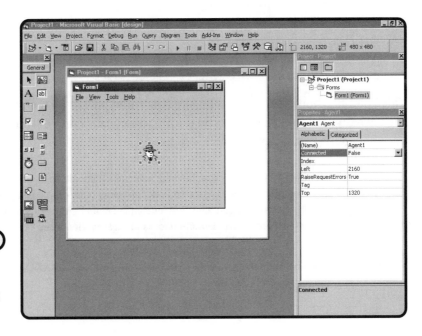

FIGURE 6.22

The Microsoft
Agent Control 2.0
in the toolbox and
on a form.

Once all the agent files are extracted and installed, you can select the Microsoft Agent Control 2.0 from the Components window, as shown in Figure 6.21.

After the agent component is added to your toolbox, you can add it to your form as you do any other Visual Basic control as depicted in Figure 6.22.

Using the Agent

Using the agent control is pretty straightforward. It has a number of methods and properties that you as the programmer can exploit to create animation and speech.

The first thing you need to do when working with agents is declare an agent variable. For the agent program, I will make the following variable form level:

```
Dim myCharacter As IAgentCtlCharacterEx
```

When the agent control is added to your form, you should see the IAgentCtlCharacterEx variable type after you type the word **As** within the variable declaration. Essentially the IAgentCtlCharacterEx type is what is known as an object data type. Though beyond the scope of this book, object data types can be used similar to other data types such as String, Boolean, or Integer.

The next step in using your agent is loading the inherit character ID of the character file into the agent control:

```
Agent1.Characters.Load "CharacterID", "Genie.acs"
```

This Load method essentially tells the control what character you will be working with. In this case, I'm explicitly telling the Agent1 control that I want to work with the genie character.

TRAP

Note that I've only specified the genie.acs filename as an argument. This implies that the genie.acs file exists in the directory where the agent program files exist. If you want the genie.acs file located in another directory, you have to explicitly tell the load method where it is, as in "c:\temp\Genie.acs".

The last step in creating an agent control is to create a reference to the character object using the keyword set:

```
Set myCharacter = Agent1.Characters("CharacterID")
```

Now we're ready to rock and roll with the genie agent character. The first thing I might want to do is display the agent with the Show method:

```
myCharacter.Show
```

Next I might want to play a specific character (genie) animation using the Play method:

```
myCharacter.Play animation name
```

HINT

Each character has a number of animation clips that you will see when you build the agent program.

Last but not least, I might want the agent to say something. I can accomplish visible and audible speech with the Speak method:

```
myCharacter.Speak string
```

When my program terminates, I want to free up any memory allocated to the agent with the following commands:

```
Set myCharacter = Nothing
Agent1.Characters.Unload "CharacterID"
```

Setting the myCharacter object to Nothing releases the memory allocated for the object. This is good practice whenever you are dealing with objects. The Unload method of the Agent1 control unloads the character (CharacterID) from the agent's character property.

Constructing the Agent Program

The agent program demonstrates the functionality of Microsoft agents and some basic human/computer interaction. After constructing the agent program, you will be able to incorporate Microsoft agents into your own programs.

The Problem

Build a program that demonstrates the features and functionalities of the agent control. Specifically, the agent program should provide the following:

- The ability to switch characters
- A list of all available animation clips for the current character
- The ability to play audible and visual text
- The option to hide the current character
- The option to stop the current animation
- The option to show the advanced properties of the agent control

Table 6.2 contains the controls and properties of the agent program.

A sample algorithm for the agent program is seen below.

1. Download and install all necessary Microsoft agent software.
2. Open a standard EXE project.
3. Add the Microsoft Agent Control 2.0 to the toolbox.
4. Add and configure all necessary controls (including menu items) to the form.
5. Write code in the form load event to set program defaults, reference a character, load all character animations in a List Box, and show the character next to the form.
6. Write code for the play command button that plays the selected animation.
7. Write code for the speak command button. The agent should use the text of the Text Box as dialog.
8. Write code in the stop command button to halt any animation.

9. Enable the change agent menu item by adding code to switch between characters.

10. Add support for the hide agent menu item.

11. Add support for the advanced properties menu item.

12. Write code to free memory used by the agent control when the program is terminated.

TABLE 6.2 CONTROLS AND PROPERTIES OF THE AGENT PROGRAM

Control	Property	Setting
frmMain	Caption	Microsoft Agents
	Border Style	1 – Fixed Single
mnuFile	Caption	&File
mnuFileExit	Caption	E&xit
mnuView	Caption	&View
mnuViewHideAgent	Caption	Hide Agent
mnuViewDash1	Caption	-
mnuViewAdvanced	Caption	Advanced Character &Options
mnuTools	Caption	&Tools
mnuToolsChangeAgent	Caption	None (Empty)
Frame1	Caption	Animations:
lstAnimations	TabIndex	0
Frame2	Caption	Text to Speech:
txtText	Text	None
	TabIndex	4
cmdPlay	Caption	&Animate
	TabIndex	1
	Default	True
cmdStop	Caption	&Stop
	TabIndex	2
cmdSpeak	Caption	Spea&k
	TabIndex	3 Agent1

The Implementation

I'm declaring a form-level variable called myCharacter as an agent to be used throughout the agent program:

```
Option Explicit
Dim myCharacter As IAgentCtlCharacterEx
```

In the form load event, I create and assign the genie character to the myCharacter variable. This lets me start using the properties and methods of the agent component:

```
Private Sub Form_Load()


'Load genie as default character
Agent1.Characters.Load "CharacterID", "Genie.acs"
Set myCharacter = Agent1.Characters("CharacterID")
```

Rather than load the animation names into the List Box from the form load event, I choose to call a procedure that I wrote specifically for this situation. I created this procedure so I could call it again if necessary during the course of the program:

```
'Change form defaults
mnuToolsChangeAgent.Caption = "&Change Agent to Merlin"
txtText.Text = "Enter a word or phrase here"


'Populate the list box
Load_Animation_Names
```

The last few lines of the form load event set the Left and Top properties of the myCharacter object to the right of the form. After which, I make the character visible through the Show method. The numbers (5500 and 900) below represent my Form's Left and Top properties. Make sure you change these to reflect your programs.

```
'Set characters starting position
myCharacter.Left = (frmMain.Left + 5500) / Screen.TwipsPerPixelX
myCharacter.Top = (frmMain.Top + 900) / Screen.TwipsPerPixelY
```

The Screen object (seen previously) is the entire Windows desktop area. Its properties can be used to manipulate a Form on a screen.

TRICK

To remove any ambiguity or confusion for other programmers looking at your code, you could change the above code to utilize the Form's Width and Height properties as seen below:

```
myCharacter.Left = (frmMain.Left + frmMain.Width) / _
Screen.TwipsPerPixelX
myCharacter.Top = (frmMain.Top + 0.5 * (frmMain.Height - _
myCharacter.Height _
* Screen.TwipsPerPixelY)) / Screen.TwipsPerPixelY
```

```
'Display the character
myCharacter.Show

End Sub
```

Notice that in the click event of the play command button, I test to make sure that an animation name is selected before playing an animation.

```
Private Sub cmdPlay_Click()

'Check to make sure an animation is selected
If lstAnimations.ListIndex = -1 Then
    cmdPlay.Enabled = False
    Exit Sub
End If

'Animation selected in the list box
myCharacter.Play lstAnimations.List(lstAnimations.ListIndex)

End Sub
```

Remembering that the agent's Speak method takes a string, I can use the Text property of a Text Box as my speak parameter:

```
Private Sub cmdSpeak_Click()
```

```
'Convert text to speech
If txtText.Text = "" Then
    Exit Sub
Else
    myCharacter.Speak txtText.Text
End If
```

I use the click event of the List Box to enable or disable the Play Command Button. If I didn't do this and a user clicked Play without an animation name selected, she would get an error:

```
End Sub


Private Sub cmdStop_Click()
myCharacter.Stop
End Sub


Private Sub lstAnimations_Click()


If lstAnimations.ListIndex <> -1 Then
    cmdPlay.Enabled = True
    cmdPlay.Default = True
End If
```

Before ending the program in the exit menu item, I free all memory used by the myCharacter object by setting it to Nothing:

```
End Sub


Private Sub mnuFileExit_Click()


Set myCharacter = Nothing
Agent1.Characters.Unload "CharacterID"
End


End Sub
```

The Load_Animation_Names() procedure uses an interesting looping technique called For Each. If you look at the looping structure carefully, you can see that "For each animation name in the list of myCharacter animation names, add an item to the List Box." The For Each looping structure is popular when dealing with control arrays and other object-based structures. I discuss arrays and control arrays in Chapter 10:

```
Public Sub Load_Animation_Names()

Dim AnimationName

lstAnimations.Clear
'Loads the names of animations into a list box
For Each AnimationName In myCharacter.AnimationNames
  lstAnimations.AddItem AnimationName
Next

End Sub
```

In the change agent menu item, I perform much of the same functionality as in the form load event with some exceptions. Depending on the current character, I unload it and load the new character. Everything else in this procedure should be familiar:

```
Private Sub mnuToolsChangeAgent_Click()

'Load the new character
If myCharacter.Name = "Merlin" Then
        Set myCharacter = Nothing
        Agent1.Characters.Unload "CharacterID"
        Agent1.Characters.Load "CharacterID", "Genie.acs"
Else
        Set myCharacter = Nothing
        Agent1.Characters.Unload "CharacterID"
        Agent1.Characters.Load "CharacterID", "Merlin.acs"
End If

Set myCharacter = Agent1.Characters("CharacterID")

'Change captions
If myCharacter.Name = "Merlin" Then
        mnuToolsChangeAgent.Caption = "&Change Agent to Genie"
```

```
Else
        mnuToolsChangeAgent.Caption = "&Change Agent to Merlin"
End If

Load_Animation_Names

'Set characters starting position
myCharacter.Left = (frmMain.Left + 5500) / Screen.TwipsPerPixelX
myCharacter.Top = (frmMain.Top + 900) / Screen.TwipsPerPixelY

myCharacter.Show

End Sub
```

Interestingly, Microsoft has already provided an advanced properties dialog window called a Property Sheet. To show the Property Sheet of the agent component, I simply set the PropertySheet's Visible property to true:

```
Private Sub mnuViewAdvanced_Click()
Agent1.PropertySheet.Visible = True
End Sub
```

In the hide agent menu item, I can call the Hide method of the myCharacter object to make the character disappear:

```
Private Sub mnuViewHideAgent_Click()
myCharacter.Hide
End Sub
```

Summary

In this chapter, you made a monumental transition from learning fundamental controls such as Labels, Text Boxes, and Command Buttons to learning more advanced controls such as menus, List Boxes, Combo Boxes, and Drive, Directory, and File List Boxes. In addition to these advanced controls, you learned about the Microsoft agent software, which can provide a rich and interactive experience to your programs. Moreover, you learned how to enhance your graphical controls and the user's experience through the application of human/computer interaction.

CHALLENGES

1. Using List Boxes and the Multimedia control, build a more intuitive CD juke-box that allows user to select from a list of CD titles in the List Box.

2. Create a quiz game that loads a number of questions into a List Box. When a user clicks on one of the questions, a message box should appear prompting him for the answer. You might want to add a second column to the List Box that holds the score information.

3. Create a more interactive quiz game that uses Microsoft agents. The agent should speak the question and alert the user whether she got it right. The agent should also have appropriate gestures or animations for presenting the question as well as responding to a correct or incorrect answer.

Debugging and Error Handling

Visual Basic provides many facilities for debugging and error handling, some of which you may have already discovered by now. In this chapter, you will learn the most common of these facilities for capturing and preventing many types of errors and how to step through and test your own code for bugs. Specifically, this chapter covers the following:

- Input validation

- Break mode and debug windows

- Building error-handling routines

- The Err object

- Constructing the mad lib game

Project: The Mad Lib Game

The mad lib game is a fun and easy-to-build program that solidifies many of the programming and Visual Basic techniques you have learned so far. Shown in Figure 7.1, the mad lib game also uses concepts that you will learn in this chapter to perform input validation for error and bug prevention.

Overview

Learning programming constructs is only half the battle in game and program development. As a programmer, you must also strive to develop sound and bug-free code. However, developing bug-free code is something of an unrealistic and misleading goal for most programmers because most, if not all, high-level languages have inherited bugs themselves.

These inherited bugs might come from the programmers who developed the IDE (Integrated Development Environment) or the developers of the operating system where the program will run.

So what's a programmer to do? Well, first and foremost, understand that debugging is the process of uncovering an error and fixing it. If your program has an error, it generally means one of two things: Either you have a syntax problem, or you don't really understand the purpose of the program or routine.

The worst way to debug or solve errors is to guess at a fix so that you keep changing code until something works. Changing code to solve an error when you have not backed up your original code is another no-no.

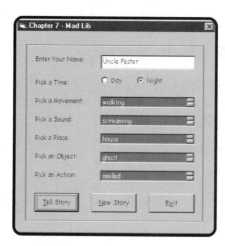

FIGURE 7.1

The mad lib game.

IN THE REAL WORLD

Most professional or corporate programming groups have some form of source-code archive. As a professional programmer, you check your program code out of a repository for making changes or enhancements and check it back in when done. These enterprise source-code repositories act as your backup in the event you need to return to the original source code.

Microsoft provides one such source-code archive and tracking tool called SourceSafe. You can find Microsoft SourceSafe under the Microsoft Visual Studio program group (providing you have purchased the Enterprise or Professional version of Visual Studio). For more information on SourceSafe, visit Microsoft's Web site at http://www.microsoft.com.

When presented with an error or bug, it is best to take a few moments and follow a scientific approach:

1. Gather data by performing multiple experiments.
2. Develop a hypothesis based on the data gathered from the experiments.
3. Repeat the first two steps until you can prove a hypothesis.
4. Back up the original source code that is performing the error.
5. Implement the fix based on the proven hypothesis.
6. Test the fix.

Providing you understand the problem and the program's purpose, implementing the fix is often the easy part. The hard part is the art or science used to find the source of the error. Most computer science students or self-taught programmers are not taught proper debugging processes or they are learning how to program in a language that does not support robust debugging facilities. Fortunately, the latter is not the case with Visual Basic because Microsoft did an excellent job when designing debugging facilities for the Visual Basic IDE.

Input Validation

Input validation is a great place to begin learning about error handling and bug fixing. Good portions of program errors come from unexpected user input or responses.

For example, what do you think would happen if a user entered a letter as an operand into a math quiz game? A better question is "How do I prevent a user from entering a letter into a Text Box intended for numbers?" What about a game that prompts a user for a level; would testing that the input is a number be enough? Probably not because most games have a limited amount of levels, so you would also need to test for a range of numbers.

In short, input validation really involves a talented programmer with enough foresight to prevent errors before they happen.

Validate Event

Most Visual Basic controls have a validate event that occurs right before the control loses focus. However, this event is not always triggered by default. To ensure it does, you can set the CausesValidation property of the control to true. To illustrate, here's an example of testing the Text property of a Text Box for a certain character:

```
Private Sub Form_Load()
Text1.CausesValidation = True
End Sub
```

In the form load event, I set the CausesValidation property of the Text Box to true. I could have also set this property during design time in the properties window of the Text Box control.

The validate event of the Text Box takes the Boolean variable Cancel as an argument:

```
Private Sub Text1_Validate(Cancel As Boolean)
If Text1.Text = "A" Then
    Cancel = False
Else
    Cancel = True
End If
End Sub
```

If the user enters the letter A into the Text Box, I set the Cancel parameter to false. This lets the user move on to the next control. However, if the user enters anything else, I set the cancel parameter to true, essentially preventing the user from going anywhere until she enters the letter A.

Checking Data Types

Sometimes, preventing input errors can be as easy as determining whether a user has entered a number or a string. You might want the user to enter his or her name, or maybe you are looking for a number such as an age. Either way, Visual Basic provides the IsNumeric function for testing such scenarios.

The IsNumeric function takes a variable or expression as a parameter and returns a Boolean value of true if the variable or expression is a number and false if it is not.

You can use the IsNumeric function in conjunction with the validate event for checking data types:

```
Private Sub Text1_Validate(Cancel As Boolean)
If IsNumeric(Text1.Text) = True Then
    Cancel = False
Else
    Cancel = True
End If
End Sub
```

In the example, you can see that by testing the value of the Text Box with the IsNumeric function, I want the user to enter a number. If the IsNumeric function returns the Boolean value false, I know that the user has entered something other than a number.

Conversely, you could use the IsNumeric function to check for a string value. Simply change the comparison operator to not equal in the If statement.

Testing a Range of Values

You might find at times that testing a value for a particular data type is not enough to prevent input errors. Sometimes, it is necessary to check for a range of values. For example, you might want to prompt a user to enter a number from 1 to 100. Or maybe you want a person to choose a letter from a to z.

As you will see, testing for a range of values involves a little more thought from the programmer. Your first thought should coincide with knowing or getting to know the range or ranges to test and whether they are numeric or character-based. Fortunately, testing ranges of values with numbers or strings uses the same programming constructs in compound conditions.

Let's take the 1-to-100 example mentioned earlier. I continue to use the validate event and the IsNumeric function as part of the overall testing for a range of numbers (1 to 100):

```
Private Sub Text1_Validate(Cancel As Boolean)
If IsNumeric(Text1.Text) = True Then
    If Val(Text1.Text) >= 1 And Val(Text1.Text) <= 100 Then
        Cancel = False
    Else
        Cancel = True
    End If
Else
    Cancel = True
End If
End Sub
```

I added another nested condition to my validation event to verify a numeric range. Specifically, if the input passes the first test (that it's a number), I check that the number is in the range of 1 to 100 with the use of compound conditions. If the input fails on the second If statement, I set the Cancel argument to false and force the user to keep trying until a valid number is entered.

Testing for a range of letters is not much different, if you remember that all characters (letters or numbers) can be represented with character code values. Let's say I want a user to enter a letter code in the range of a through m. I can still use the validate event and the IsNumeric function to help me out, but I need to perform some additional tests:

```
Private Sub Text1_Validate(Cancel As Boolean)
If IsNumeric(Text1.Text) <> True Then
    If Asc(UCase(Text1.Text)) >= 65 And Asc(UCase(Text1.Text)) _
<= 77 Then
        Cancel = False
    Else
        Cancel = True
    End If
Else
    Cancel = True
End If
End Sub
```

The first thing I did in my validate event was change the comparison operator in the first condition to not equals. (In other words, I'm looking for the IsNumeric function to return a false value, which means the input was not a number.) Next I use the Asc function, which converts a character to its corresponding character code value.

Using compound conditions, I specifically look for a range of 65 through 77, which represents the capital letters A through M. You might also notice that I use the function UCase in association with the asc function. The UCase function converts lowercase letters to uppercase letters. If I do not convert the characters to uppercase, I have to check for the lowercase letters as well (with numbers 97 to 109).

For more information on character codes, please see Appendix A, "Common ASCII Codes."

Break Mode and Debug Windows

You might remember from Chapter 1 that Visual Basic contains three modes of program operation:

- Design time is the mode by which you add controls to containers (such as forms) and write code to respond to events.

- The runtime environment allows you to see your program running the same way a user would. During runtime, you can see all your Visual Basic code, but you cannot modify it.

- Break mode allows you to pause execution of your Visual Basic program (during runtime) to view, edit, and debug your program code.

By now you should be fairly comfortable with the Visual Basic design time and runtime environments. You may have also discovered the break mode environment, but if not, this is a good starting point for you to begin learning about Visual Basic debugging.

Inserting Breakpoints

Visual Basic allows you to step through your program code one line at a time. Known as *stepping* or stepping into, this process allows you to graphically see what line of code is currently executing as well as the values of current variables in scope.

Definition

Stepping, or stepping into, is the process of executing one Visual Basic statement at a time.

Using function keys or menu items, you can navigate through program code with ease. For example, once in break mode, you can press the F8 key to skip to the next line.

During break mode, it is also possible to step over a procedure without having to execute the procedure's statements one at a time. Known as *procedure stepping* or stepping over, this process is available during break mode if you press Shift+F8.

Sometimes, you might want to skip ahead in program code to a predetermined procedure or statement. Visual Basic provides this functionality through the use of breakpoints.

You can insert *breakpoints* into your Visual Basic procedures during design time or break mode, as shown in Figure 7.2. To create or remove a breakpoint, simply click in the left margin of the code window at the program statement where you want program execution to pause. Breakpoints can also be inserted or removed through the F9 function key.

To skip to the next breakpoint (or to the end of the program), simply press the function key F5.

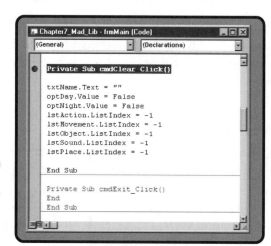

FIGURE 7.2

Pausing program execution through the use of breakpoints.

Sometimes you want to go back in time and re-execute a particular program statement without having to halt the entire program and re-run it.

Believe it or not, Visual Basic provides a facility for traveling back in time while in break mode. To do so, simply click the yellow arrow in the left margin of the code window (as shown in Figure 7.3) and drag it to a previous program statement.

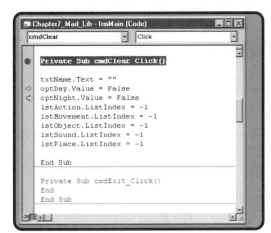

FIGURE 7.3

Going back in time to re-execute program statements while in break mode.

The Immediate Window

During testing or debugging, it is not always desirable to change the values of variables and properties by modifying program code because you might forget what you have changed and for what reason. A safer way of testing program code is through the use of the Immediate window. Shown in Figure 7.4, the Immediate window allows you to verify and change the values of properties and variables.

You can use the Immediate window during design time or break mode. Most popular in break mode, the Immediate window is available if you press Ctrl+G or choose Immediate Windows from the View menu.

You can type statements that do not directly correspond with your current program's execution. For example, in Figure 7.4, I entered the expression

```
print 25 + 25
```

into the Immediate window. After I press the Enter key, the Immediate window produces the result of my expression, in this case 50. The keyword print tells the Immediate window to print the expression's result to the Immediate window's screen.

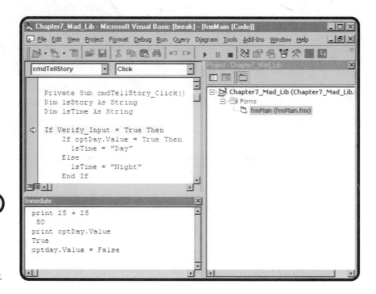

Changing a
property's value
through the
Immediate window.

I used the Immediate window in Figure 7.4 to change the value of an option button:

```
print optDay.Value
True
optday.Value = False
```

The first statement generates the result "true," which is the current value of the option button. In the next statement, I change the value of the option button to false.

 HINT   You can re-execute a statement in the Immediate window by moving the cursor to the line and pressing Enter.

In addition to calculations and property settings, the Immediate window is also useful for viewing or changing variables.

The Watch Window

In addition to breakpoints, the Watch window, shown in Figure 7.5, can aid you in troubleshooting or debugging program code. Accessed from the View menu, the Watch window can track the values of expressions and break when expressions are true or have been changed.

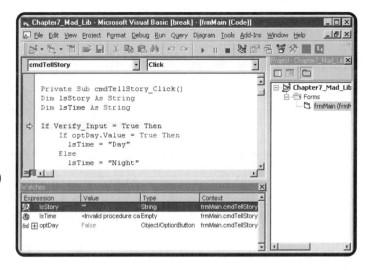

FIGURE 7.5

Tracking expressions through the use of the Watch window.

A basic watch expression allows you to graphically track the value of an expression throughout the life of a program. Moreover, you can create a watch expression that pauses program execution when an expression has been changed or is true.

For example, let's say that you know a bug occurs in your program because the value of a variable is being set incorrectly. You know the value of the variable is changing, but you do not know where in the code it is being changed. Using a watch expression (as shown in Figure 7.6), you can create an expression that pauses program execution whenever the value of the variable in question changes.

 Although you can create watch expressions within the Watch window, it is much easier to create them by right-clicking a variable or control name in the code window and choosing Add Watch.

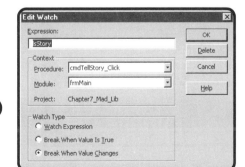

FIGURE 7.6

Pausing program execution with a break expression.

The Locals Window

The Locals window, shown in Figure 7.7, provides valuable information about variables and control properties in current scope.

Accessed from the View menu, the Locals window not only supplies information on variables and properties, but also lets you change control property values.

Building Error-Handling Routines

Whenever your program interacts with the outside world, you should provide some form of error handling to counteract various unexpected inputs or outputs. One way of providing error handling is writing your own error-handling routines.

Error-handling routines are the maintenance crew of your program. They can handle any kind of programming or HCI (human/computer interaction) errors you can think of. Like any good maintenance crew, error-handling routines should not only identify the error, but also try to fix it or at least give the program or interacting human a chance to.

Use the On Error GoTo statement to signify that you are going to use an error-handling routine in your procedure:

```
On Error GoTo ErrorHandler
```

This statement can go anywhere in your procedure but should appear toward the top, generally right after any procedure-level variable declarations.

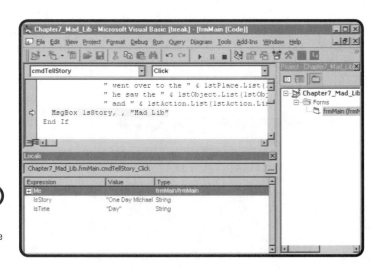

FIGURE 7.7

Providing variable information with the Locals window.

ErrorHandler is the name I give my error-handling routine. (You can call it whatever you like.)

Once an error handler is declared, errors generated in the procedure are directed to the error-handling routine:

```
Public Function Verify_Input() As Boolean
On Error GoTo ErrorHandler
'Get input from user
Exit Function
ErrorHandler:
    MsgBox ("An error has occurred.")
    Resume
End Function
```

It is customary to execute the Exit Function or Exit Sub statements before program execution enters the error-handling routine. Without these statements, a procedure that executes without any errors will execute the error handler as well.

The error handler begins by calling the name of the error handler followed by a colon. Within the error handler, you write code to respond to the error. In the example, I simply use a message box to denote an error has occurred.

The Resume keyword takes program execution back to the statement where the error occurred. Note the three possible ways for returning program control back to the procedure:

- Resume
- Resume Next
- Resume label

By itself, the keyword Resume returns program control to where the error occurred. The Resume Next statement returns program control to the statement after the statement where the error occurred. The Resume label statement returns program control to a predetermined line number, as in the following code:

```
Public Function Verify_Input() As Boolean
On Error GoTo ErrorHandler
'Get input from user
BeginHere:
Exit Function
ErrorHandler:
    MsgBox ("An error has occurred.")
    Resume BeginHere:
End Function
```

Generally speaking, a message box is a good way to let a user know that an error has occurred. However, it is not enough to let a user know that an error has occurred; you should also let the user know what caused the error and what his options are for resolving the error.

In the next section, you will learn how to identify specific and custom errors using the Err object.

The Err Object

When a user encounters an error in your program, she should be provided with a clear and precise description of the problem and a resolution. The Err object provides Visual Basic programmers an accessible means for finding or triggering Windows-specific errors.

Essentially, the Err object maintains information about errors that occur in the current procedure. This information is stored in the form of properties. The most common of its properties follow:

Source	Name of object that generated the error
Number	The error number of the current error (0 to 65,535)
Description	A description of the current error

TABLE 7.1 COMMON ERROR NUMBERS AND DESCRIPTIONS

Error Number	Error Description
11	Division by zero
13	Type mismatch
53	File not found
61	Disk full
70	Permission denied
71	Disk not ready
76	Path not found
482	Printer error

Here's a bit of code that prompts a user for a file. If there are problems accessing the file, an error is generated and the error-handling routine is called:

```
Public Sub Get_File()
On Error GoTo FileError
'Get file from user
Exit Function
FileError:
    Select Case Err.Number
Case 53
        'File not found
Case 71
        'Disk not ready
Case 76
        'Path not found
End Select
Resume
End Sub
```

I simply used a Select Case structure to check the Err Number property for some common file access errors.

Sometimes an error in your program is similar to that of a given Err object Description but does not trigger the specific Err Number. You can provide the ability to trigger errors through the Err object's Raise method.

The Raise method allows you to trigger a specific error condition, thus displaying a dialog box to the user. The Raise method takes a number as a parameter. For example, you can use the following to trigger a "Disk not ready" dialog box:

```
Err.Raise 71
```

TRAP

You can check the Err's Description property in a condition that looks for a specific error. However, it is possible that error descriptions change from one version of Visual Basic to another. Thus, it is advisable to use the Err's Number property rather than the Description property to match error conditions.

Constructing the Mad Lib Game

You can now put your newly acquired debugging and error-handling skills to the test with a game called mad lib. The main programming concept in the mad lib game is to prevent unwanted results (in other words, bugs). To do so, I apply the input validation skill sets you learned earlier in this chapter.

The Problem

Build a mad lib game. The game should allow a user to enter information via Text Boxes, Radio Buttons, and List Boxes. After that, the game should generate and output a unique story to the player.

Table 7.2 lists the controls and properties of the mad lib game.

A draft algorithm for the mad lib game is shown below.

1. Open a new standard EXE project.
2. Create the user interface.
3. Write code to populate the List Boxes at form load.
4. Create a function that validates the user's input prior to story generation.
5. Write code that generates a story based upon user input.
6. Write code for starting a new story. (Clear text boxes and input boxes.)
7. Write code to quit the game.

The Implementation

During form load, I call a procedure I wrote for populating all List Boxes:

```
Option Explicit
```

```
Private Sub Form_Load()
Fill_ListBoxes
End Sub
```

I test the return value of a function called Verify_Input before creating and displaying the mad lib story:

```
Private Sub cmdTellStory_Click()
Dim lsStory As String
Dim lsTime As String


If Verify_Input = True Then
```

TABLE 7.2 CONTROLS AND PROPERTIES OF THE MAD LIB GAME

Control	Property	Setting
frmMain	Caption	Chapter 7 – Mad Lib
	Border Style	1 – Fixed Single
Frame1	Caption	Nothing
lblName	Caption	Enter Your Name:
txtName	Text	Nothing
lblTime	Caption	Pick a Time:
optDay	Caption	Day
optNight	Caption	Night
lblMovement	Caption	Pick a Movement:
lstMovement		
lblSound	Caption	Pick a Sound:
lstSound		
lblPlace	Caption	Pick a Place:
lstPlace		
lblObject	Caption	Pick an Object:
lstObject		
lblAction	Caption	Pick an Action:
lstAction		
cmdTellStory	Caption	&Tell Story
cmdClear	Caption	&New Story
cmdExit	Caption	E&xit

Using concatenation and user input, I create a unique mad lib story, which is outputted to the user through the use of a Message Box:

```
If optDay.Value = True Then
    lsTime = "Day"
Else
    lsTime = "Night"
End If
lsStory = "One " & lsTime & " " & Trim(txtName.Text) & _
    " was " & lstMovement.List(lstMovement.ListIndex) & _
    " down the street when he heard a " & _
    lstSound.List(lstSound.ListIndex) & " sound " & _
    "coming from the " & lstPlace.List(lstPlace.ListIndex) & _
    " next door.  " & Trim(txtName.Text) & " paused for a moment " & _
    "to see what was making the " & _
    lstSound.List(lstSound.ListIndex) & _
    " sound.  When " & Trim(txtName.Text) & _
    " went over to the " & lstPlace.List(lstPlace.ListIndex) & _
    " he saw the " & lstObject.List(lstObject.ListIndex) & _
    " and " & lstAction.List(lstAction.ListIndex) & "."
    MsgBox lsStory, , "Mad Lib"
End If
```

The procedure Fill_ListBoxes uses the AddItem method to add items to each List Box: (Assume that the other list boxes are populated in this procedure as well; the complete code appears on the CD.)

```
End Sub

Public Sub Fill_ListBoxes()
lstAction.Clear
lstAction.AddItem "ran away"
lstAction.AddItem "smiled"
lstAction.AddItem "shouted"
End Sub
```

The Verify_Input function is the maintenance crew of my mad lib game. In this function, I check all possible inputs for existence. If any of the inputs are invalid, I return a false to the calling procedure (in this case the Command Button's click event):

```
Public Function Verify_Input() As Boolean

If txtName.Text = "" Then
    MsgBox "Please enter your Name.", , "Error"
```

```
        Verify_Input = False
        Exit Function
    ElseIf optDay.Value = False And optNight.Value = False Then
        MsgBox "Please select a Time.", , "Error"
        Verify_Input = False
        Exit Function
    ElseIf lstMovement.ListIndex = -1 Then
        MsgBox "Please select a Movement.", , "Error"
        Verify_Input = False
        Exit Function
    ElseIf lstSound.ListIndex = -1 Then
        MsgBox "Please select a Sound.", , "Error"
        Verify_Input = False
        Exit Function
    ElseIf lstPlace.ListIndex = -1 Then
        MsgBox "Please select a Place.", , "Error"
        Verify_Input = False
        Exit Function
    ElseIf lstObject.ListIndex = -1 Then
        MsgBox "Please select an Object.", , "Error"
        Verify_Input = False
        Exit Function
    ElseIf lstAction.ListIndex = -1 Then
        MsgBox "Please select an Action.", , "Error"
        Verify_Input = False
        Exit Function
    Else
        Verify_Input = True
    End If

End Function
```

The click event of the Clear Command Button starts a new mad lib by setting various control properties.

```
Private Sub cmdClear_Click()

txtName.Text = ""
optDay.Value = False
optNight.Value = False
lstAction.ListIndex = -1
lstMovement.ListIndex = -1
lstObject.ListIndex = -1
lstSound.ListIndex = -1
```

```
1stPlace.ListIndex = -1

End Sub
```

The last subprocedure exits the mad lib game with the keyword End.

```
Private Sub cmdExit_Click()
End
End Sub
```

Summary

In this chapter, you learned how to validate input from a user. Specifically, you learned how to test for numbers, characters, and ranges of each. In addition, you learned new tricks for navigating through break mode with debugging tools such as breakpoints and the Local, Immediate, and Watch windows. Finally, you learned how to build custom error-handling routines with the On Error GoTo statement and the Err object.

I hope this chapter has broadened your perspective on programming and human/computer interaction. You should always strive to build bug-free code, but in the event that an error or bug does occur, you should know how to deal with it.

CHALLENGES

1. Build a custom error-handling routine for the math quiz program (from previous chapters). The error-handling routine should use the Err object to look for Err Number 11 (division by zero).

2. Further modify the math quiz program to use input validation to verify that a user has entered a number and not a string.

3. Create a custom error-handling routine for the image preview program (Chapter 6) that uses the Err object to look for disk, path, and file access errors.

4. Create a number-guessing game that prompts a user for a number in a range. Use input validation to verify the user has entered a valid number in the corresponding range.

Data Files and File Access

So far, you have learned various programming techniques that make Visual Basic a popular programming language for beginners and experienced programmers alike.

This chapter covers the following topics:

- Data files

- Sequential access files

- Random access files

- Constructing the quiz game

IN THE REAL WORLD

Most programming languages include some forms of libraries or functions for handling file I/O. Some languages provide powerful and fast programming constructs to build and manage file I/O. Some of these languages are closely tied to the operating system, such as C or Assembly language and can be difficult to learn and master.

Generally speaking, other, high-level languages provide easy-to-learn and quick-to-build file I/O routines. Visual Basic is one such language.

Some of Visual Basic's more popular programming facilities are

- Rapid application development
- GUI design and prototyping
- Event-driven model
- String manipulation
- Debugging and error handling

The list could be much larger but would move beyond the scope of this book. You will, however, learn about another popular programming facility in Visual Basic known as file I/O or file input/output.

Visual Basic has many techniques for building and managing file I/O routines. You will specifically learn how to build and use sequential and random file access.

Project: The Quiz Game

Shown in Figure 8.1, the quiz game uses a sequential access file to keep what is known as persistent data. Using *persistent data*, the quiz game prompts the user with questions read from a file generated by you.

After successfully answering a question, the quiz game determines whether the user's response was correct based on answers stored in the file.

Definition

Unlike data stored in variables during program execution, *persistent data* is stored in files that maintain their values when your computer's power is turned off.

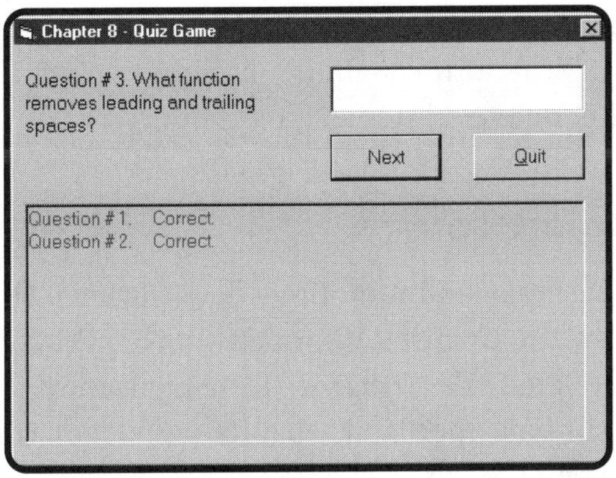

FIGURE 8.1

Demonstrating
file I/O with the
quiz game.

Data Files

It is safe to assume that in one way or another, all the elements of an operating system (also known as a file system) are files. You can think of them as everything from the brick and mortar to the paint and wall décor of an operating system.

Files serve many different purposes:

> Page files
>
> Routing tables
>
> Configuration files (config.sys)
>
> Initialization files (.ini files)
>
> Registry files
>
> Log files
>
> Setup files
>
> Executable files
>
> Database files
>
> Document files
>
> Spreadsheets
>
> Email
>
> Pictures

This list is only a small sample of file types located on your hard drive. The important thing to note is everything that makes a functional operating system is constructed with files.

How are these files built, accessed, and managed? The simple answer is with other files. Specifically, programmers build programs (which themselves are files) to build, write, save, delete, and manage other files.

Data File Organization

Each file type contains a unique and sometimes proprietary format. For example, a Microsoft operating system such as Windows 98, Windows NT, or Windows 2000 consists of many related files, each with its own unique and proprietary makeup. Although the files may perform separate tasks, they come together as a whole to build an operating system.

Fortunately for us, data files as they relate to this chapter are not proprietary and are a great starting point for learning file organization.

 Data files that you create can be viewed and edited through Microsoft text editors such as Notepad and WordPad.

Used for storing and retrieving data, data files consist of three main components:

Files   A related collection of data

Records   Rows of data that make a file

Fields   Elements composing a record

For example, a data file that contains question information for a quiz might look like Figure 8.2.

As shown in Figure 8.2, the question.dat file contains three records, and each record contains three fields (question number, question, and answer).

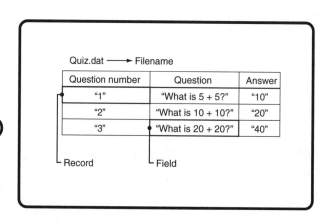

FIGURE 8.2

The data file question.dat consists of records and fields.

The question-number field is unique from the other fields because it provides the organizational manner for the data file. Organization in data files is obtained through *key fields* (such as the question-number field), which uniquely identify a row.

Definition

Key fields consist of one or more fields that uniquely identify a row of data.

Sequential Access Files

Data files created with sequential file access have records stored in one file after another in sequential order. When accessing data files with sequential file access, a program must read records in the same order they were written to the file. In other words, if you want to access the 20th record in a data file, you first must read records 1 to 19.

 TRAP Sequential file access is useful and appropriate for small data files. If you find that your sequential file access program is starting to run slowly, you might want to change file access to random file access, or better yet, migrate to a relational database management system. Visit Microsoft's Web site (http://www.microsoft.com) for more information on relational database management systems.

Opening a Sequential Data File

The first step in creating or accessing a data file is opening it. Microsoft provides an easy-to-use facility for opening a data file through the Open function:

```
Open "Filename" For {Input | Output | Append} As #Filenumber _
[Len = Record Length]
```

The Open function takes three parameters: Filename describes the name or path of the file you want to open or create. Input\Output\Append is a selection list described in Table 8.1, and you pick the action to use. #Filenumber is a number

TABLE 8.1 SEQUENTIAL ACCESS MODES

Mode	Description
Input	Reads records from a data file
Output	Writes records to a data file
Append	Writes or appends records to the end of a data file

from 1 to 511 used for referencing the file, and Len is an optional parameter that can control the number of characters buffered.

For example, I use the Open method to create a new file for output called quiz.dat:

```
Open "quiz.dat" For Output As #1
```

The filename attribute can contain paths in addition to filenames. For example, if you want to create employee records in a file named employee.dat on a floppy disk, you can use the following syntax:

```
Open "a:\employee.dat" For Output As #1
```

The result of the Open function varies depending on the initial action. If you use the input parameter, the Open function searches for the filename and creates a *buffer* in memory. If the file is not found, Visual Basic generates an error.

> ### Definition
>
> A *buffer* is an area of storage (computer memory) where data is temporarily stored.

The result of the Open function for append and output is similar to that of input with one main exception: If the file specified is not found, a new file is created using the filename parameter as the filename.

Note that the output mode always overwrites an existing file.

Once you successfully open a data file, you can read from it, write to it, and close it.

Writing Sequential Data to a File

To write data to a sequential file, you want to use either the output mode, which creates a new file for writing, or the append mode, which writes records to the end of a data file. After opening the file, you can use the Write function to write records:

```
Write #Filenumber, Fields
```

The Write function takes two parameters, #Filenumber and a list of fields. The #Filenumber denotes the file number used in the Open function, and the fields parameter is a list of strings, numbers, variables, or properties that you want to use as fields.

For example, if I want to create a data file and write quiz records to it, I can use the following syntax:

```
Open "quiz.dat" For Output As #1
Write #1, 1, "Is Visual Basic an Event Driven language?", "Yes"
```

I can also use variable names for my fields list:

```
Write #1, liQuestionNumber, lsQuestion, lsAnswer
```

Either way, Visual Basic outputs numbers as numbers and strings as strings surrounded with quotation marks.

Reading Data from a Sequential File

If you want to read records from a data file, you must use the input parameter with the Open function:

```
Input #Filenumber, Fields
```

Like the Write function, the Input statement takes two parameters, the #Filenumber and a list of fields. For example, if you want to read the first record in a data file called quiz.dat (assuming quiz.dat contains three fields for each record), you can use the following syntax:

```
Dim liQuestionNumber as Integer
Dim lsQuestion as String
Dim lsAnswer as String
Open "quiz.dat" For Input As #1
Input #1, liQuestionNumber, lsQuestion, lsAnswer
```

Notice that I pass three variables as the field list to the input statement. These variables hold the contents of the first record found.

By now, you might be thinking, so far, so good, but how do I read all the records in a data file? The answer involves something new and something old. First, you have to use a loop to search through the data file. Second, your loop's condition should use the EOF function.

The EOF (end of file) function tests for the end of the data file. It takes a file number as a parameter and returns a true if the end of the file is found or false if the end of file is not reached.

To test for the end of file, the EOF function looks for an EOF marker that is placed at the end of a file by the Close function:

```
Dim liQuestionNumber as Integer
Dim lsQuestion as String
Dim lsAnswer as String
Open "quiz.dat" For Input As #1
Do Until EOF(1)
   Input #1, liQuestionNumber, lsQuestion, lsAnswer
   picOutput.Print "Question number: " & liQuestionNumber & lsQuestion
Loop
```

This loop iterates until the EOF function returns a true value. Inside the loop, each record is read one at a time. After a record is read, the Print method of a Picture Box control outputs two of the fields (liQuestionNumber and lsQuestion) for display.

Closing a Sequential Data File

Remember when your mom used to say "Put away your toys after you play with them?" Well, I do. Working (or playing with) data files requires similar attention to cleanup. It is always good practice to close your data files when you are done working with them.

Closing a data file performs important housekeeping not to mention the actual creation of your data file. Specifically, closing a data file performs the following operations:

- It writes the EOF marker.
- In output or append mode, closing a data file writes records to the physical file in the sequential order in which they were created.
- It releases the file number and buffer for memory conservation.

The Close function takes the file number as its only parameter:

```
Close #FileNumber
```

For example, to close the file quiz.dat after writing one record, I can use the Close function in the following way:

```
Open "quiz.dat" For Output As #1
Write #1, 1, "Is Visual Basic an Event Driven language?", "Yes"
Close 1
```

HINT If you use the Close function without any parameters, it closes all open sequential data files.

Figure 8.3 shows a small program called the quiz creator, which uses most of the sequential file access techniques you have learned so far. Its main purpose is to create a data file containing question-related records. Each time the program is executed, it overwrites any previous file. The quiz creator can be useful to you when building the quiz game at the end of this chapter.

As shown in Figure 8.4, the result of the quiz creator is a data file containing records and fields that you can view by opening it in an editor such as Notepad or WordPad.

Throughout the program's procedures, the fiQuestionNumber form-level variable keeps track of the current question:

```
Option Explicit
Dim fiQuestionNumber As Integer
```

I open the quiz.dat data file in the form load event and assign the caption property of a label control to that of the current question number:

```
Private Sub Form_Load()
Open "quiz.dat" For Output As #1
fiQuestionNumber = 1
lblQuestionNumber.Caption = "Question # " & fiQuestionNumber
End Sub
```

FIGURE 8.3

The quiz creator creates quiz records based on user input.

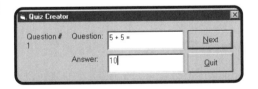

FIGURE 8.4

A data file created with the quiz creator program.

Note that I provide the question number to the user throughout the life of the program. This ensures that the question numbers are sequential.

Before adding a question record, I check that the user has entered a question and answer. If the user has entered a question and corresponding answer, I use the Write statement to add the record. After that, I increase the current question number by 1 and update the label's caption property with the new question number:

```
Private Sub cmdNext_Click()
If txtQuestion.Text = "" Or txtAnswer.Text = "" Then
  MsgBox "Both question and answer are required.", , "Error!"
  Exit Sub
Else
  Write #1, fiQuestionNumber, txtQuestion.Text, txtAnswer.Text
  fiQuestionNumber = fiQuestionNumber + 1
  lblQuestionNumber.Caption = "Question # " & fiQuestionNumber
  txtQuestion.Text = ""
  txtAnswer.Text = ""
  txtQuestion.SetFocus
End If
End Sub
```

Last but not least, I close the sequential file with the Close statement in the click event of the quit Command Button:

```
Private Sub cmdQuit_Click()
Close #1
End
End Sub
```

Random Access Files

Sometimes, you want to find a specific row or record in a data file. To accomplish this in sequential file access; you have to read all the records before the record you are looking for. If the file is quite large and the record being sought after is close to the end of the file, this can be a time-consuming process and a frustrating endeavor for your users.

Random access provides an alternative to sequential file access and a solution to the problem. Containing a similar record structure as sequential access files, random access also uses records and fields to store information.

Although random access uses similar concepts, such as files, records, and fields, its process for storing record information is quite different from sequential access. Whereas sequential access uses a form of delimiters (such as commas) to separate fields, random access uses what's known as fixed record lengths. In other words, for random access to work properly, all records in a data file must maintain the same record length.

Fixed record lengths are easily maintained with numbers because all numbers have fixed byte counts. For example, integers are stored as 2 bytes and single precision numbers are stored as 4 bytes. Strings, on the other hand, are unpredictable. String data types shrink and grow as needed. You can, however, force a string data type to become a predetermined size, through the use of fixed string lengths.

The following syntax dimensions a variable with a fixed string length of 100 characters:

```
Dim VariableName As String * 100
```

To create a fixed string length, simply use the asterisk (*) symbol followed by an integer number.

TRAP Data will be truncated if you assign a string value larger than the size of a fixed string length variable.

User-Defined Types

Known as structs in C, user-defined types are special variables that allow you to create a collection of variables not limited to one variable type.

You create user-defined types in Visual Basic with the keyword Type. For example, I can use the following syntax to create a user-defined type called quiz:

```
Type Quiz
    QuestionID As Integer
    Question As String * 100
    Answer As String * 100
End Type
```

Depending on the desired accessibility or scope, you can declare your user-defined type as Public or Private:

```
'Public scope
```

```
Public Type Quiz
    QuestionID As Integer
    Question As String * 100
    Answer As String * 100
End Type
'Private scope
Private Type Quiz
    QuestionID As Integer
    Question As String * 100
    Answer As String * 100
End Type
```

When located in Forms modules, user-defined types must be declared Private in form-level scope (like a form-level variable). Form-level user-defined types are only accessible to procedures in that Form module. User-defined types, however, can also be declared in standard code modules (covered in Chapter 9), where they can take Private or Public scope. User-defined types declared as Private in standard code modules are only available to that module. Declared as Public, however, they become available to the entire Visual Basic project.

Once you create your user-defined data type, it is time to create instances of its object type. Do what? You see, when you create a user-defined type, it is only a shell or blueprint of an object or entity. To actually use the user-defined type, you create an instance of it through other variables. For example, to use the quiz user-defined type created earlier, I declare a variable as type quiz (as you would create a variable of type Integer or String or Boolean):

```
Dim myQuiz As Quiz
```

Now I can access the elements of the quiz type by referencing the myQuiz variable. Specifically, I can use *dot notation* to gain access to a user-defined type's element:

> **Definition**
>
> *Dot notation* uses periods after an object's name to create accessibility to its properties and methods.

```
myQuiz.QuestionID = 10
myQuiz.Question = "Is Visual Basic an Event
Driven language?"
myQuiz.Answer = "Yes"
```

Don't worry if the concept of user-defined types doesn't sink in right away. I promise that if you work with them a little, they will eventually grow on you. Besides, if you plan to add object-oriented programming to your bag of tricks, the concept of objects and instances will be important.

Opening Random Access Files

As with sequential access, you must first open a data file for random access before you can use it. With some minor differences from sequential access files, you use the Open statement to open random access files:

```
Open PathName [For Random] As FileNumber Len = RecLength
```

PathName is the location of the data file. [For Random] is not required because it is the default access type. FileNumber is the data file number that's used for reference (similar to sequential access files). Len = RecLength is the size of each record in bytes.

 TRAP An error is generated if the record length in the data file is larger than the RecLength argument.

Here are some functions you will find useful when dealing with random access files:

- LenB—Returns a long number containing the size of a variable in bytes or the number of characters in a string.
- FreeFile—Returns an integer number representing the next available file number for use in an Open statement.

Using the Open statement and my newly found friends, I can open a quiz.dat data file for random access:

```
Dim FileNumber As Integer
Dim TypeSize As Long
Dim myQuiz As Quiz
TypeSize = LenB(myQuiz)
FileNumber = FreeFile
Open "Quiz.dat" For Random As FileNumber Len = TypeSize
```

Reading Data from Random Access Files

Reading records from random access files is surprisingly easy. Simply use the Get statement to store the record in your previously created user-defined type:

```
Get FileNumber, RecordNumber, UserDefinedType
```

The FileNumber represents the file number previously assigned in the Open statement; the RecordNumber is the desired record number for reading; and the UserDefinedType houses the corresponding record's elements.

Here's another example of the Get statement that retrieves the first record in a quiz.dat data file:

```
Get FileNumber, 1, myQuiz
```

Each field in the first record is stored in the corresponding user-defined type's elements (providing you built your user-defined type with elements that directly correspond to the fields in the quiz.dat records).

You can now access the elements of the myQuiz user-defined type, which holds the fields in the first record of the quiz.dat data file. For example, if I want to print the elements of myQuiz to a Picture Box control, I use the following dot notation in conjunction with the Print method:

```
picOutput.Print myQuiz.QuestionID
picOutput.Print myQuiz.Question
picOutput.Print myQuiz.Answer
```

Editing and Creating Data in Random Access Files

One of the key benefits of using random access files is the ability to directly access one record anywhere in a data file and edit it. To do so, use the Put statement:

```
Put FileNumber, RecordNumber, UserDefinedType
```

As with the Get statement, you work with a user-defined type to edit and save a record.

Here's another example, where I assign values to the myQuiz user-defined type and write them to the fifth record in the random access file:

```
myQuiz.QuestionID = 5
myQuiz.Question = "What function returns the next _
available file number?"
myQuiz.Answer = "FreeFile"
Put FileNumber, 5, myQuiz
```

To append a record to the end of a random access file, simply add 1 to the number of the last record in the file. Use the LOF function (as demonstrated in the next section) to find the number of the last record in a file.

You can use the LOF (length of file) function to determine the length of an opened data file in bytes:

```
LOF(FileNumber)
```

Moreover, the LOF function is particularly useful for determining how many records exist in a random access file. Take the length of an opened random access file and divide it by the length of your user-defined type:

```
Dim llRecordCount As Long
llRecordCount = LOF(FileNumber) / Len(myQuiz)
```

Another useful tool in the world of file access is the Seek function. The Seek function returns a long number representing the next record in a random access file:

```
Seek(FileNumber)
```

Closing a Random Access File

Just like sequential access files, random access uses the Close statement for closing a data file:

```
Close #FileNumber
```

Figure 8.5 shows a complete random access file program that creates quiz records.

The first part of the code creates form-level variables and one user-defined type called Quiz.

```
Option Explicit
Private Type Quiz
    QuestionNumber As Integer
    Question As String * 100
    Answer As String * 100
End Type
Dim myQuiz As Quiz
Dim flFileNumber As Long
Dim flTypeSize As Long
Dim flRecordNumber As Long
```

FIGURE 8.5

Creating persistent quiz records through random access files.

With a little help from the LenB and FreeFile functions I open my data file (quiz2.dat) for random access in the form load event.

```
Private Sub Form_Load()
flFileNumber = FreeFile
flTypeSize = LenB(myQuiz)
Open "quiz2.dat" For Random As flFileNumber Len = flTypeSize
flRecordNumber = 0
End Sub
```

To add a record, I first check that the user has entered relevant information. After which, I assign data to the user-defined type and insert one record into the file with the Put statement.

```
Private Sub cmdAdd_Click()
If txtQuestionNumber.Text = "" Then
    MsgBox "Please enter a question number."
    txtQuestionNumber.SetFocus
    Exit Sub
ElseIf txtQuestion.Text = "" Then
    MsgBox "Please enter a question."
    txtQuestion.SetFocus
    Exit Sub
ElseIf txtAnswer.Text = "" Then
    MsgBox "Please enter an answer."
    txtAnswer.SetFocus
    Exit Sub
End If

myQuiz.QuestionNumber = Val(txtQuestionNumber.Text)
myQuiz.Question = txtQuestion.Text
myQuiz.Answer = txtAnswer.Text
flRecordNumber = flRecordNumber + 1
Put flFileNumber, flRecordNumber, myQuiz
txtQuestionNumber.Text = ""
txtQuestion.Text = ""
txtAnswer.Text = ""
txtQuestionNumber.SetFocus
End Sub
```

Before ending the program, I close the file with the Close statement.

```
Private Sub cmdQuit_Click()
Close flFileNumber
```

```
End
End Sub


Private Sub Form_QueryUnload(Cancel As Integer, UnloadMode _
As Integer)
cmdQuit_Click
End Sub
```

Error Trapping for File Access

Error trapping is always a must when dealing with file I/O, or specifically, data files. Why? Well, have you ever tried to access your floppy disk from Windows Explorer only to get an error message because there is no floppy disk in the drive? Or what if the disk is in the drive, but the file is not found, or better yet, the file is there but it is corrupt?

As you see, you face all types of potential errors when dealing with sequential or random access files. Your best bet is to plan ahead and create error trapping or error-handling routines. In fact, it is safe to promote error trapping in any procedure that opens, writes, reads, appends, or closes files.

Your best bet for capturing file I/O errors is using Visual Basic's Err object. The Err object contains preexisting codes for various known errors such as "file not found," "disk not ready," and many more that you can use to your advantage.

Here's an error-handling routine from the quiz game that uses the Err object to check for specific errors when the game attempts to open a file in the form load event. As in any other error-handling routine, I start off my procedure by declaring my error-handling label with an On Error GoTo statement:

```
Private Sub Form_Load()
On Error GoTo ErrorHandler:
```

This strange fellow (BeginHere:) is just another label:

```
cmdBeginNext.Caption = "Start"
fiQuestionNumber = 1
BeginHere:
```

You can actually put unique labels throughout your code, but it is not advised because your code will turn into spaghetti. Nevertheless, they can serve useful purposes as long as you keep their existence minimal and easy to follow. As you will see later in the code, I choose the BeginHere label as a good starting point in this procedure.

After opening the sequential data file, the procedure is exited, providing no errors have occurred:

```
Open "quiz.dat" For Input As #1
Exit Sub
```

But if an error does occur in opening the file, my guess is that it will be one of the following error conditions (error codes). You can see that I'm using the Select Case structure to check for specific Err object codes. If an error code is found, the user is prompted with an opportunity to fix the problem. If she chooses to retry the operation, the program resumes execution at the BeginHere label:

```
ErrorHandler:
    Dim liResponse As Integer
    Select Case Err.Number
        Case 53
            'File not found
            liResponse = MsgBox("File not found!", vbRetryCancel, "Error!")
            If liResponse = 4 Then 'Retry
                Resume BeginHere:
            Else
                cmdQuit_Click
            End If
        Case 71
            'Disk not ready
            liResponse = MsgBox("Disk not ready!", vbRetryCancel, "Error!")
            If liResponse = 4 Then 'Retry
                Resume BeginHere:
            Else
                cmdQuit_Click
            End If
        Case 76
            liResponse = MsgBox("Path not found!", vbRetryCancel, "Error!")
            If liResponse = 4 Then 'Retry
                Resume BeginHere:
            Else
                cmdQuit_Click
            End If
        Case Else
            MsgBox "Error in program!", , "Error"
            cmdQuit_Click
    End Select
End Sub
```

TRICK

The above error handler can be refined to simply display the Err object's number and description in one simple message. Once the message is generated, the user's response is evaluated:

```
Dim Message as String
If Err.Number <> 0 Then
    Message = "Error # " & Str(Err.Number) & ", " &
Err.Description
    liResponse =MsgBox(Message, vbRetryCancel, "Error",
Err.HelpFile, Err.HelpContext)
    If liResponse = 4 Then
        Resume BeginHere:
    Else
        CmdQuit_Click
    End If
End If
```

Constructing the Quiz Game

Using persistent data stored in a sequential file, the quiz game prompts a user with a predetermined number of questions as seen in Figure 8.6. After each question is answered, the quiz game evaluates the answer and outputs the corresponding score.

You can generate quiz records by hand through a text editor such as Notepad or WordPad. Better yet, you can create them through a record creator such as the one shown in the section "Sequential Access Files" earlier in this chapter.

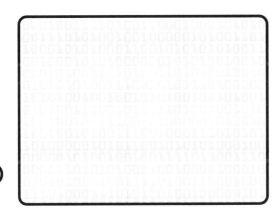

FIGURE 8.6

The quiz game.

The Problem

Create a quiz game that prompts a user with questions read from a sequential access file. After a question is answered, the quiz game should evaluate the answer and output the score to a Picture Box.

Figure 8.6 depicts the quiz game with its controls and properties listed in Table 8.2.

A sample algorithm for the quiz game:

1. Create a sequential access file based on a predetermined record type.
2. Create a new standard EXE project.
3. Write code in the form load event to open an existing sequential access file. The form load event should also contain error-handling routines to handle file I/O problems.
4. Write code to start the quiz game. This code should read the first record in the sequential access file and then stop and wait for the player to answer the question.
5. Write code that responds to the user prompting for the next question. This routine should score the current question, output the score to a Picture Box, and then read the next available record.
6. Keep reading records, displaying questions, and scoring question and answers until the end of file (EOF) is reached.
7. Write code to close the sequential access file when the quiz is completed.

TABLE 8.2 CONTROLS AND PROPERTIES OF THE QUIZ GAME

Control	Property	Setting
frmMain	Caption	Chapter 8 – Quiz Game
	Border Style	1 – Fixed Single
lblQuestion	Caption	Empty
txtAnswer	Text	Empty
cmdBeginNext	Caption	Command1
	Default	True
cmdQuit	Caption	&Quit
picScoreSheet		

The Implementation

The quiz game starts by declaring two form-level variables in the general section and opening a data file for input in the form load event. An error handler also exists in the form load event to catch any file I/O or program errors.

```
Option Explicit
Dim fiQuestionNumber As Integer
Dim fsCurrentCorrectAnswer As String


Private Sub Form_Load()
On Error GoTo ErrorHandler:
cmdBeginNext.Caption = "Start"
fiQuestionNumber = 1
BeginHere:
Open "quiz.dat" For Input As #1
Exit Sub


ErrorHandler:
    Dim liResponse As Integer

    Select Case Err.Number
       Case 53
           'File not found
           liResponse = MsgBox("File not found!", vbRetryCancel, "Error!")
           If liResponse = 4 Then 'Retry
              Resume BeginHere:
           Else
              cmdQuit_Click
           End If
       Case 71
           'Disk not ready
           liResponse = MsgBox("Disk not ready!", vbRetryCancel, "Error!")
           If liResponse = 4 Then 'Retry
              Resume BeginHere:
           Else
              cmdQuit_Click
           End If
       Case 76
           liResponse = MsgBox("Path not found!", vbRetryCancel, "Error!")
           If liResponse = 4 Then 'Retry
```

```
                    Resume BeginHere:
                Else
                    cmdQuit_Click
                End If
            Case Else
                MsgBox "Error in program!", , "Error"
                 cmdQuit_Click
        End Select
    End Sub
```

The BeginNext Command Button takes care of calling procedures to read the first and subsequent questions and scoring the user's answer.

```
Private Sub cmdBeginNext_Click()

If cmdBeginNext.Caption = "Start" Then
    txtAnswer.Text = ""
    If Get_Question = True Then
        cmdBeginNext.Caption = "Next"
        txtAnswer.SetFocus
    End If
Else 'Quiz is in progress
        'verify input
        If txtAnswer.Text = "" Then
            MsgBox "Enter an answer.", , "Error"
        txtAnswer.SetFocus
            Exit Sub
    Else
        'Score previous question
        Score
        If Get_Question = True Then
            cmdBeginNext.Caption = "Next"
            txtAnswer.Text = ""
            txtAnswer.SetFocus
        End If
    End If
End If

End Sub
```

The Get_Question function reads a data file for a question and a corresponding answer. If no more question records exist, the function stops the game by setting properties and returning false to the calling procedure.

```
Public Function Get_Question() As Boolean

Dim liQuestionNumber As Integer

If EOF(1) <> True Then
    Input #1, liQuestionNumber, fsCurrentQuestion, _
fsCurrentCorrectAnswer
    lblQuestion.Caption = "Question # " & liQuestionNumber & _
". " & fsCurrentQuestion
    If fiQuestionNumber <> liQuestionNumber Then
        fiQuestionNumber = fiQuestionNumber + 1
    End If
    Get_Question = True
Else
    Get_Question = False
    cmdBeginNext.Enabled = False
    txtAnswer.Enabled = False
    lblQuestion.ForeColor = vbBlue
    lblQuestion.Caption = "Quiz Completed"
End If

End Function
```

The Score subprocedure evaluates the user's response to the actual answer as reported by the data file.

```
Public Sub Score()
If Trim(UCase(txtAnswer.Text)) = UCase(fsCurrentCorrectAnswer) Then
    picScoreSheet.Print "Question # " & fiQuestionNumber & _
".      " & "Correct. "
Else
    picScoreSheet.Print "Question # " & fiQuestionNumber & _
".      " & "Incorrect. Correct Answer: " & fsCurrentCorrectAnswer
End If
End Sub
```

The last two procedures handle closing the data file and ending the game.

```
Private Sub cmdQuit_Click()
Close #1
End
End Sub


Private Sub Form_QueryUnload(Cancel As Integer, UnloadMode _
As Integer)
cmdQuit_Click
End Sub
```

Summary

In this chapter, you learned how to build file access programs using sequential access files that read one record at a time in sequential order. You also learned how to create more dynamic file access programs using random access files that use fixed record lengths and user-defined types to navigate through records and fields. In addition to building file access programs, you learned how to prevent file I/O errors using the Err object and labels.

Moreover, this chapter covered an important computer science concept called file structures. File structures and file organization are key components to building and managing programs such as games, applications, databases, and operating systems.

CHALLENGES

1. Using any sequential access file, build a program that populates one or more List Boxes with fields from records. Hint: You need to use a looping construct to iterate through the sequential file until the EOF marker is found. While looping through the file, use the AddItem method of the List Box control to add fields as items to the List Box.

2. Create a random access program that allows a user to navigate through an existing random access file. The program should also allow a user to make edits (changes) to any record found.

3. Modify the quiz game to allow the player to start the quiz over again.

4. Migrate the quiz game from sequential access to random access.

Standard Code Modules, Multiple Forms, and Encryption

T his chapter shows you how to add multiple forms to your projects to create about boxes and splash screens. You will then learn about code modules and an intriguing and sometimes controversial computer science topic called encryption. Specifically, I show you how to encrypt data with a basic encryption algorithm using Visual Basic functions in code modules. This should be an exciting and intriguing chapter, so get your pop or coffee ready, and let's go.

This chapter covers the following topics:

- Creating and using multiple Forms

- Code modules

- Encryption

- Constructing the enhancements for the quiz game

Project: Enhancing the Quiz Game with Encryption and Multiple Forms

Although functional, the quiz game from Chapter 8 contained one major security flaw. Any player sophisticated enough to open the sequential file can find the answers to the questions. The enhanced quiz game in this chapter solves this security problem by implementing encryption.

In addition to encryption, the enhanced quiz game, shown in Figure 9.1, implements an about box and splash screen to add a custom and more professional feel to the program.

Creating and Using Multiple Forms

Life would be simple if you could write all Visual Basic programs with just one Form. Or would it be? Sometimes programs are actually easier to build and use with multiple Forms. This might be the case if your program requires a number of controls. For example, your program might be easier for users if you distribute functionality to multiple Forms rather than cram all the controls and functionality onto one Form.

With an ATM (automated teller machine), the first object you see is a login screen. After successfully logging into the bank's system, you are prompted with another screen that displays a menu of choices. For each menu item selected, a new screen appears. You can probably imagine a painful human-to-computer interaction if an ATM conducted all of its functionality on one screen. Now that would be messy!

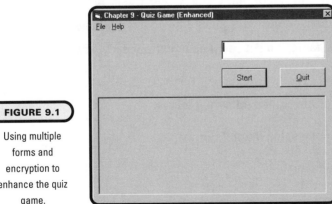

FIGURE 9.1

Using multiple forms and encryption to enhance the quiz game.

Visual Basic makes it easy for you to create and manage multiple Forms in one project. Hey, it's not rocket science; it's computer science! Okay, in all seriousness, what other circumstances might require the use of multiple Forms? Well, so far the ATM example is good, but what about an options screen in your game? Maybe you want your players to click on a menu item that launches another Form (screen) where they can make decisions on the game's options. Or maybe a high-scores screen appears after a player has reached a certain amount of points, at which time the player can enter his or her name.

If you find yourself reaching for a scenario where your program should use multiple Forms, there might not be a need for more than one Form. After you have some experience in designing applications (and receiving user feedback), you will find that during design phase, programs speak to you about how their layout and design should look and feel.

Although this chapter covers multiple Forms as they pertain to splash screens and about boxes, the process for loading Forms and accessing their control's properties and methods is the same.

Creating an About Box

As a software developer, you might want to display specific information pertaining to your application and company to users or customers. Such information could contain a company logo, address, contact information, software version, and copyright information. In the software world, this type of information is generally contained in a Form called an about box.

To add an about box to an existing standard EXE project, simply click on the Project menu item and select Add Form, as shown in Figure 9.2.

A dialog box appears, prompting you with multiple choices on Form types. Simply select the Form icon and press Open.

 HINT **Visual Basic provides a customizable about box template, the icon for which (About Dialog) is shown in Figure 9.3.**

Once the Form is added to your existing project, you might notice that it looks and feels just like the default Form that is loaded when a new standard EXE project is created. The newly added Form is the same as the default Form in a standard EXE project. Both Forms contain the same properties and methods.

Add Form menu item

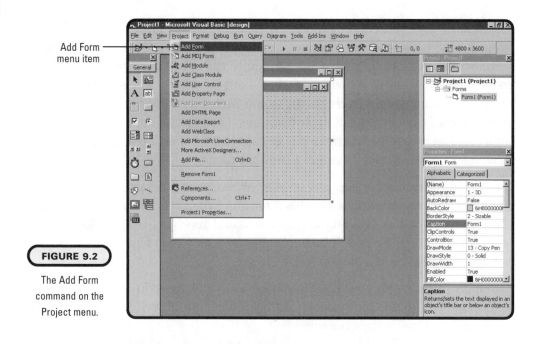

FIGURE 9.2

The Add Form command on the Project menu.

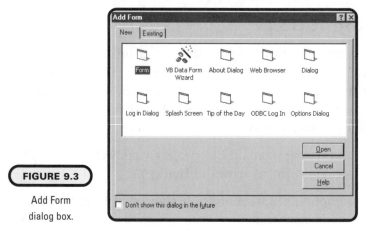

FIGURE 9.3

Add Form dialog box.

You may also notice that your Project Explorer window contains two entries under the Forms section. You can use the Project Explorer window to navigate between Forms by double-clicking the Form icon, as shown in Figure 9.4.

You can now add controls to your second Form. Remember that because this is an about box, you should add information or graphics that pertain to your company, you the programmer, and the program itself. For example, Figure 9.5 depicts a Form I used as an about box for the enhanced quiz game.

After you add controls to your Form, you can write code to access it from any other Form in your project. With the enhanced quiz game, I wanted users to access the about box from a menu item. To call the about box (or any other Form, for that matter), I simply called the Show method of the Form:

```
Private Sub mnuHelpAbout_Click()
frmAbout.Show
End Sub
```

The Project Explorer window

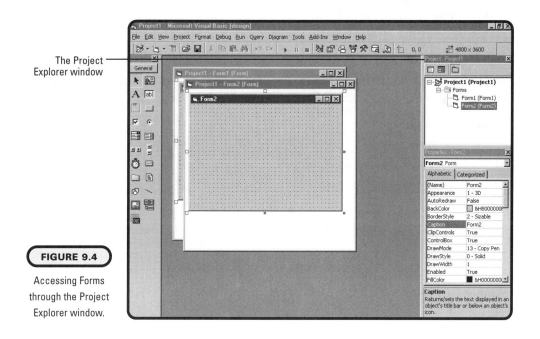

FIGURE 9.4

Accessing Forms through the Project Explorer window.

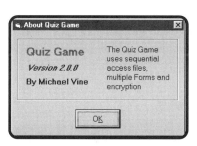

FIGURE 9.5

An about box for the enhanced quiz game.

The Show method can also take an argument as its display type. In Visual Basic, Forms are shown as modal or modeless (default). A Form displayed in modal form prevents the user from accessing any other Forms in the current program (project) until she has responded to the active Form:

```
Private Sub mnuHelpAbout_Click()
frmAbout.Show vbModal
End Sub
```

Forms shown with the modeless type do not prevent the user from switching to other Forms in the application:

```
Private Sub mnuHelpAbout_Click()
frmAbout.Show vbModeless
End Sub
```

When creating about boxes, you have only one more piece of code to write. You should have code written to unload the Form when a user decides to close your about box. You use the Unload Me statement:

```
Private Sub cmdOK_Click()
Unload Me
End Sub
```

The Unload keyword essentially removes a Form or control from memory. You use the Me keyword to reference the current active object (in this case, the about form). Note that you can also simply reference the Form followed by the Unload method as seen next.

```
Private Sub cmdOK_Click()
frmAbout.Unload
End Sub
```

You can also use the Me keyword to access the current object's controls, properties, and methods. To do so, simply type the keyword Me followed by a period (the dot notation). Visual Basic provides you a list of controls, properties, and methods to choose from.

Creating Splash Screens

Splash screens are tools software developers sometimes use to trick a user into thinking a large program is loading faster than it would if there were no splash screen. For instance, a large accounting program that connects to a database, performs transactions, and reads initialization strings during program load might take a few moments to complete before showing its main Form. A user could become impatient while the program loads, or he could even misinterpret the application as not responding. Adding a splash screen to the accounting program can distract the user by giving him something to look at while the program finishes loading.

Some splash screens are displayed while the program's processes are loading and disappear once the loading processes have completed. Other splash screens stay visible until the user does something.

Essentially, there are two ways to create splash screens. In the first way, you simply add a Form to your project just as you would for an about box. After adding the new Form, you place code in various events to show and unload the splash screen (again, similar to the about box).

In the second way, you can use a Visual Basic template to assist you. To find the splash screen template, simply add a new Form to your project by clicking the Project menu item and selecting Add Form (see Figure 9.6).

The splash screen template provides a number of built-in, ready-to-use controls and procedure code. As shown in Figure 9.7, I used a splash screen template for the enhanced quiz game.

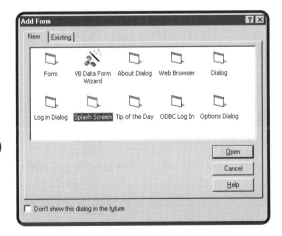

FIGURE 9.6

Splash screen template icon in the Add Form dialog box.

FIGURE 9.7

The splash screen
for the enhanced
quiz game.

Before modifying any default controls provided in the splash screen template, you should first look at the default procedure code provided by the template:

```
Option Explicit
Private Sub Form_KeyPress(KeyAscii As Integer)
    Unload Me
End Sub
Private Sub Form_Load()
    lblVersion.Caption = "Version " & App.Major & "." & _
App.Minor & "." & App.Revision
    lblProductName.Caption = App.Title
End Sub
Private Sub Frame1_Click()
    Unload Me
End Sub
```

First, notice that Visual Basic added code to unload the Form from memory in the frame click event and form KeyPress event. What this means is that the splash screen stays visible until a user clicks anywhere on the Frame control or presses any key. In addition, Visual Basic adds default code for you in the splash screen's form load event. This code uses various App properties to dynamically assign caption properties. To customize the App object's properties, simply right-click your project in the Project Explorer window and choose Project Properties.

The App keyword refers to the global App object. It can be used to access the application's version, title, path, and names of its executable and help files.

From the Project Properties window, shown in Figure 9.8, you can change some of the project settings as they directly apply to the splash screen templates procedure code (such as version numbers). Once you modify the project properties to reflect your current application, they are displayed on your splash screen.

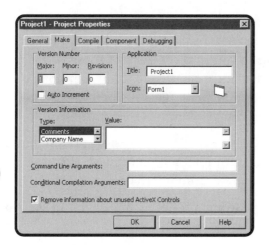

FIGURE 9.8

Project properties
in the Project
Properties window.

One piece of code not provided by Visual Basic's splash screen template is the process by which the splash screen appears. Normally, splash screens appear at the beginning of an application, or in other words, before any other Form in the project appears. You can set this up through the Project Properties window. Simply change the startup object from the Startup tab to that of the splash screen, as shown in Figure 9.9.

Code Modules

You can think of modules as containers for all Visual Basic code. The way a module is implemented depends on its type. Visual Basic provides three types of modules (one of which you already know about): Form, Standard, and Class.

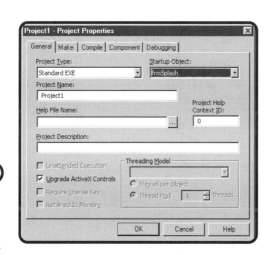

FIGURE 9.9

Changing the
startup object
from the Project
Properties window.

For example, in a small application, you might have only one Form. All of your code for this small application resides in the one Form module. Over time, you might add other Forms to your project. Each of those Forms modules will have its own code. You may at some time need to share common procedures or global variables among your Form modules. This is when you can decide to add a standard module to your project.

Standard modules (which have the *.bas extension) are similar to Form modules because they can have declarations and procedures. However, unlike Form modules, a standard module contains no interface.

To add a standard module to your project, simply click on the Project menu item and select Add Module (see Figure 9.10).

An Add Module dialog box appears, as in Figure 9.11, so you can select your module.

Once you add the standard module, you can access it from the Project Explorer window under the Modules section. In Figure 9.12, note that the newly added standard module contains only a code window. There is no user interface.

To see how standard code modules are implemented with other modules such as Forms, I've built a small program that displays application information into a Picture Box as seen in Figure 9.13.

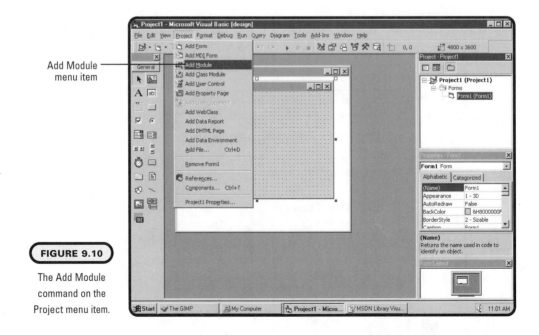

Add Module menu item

FIGURE 9.10

The Add Module command on the Project menu item.

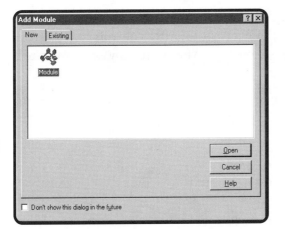

FIGURE 9.11

Selecting the
module from
the Add Module
dialog box.

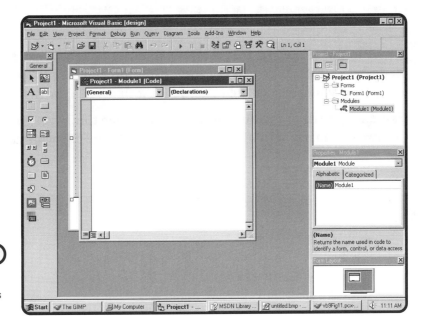

FIGURE 9.12

Viewing the
standard module's
code window.

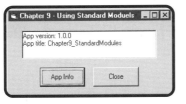

FIGURE 9.13

Using standard
code modules.

To build this program, first create a new standard EXE project and add the applicable controls as seen in Figure 9.13. After controls have been added to the Form, add a standard code module to the project by selecting the Add Module item from the Projects menu item.

Open the standard code module's window (if it's not already open) and add a new public subprocedure as seen here:

```
Option Explicit


Public Sub GetAppInfo()
frmMain.picOutput.Cls
frmMain.picOutput.Print "App version: " & App.Major & "."; App.Minor &
"." & App.Revision
frmMain.picOutput.Print "App title: " & App.Title
End Sub
```

Notice in the code above that control names are preceded with the Form name, in this case frmMain. To access a Form's controls and their properties and methods from a standard code module, you must first qualify with a Form name.

Save and close the standard code module and open the Form's code window. Find the two Command Button's click events and add the following code:

```
Option Explicit


Private Sub cmdGetAppInfo_Click()
GetAppInfo
End Sub


Private Sub cmdClose_Click()
End
End Sub
```

In the click event of the app info Command Button I need to reference the standard code module's subprocedure name to execute its statements. But, why did I not need to precede the procedure's name with the name of the module? Simply put, scope is why. As seen below, the standard code module's procedure is declared as Public.

```
Public Sub GetAppInfo()
```

This means that it becomes available to other modules in the application as if they were intrinsic (built-in) to each module. If, on the other hand, the procedure was declared as Private, the program would no longer work. Procedures or variables declared as Private are only available to the module in which they were created.

Encryption

Cryptography is the science of encoding and protecting data from those whom you do not trust. Cryptography uses a broad spectrum of technologies, such as encryption, digital signatures, watermarks, cryptograms, algorithms, and mathematics, to name just a few.

Depending on the sensitivity of the information, cryptography can be simple to design (and break) or complicated and near break-proof. In fact, the best cryptography in this country is restricted from going overseas. Not surprisingly, the United States is not the only country concerned about controlling cryptography; most countries have developed some forms of laws and security agencies for securing and monitoring cryptography.

But what is cryptography? Simply put, cryptography provides a solution to a problem. What is the problem? Is it how to encrypt messages? Not really; the problem goes deeper than just encrypting messages.

Technologists and security analysts know that you cannot always prevent someone from getting your data. For example, if you send encrypted information over the public Internet, you are always—I mean *always*—in danger of someone capturing the encrypted data.

The problem for the person who captures the encrypted data is how to hack the algorithm that decrypts the message. This is the root problem of cryptography.

IN THE REAL WORLD

Every culture and subculture has a group of persons that attempt to misuse a product or steal information. In the world of computers, these people are known as hackers.

The term hacker was not always synonymous with someone who committed computer crimes. Originally, the term hacker represented someone who knew a little more about a particular computer system than the average user. Hackers were considered the technologists who always knew how to figure out a problem on a computer. If they didn't know the solution off-hand, they would spend the time necessary to hack it out.

How can you protect data once it has been received or stolen by the wrong person? In other words, what kind of algorithm will take so long to hack that it is not feasible with current technology or a realistic amount of time?

How do you disguise a message? Well, the simple answer is to take the original message, called *plaintext*, and disguise it with *ciphertext*.

> **Definition**
>
> *Plaintext* is a readable message. *Ciphertext* is an unreadable message in encrypted form.

For example, let's say I want to send you the phrase "Top Secret" as ciphertext. Well, first I have to come up with a *key* (or algorithm) for encrypting the message and then a key for decrypting the message.

Using the alphabet and a swapping pattern, I can encrypt a message by replacing one character for another. I'll call this swapping pattern *move by n*, where *n* is the number of moves to make.

> **Definition**
>
> *Keys*, like their physical counterparts, lock and unlock something. Keys normally refer to an algorithm for encrypting a message or decrypting a message.

For instance, if I use a move-by-2 pattern, the plaintext letter a is replaced by the letter c, the letter b is replaced by the letter d, and so on.

My plaintext message "Top Secret" now becomes "Vqr Ugetgv." Hey, that was pretty cool! Now, unless you know the key, move by 2, the message seems useless and unreadable.

Numbering Systems

As you saw earlier, there are ways to encrypt data without using computers. But in reality, all modern cryptography happens with some form of technology or computers. Because this is a computer book, I show you how to create applied encryption and decryption using Visual Basic. Before you dive into applied cryptography and encryption, you need to learn some basics about computer numbering systems.

At the lowest level, computer hardware such as digital circuitry uses electrical signals to represent data or decisions. Computer software can recognize these electrical signals as either off or on. These off and on patterns are translated into binary digits (1 for on and 0 for off), which can then be translated into an integer equivalent number. These integer equivalents are known as ASCII (American Standard Code for Information Interchange) codes that can represent keyboard characters.

ASCII uses 8 bits to represent one character and can encode a total of 256 characters ($2^8 = 256$) ranging 0 to 255. Although the process of converting binary code into ASCII code is beyond the scope of this book, you can get a feel for numbering systems by looking at Table 9.1.

ASCII codes 0 to 127 appear in Appendix A. For a complete list of ASCII codes (0 to 255), visit Microsoft's Web site at http://www.microsoft.com or enter keyword "ASCII" in your copy of MSDN Library.

What if we want the number 97 and not the letter a? Does the binary code 01100001 represent both? Yes, it does represent both. The only way a computer knows how to represent binary codes is in the way you use it.

TABLE 9.1 SAMPLE CONVERSIONS

Binary Code	ASCII Code	Keyboard Character
00110000	48	0
00110001	49	1
00110010	50	2
00110011	51	3
00110100	52	4
00110101	53	5
00110110	54	6
00110111	55	7
00111000	56	8
00111001	57	9
01100001	97	a
01100010	98	b
01100011	99	c
01100100	100	d
01100101	101	e
01100110	102	f
01100111	103	g
01101000	104	h
01101001	105	i
01101010	106	j

You might remember the functions *Str* and *Val* from earlier chapters. These functions are good examples of how you control what the computer displays or returns.

Simple Encryption Algorithm

Using Visual Basic, you are ready to take what you know about cryptography and computer numbering systems and build a simple encryption algorithm. Before you begin, let me refresh you with the definition of an algorithm: An algorithm is a finite, step-by-step process for solving a problem.

With that in mind, what kind of algorithm can we write to encrypt any plaintext message? Well, I start off with a non-technical algorithm similar to the move-by-*n* key discussed earlier:

1. Create a plaintext message.
2. Begin a looping process that looks at each character in the plaintext message.
3. For each character found, replace it with a different character.
4. Output a completed ciphertext message.

So far, so good; but what characters will I replace the plaintext characters with? Knowing what you now know about numbering systems, you could replace plaintext characters with ASCII codes. Here's another more refined algorithm with a little more technical detail:

1. Create a plaintext message.
2. Pass the plaintext message to an encrypt function.
3. Within the encrypt function, begin a looping process through the entire plaintext message starting with the first character.
4. For each character found, replace it with its corresponding character code (ASCII) value.
5. Output a completed ciphertext message.

Okay, this algorithm is a little more precise but still lacks a good key. In other words, anyone understanding computer-numbering systems can translate each ASCII value to a corresponding plaintext character. That's no good!

A better approach to this key adds a little randomization to the algorithm. The process of adding randomization to a key is, well, only limited by your imagination or creativity.

One way to add randomization to the algorithm is to take the length of the incoming string (plaintext message) and add that number to the character's corresponding ASCII value. After that, I can take the ASCII code and find its new corresponding character value. Although certainly not hack-proof, this key is starting to sound a little more cryptic in nature. Here's the revised algorithm:

1. Create a plaintext message.

2. Pass the plaintext message to an encrypt function.

3. Acquire the length of the incoming string.

4. Within the encrypt function, begin a looping process through the entire plaintext message starting with the first character.

5. For each character found, add the length of the string to its corresponding character code (ASCII) value.

6. Convert the new ASCII value to its corresponding character value.

7. Output a completed ciphertext message.

Now let me show you how I implemented this algorithm in Visual Basic.

With the exception of the do while loop's contents, everything in the code should look familiar to you:

```
Public Function Encrypt(inString As String) As String


Dim liCurrentPosition As Integer
Dim liStringSize As Integer
Dim lsTempString As String
Dim lsCurrentCharacter As String


liCurrentPosition = 1
lsTempString = ""
liStringSize = Len(inString)


Do While liCurrentPosition <= liStringSize
    lsCurrentCharacter = Chr(Asc(Mid(inString, liCurrentPosition, _
1)) + liStringSize)
    liCurrentPosition = liCurrentPosition + 1
    lsTempString = lsTempString & lsCurrentCharacter
Loop
Encrypt = lsTempString


End Function
```

In the loop, I first use the Mid function to acquire all characters, one at a time in the plaintext message. Next, I use the *Asc* function to convert the character into its corresponding character code (ASCII value). Finally, I add the incoming string length to the character code before using the *Chr* function to convert an ASCII value into a character.

> ### Definition
>
> The *Asc* function takes a string value as its argument and returns the corresponding character code.
>
> ```
> Asc(String)
> ```
>
> The *Chr* function takes a character code (ASCII value) as its parameter and returns a string containing the corresponding character value.
>
> ```
> Chr(CharacterCode)
> ```

Now you've seen the key implemented as an encryption function. Can you guess what the decryption key would look like? All right, I won't keep you in suspense. Here's the other key that unlocks the decrypted message:

```
Public Function Decrypt(inString As String) As String

Dim liCurrentPosition As Integer
Dim liStringSize As Integer
Dim lsTempString As String
Dim lsCurrentCharacter As String

liCurrentPosition = 1
lsTempString = ""
liStringSize = Len(inString)

Do While liCurrentPosition <= liStringSize
    lsCurrentCharacter = Chr(Asc(Mid(inString, liCurrentPosition, _
1)) - liStringSize)
    liCurrentPosition = liCurrentPosition + 1
    lsTempString = lsTempString & lsCurrentCharacter
Loop
Decrypt = lsTempString

End Function
```

After looking at the decrypt function, you may notice that the only difference between the two keys is the way the functions treat the length of the incoming messages.

To be more exact, the encryption key adds the length of the incoming plaintext message to the character code, and the decryption key subtracts the length of the incoming ciphertext message from the character code. Voilà, that's it! Two keys are created in Visual Basic, one to close the door and one to open it.

The graphical output of the encrypt/decrypt program appears in Figures 9.14 and 9.15.

Login Dialog Box and Passwords

As you've seen, cryptography and encryption can be important security tools in sending messages. Sometimes, however, the display of data (or the lack thereof) can be as important as the key used to encrypt it. Passwords, for example, should always be encrypted. But it would be cumbersome for us as users to enter an encrypted password every time we want access to a particular system.

Wouldn't it be easier if you could just enter your password as plaintext and leave the encryption/decryption to the operating system? Sure it would. In fact, that is how most (if not all) operation systems work today. You never enter an encrypted password into a login screen. You simply enter your plaintext password for

FIGURE 9.14

The encrypt/decrypt program ready to encrypt a plaintext message.

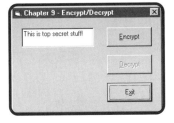

FIGURE 9.15

A ciphertext message encrypted with the encrypt/decrypt program.

system access, and the operating system stores your password for future lookup in a ciphertext (encrypted) format.

There is, however, a catch to entering plaintext passwords. Characters entered for passwords on most login screens are converted to a mask. The mask generally consists of a pattern using one character, such as an asterisk (*). Visual Basic provides this masking technique for all Text Box controls in the form of the PasswordChar property. The PasswordChar property dictates the character shown for each character entered into the Text Box.

In addition to password masking, Visual Basic provides the MaxLength property for controlling the length of passwords. The MaxLength property takes an integer number representing the allowed length of the Text property.

Creating login screens in Visual Basic is easy. You can create your own with a Form, or you can use Visual Basic's standard login dialog template. To access Visual Basic's login dialog template, simply click the Project menu item and select Add Form. When the Add Form dialog appears, choose the Log in Dialog, as shown in Figure 9.16.

After adding the Log in Dialog template to your project, you can customize it (code) and its controls as needed (see Figure 9.17).

Constructing the Enhancements for the Quiz Game

As seen in Figure 9.18, the enhanced quiz game offers new features such as a splash screen about box and encryption.

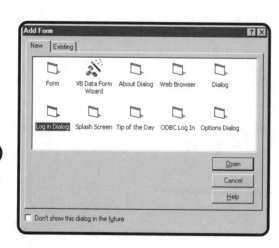

FIGURE 9.16

Selecting the Log in Dialog template from the Add Form dialog.

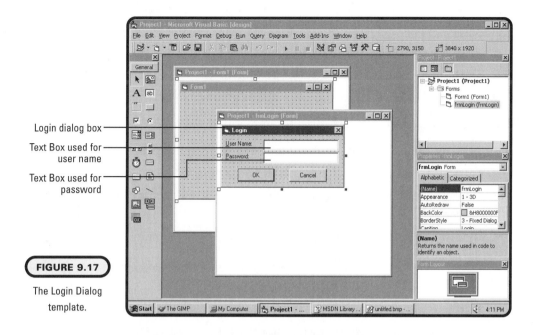

Login dialog box ——

Text Box used for —
user name

Text Box used for —
password

FIGURE 9.17

The Login Dialog
template.

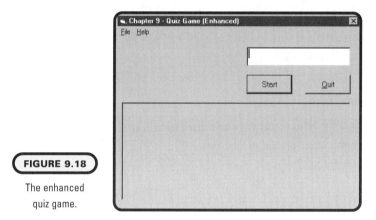

FIGURE 9.18

The enhanced
quiz game.

The Problem

Enhance the quiz game from Chapter 8 to include a splash screen, about box, and encryption for stored answers.

Necessary tools for enhancing the quiz game:

- One about box template
- One splash screen template
- One standard module

The following steps are the algorithm for adding the about box:

1. Add one about box template to the existing quiz game project.
2. Customize controls on the about box form.
3. Write code to open and close the about box.

Here's how you add the splash screen template:

1. Add one splash screen template to the existing quiz game project.
2. Customize controls on the splash screen form.
3. Change the startup object under Project Properties to that of the splash screen.
4. Modify the splash screen's default procedure code to show the main quiz game after it has unloaded.

Follow these steps to add encryption to the quiz game:

1. Add one standard module to the quiz game project.
2. Implement a decryption key (as shown in the section "Simple Encryption Algorithm" earlier in this chapter) in the standard code module.
3. Modify the quiz game's code to pass the stored answer to the decryption function prior to scoring an item.

The Implementation

The first code segment is the form module code for the about box:

```
Option Explicit


Private Sub cmdOK_Click()
Unload Me
End Sub
```

Next, you write the form module code for the splash screen:

```
Option Explicit


Private Sub Form_KeyPress(KeyAscii As Integer)
        Unload Me
        frmMain.Show
End Sub


Private Sub Form_Load()
        lblVersion.Caption = "Version " & App.Major & "." & App.Minor _
```

```
& "." & App.Revision
        lblProductName.Caption = App.Title
End Sub


Private Sub Frame1_Click()
        Unload Me
        frmMain.Show
End Sub
```

Following is the standard module code for the decryption key:

```
Option Explicit


Public Function Decrypt(inString As String) As String


Dim liCurrentPosition As Integer
Dim liStringSize As Integer
Dim lsTempString As String
Dim lsCurrentCharacter As String


liCurrentPosition = 1
lsTempString = ""
liStringSize = Len(inString)


Do While liCurrentPosition <= liStringSize
    lsCurrentCharacter = Chr(Asc(Mid(inString, liCurrentPosition, _
1)) - liStringSize)
    liCurrentPosition = liCurrentPosition + 1
    lsTempString = lsTempString & lsCurrentCharacter
Loop
Decrypt = lsTempString


End Function
```

The last segment contains the modified form module code for the quiz game:
(For a complete list of quiz game program code, see Chapter 8.)

```
Public Sub Score()
If Trim(UCase(txtAnswer.Text)) = _
UCase(Decrypt(fsCurrentCorrectAnswer)) Then
    picScoreSheet.Print "Question # " & fiQuestionNumber & _
".      " & "Correct. "
Else
    picScoreSheet.Print "Question # " & fiQuestionNumber & ".      " _
```

```
        & "Incorrect. Correct Answer: " & Decrypt(fsCurrentCorrectAnswer)
    End If
End Sub
```

Summary

This chapter showed you how to work with multiple Forms in Visual Basic. You specifically learned that Visual Basic already provides some easy-to-use Form templates such as about boxes, splash screens, and login dialogs.

You also made a transition from thinking about Forms as control containers to Form modules as control and code containers. This concept was presented with the idea of using standard modules for sharing global variables and procedures across a project.

Beyond modules, this chapter introduced the exciting premise and application of cryptography and encryption. You specifically learned that cryptography is the art, science, and technology behind safeguarding messages. You also saw how you can design basic encryption keys through algorithms and implement them in programming languages such as Visual Basic.

CHALLENGES

1. Add your own custom about boxes and splash screens to previous games or programs you have built.

2. Create a new quiz creator program that encrypts the answer associated with the question. Use the quiz creator program from Chapter 8 to aid you in program design.

3. Add a login dialog to the new quiz creator program. The login dialog should allow only authorized users into the quiz creator. When a user name and password are entered, the login dialog should check the string values against an existing encrypted sequential file of user names and passwords.

4. Modify the encryption/decryption keys in this chapter to use other random criteria. For example, instead of using the length of the incoming string, you could use the time of day, day of week, the rnd function, or anything else that appears random. Hint: If you use a random number such as time of day, you need to include that number somehow into your ciphertext. Otherwise, you have no way of knowing what was used in the encryption key during the decryption process.

Arrays

In this chapter, you will increase your computer science, programming, and Visual Basic skills to include a new structure called arrays. You will become familiar with array concepts such as multidimensional arrays, control arrays, dynamic arrays, upper and lower bounds, and the PictureClip control. The array topics covered in this chapter take you from basic array concepts to a fully functional game program called video poker. Specifically, this chapter covers the following topics:

- Arrays

- Control arrays

- PictureClip control

- Constructing the blackjack game

Project: Video Poker (Blackjack) Game

The video poker game uses arrays and a PictureClip control to simulate a popular card game known as blackjack or 21. Figure 10.1 shows the video poker game.

Arrays

Don't worry if you find this chapter to be a bit complex at first. Most beginning programmers find array structures a difficult concept to master. Nevertheless, arrays are an integral component of any programming language, and you should implement them whenever possible.

The first thing to learn about arrays is that *arrays* are just variables. However, they are special variables that contain a group of like data types. Like variables, arrays can be classified into various data types. For instance, you could have an array of integers, an array of strings, an

> **Definition**
>
> *Arrays* are a grouping of memory locations containing the same name and data type.

> **IN THE REAL WORLD**
>
> To array or not to array: Believe it or not, most programmers use arrays to simplify their program code. Arrays provide a mechanism for keeping like data types together and for accessing them. Surprisingly, using arrays in program code generally produces cleaner and smaller code. The tricky part, however, is identifying when to use arrays. Generally speaking, whenever you have a number of like data-types serving the same function, you might want to use an array.

FIGURE 10.1

Using arrays and the PictureClip control to create the video poker game.

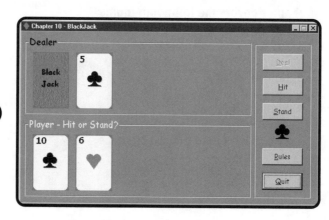

array of doubles, or even an array of arrays (yikes). Unlike variables that contain one data type element, arrays can contain many variable elements of the same type.

You may remember that variables are placeholders for memory addresses that contain the location of data. As seen in Figure 10.2, an integer variable called myInteger points to a location in memory 4 bytes long where the integer value lives.

Arrays, on the other hand, can contain multiple contiguous memory segments using just one variable name. As seen in Figure 10.3, an array of integers called myArray(4) points to a location in memory containing five contiguous 4-byte integer data types.

You can access the individual memory locations of an array through the use of element numbers, such as myArray(2).

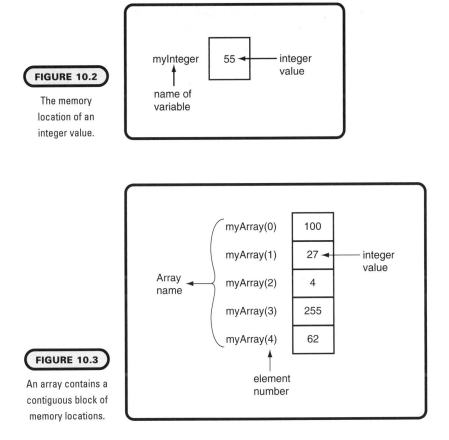

FIGURE 10.2

The memory location of an integer value.

FIGURE 10.3

An array contains a contiguous block of memory locations.

Declaring Arrays

Arrays have what is known as upper and lower bounds. This essentially means that an array has a starting element number and an ending element number. To declare an array, simply dimension the array name followed by parentheses containing its upper bound:

```
Dim ArrayName(Number of Elements) As DataType
```

For example, if I want to create an integer array called myArray that contains five elements, I use the following syntax:

```
Dim myArray(4) As Integer
```

Notice that my element number is 4 instead of 5. This is because array elements start with the element number zero (0). In other words, the lower bound is 0, and the upper bound is 5. You can, however, specify a lower bound for an array in its declaration:

```
Dim myArray(1 To 5) As Integer
```

Explicitly declaring a lower bound element number and upper bound element number allows me to access the first element in myArray with element number 1.

TRAP

Beginning and even experienced programmers face the notorious off-by-one error every now and then. The off-by-one error generally represents a program statement trying to access an array element that either does not exist or does exist and returns an unintentional value. These off-by-one errors happen because the programmer forgot the array's upper and lower bounds.

HINT

As with other variables, you can declare arrays using the keywords public and private depending on the desired scope.

It is worthy to mention that when creating fixed-size arrays, Visual Basic allocates the number of bytes necessary to hold all array elements. Being memory-conscious, you should have a pretty good idea of how many elements the array will use throughout the life of your program. This prevents you from having to create unnecessary element numbers and thus saves memory. However, there is a way to create arrays that will allocate elements as needed. See the section "Dynamic Arrays" later in this chapter for more information on dynamic element allocation.

TRICK

The default lower bound for arrays is 0. You can, however, change the default lower bound with the Option Base statement. The Option Base statement is used at the module level outside of any procedures:

```
Option base 1
```

Using the above statement provides arrays (except for arrays that are declared with a different lower bound) with the default lower bound of 1.

Single Dimension Arrays

The arrays you have seen so far are known as single dimension arrays. A single dimension array contains a single row of like data. The best way to understand arrays and their elements is to build and use them. Figure 10.4 shows a small program that uses a single dimension array to print the contents of its elements.

I declared a form-level single dimension array called myArray to contain 10 integer elements:

```
Option Explicit
Dim myArray(9) As Integer '10 elements
```

In the form load event, I use a For loop to assign an incrementing integer value to each element in the array. Notice that I can use a number variable to reference an element of the array: (In this case, x is an integer variable representing an element number.)

```
Private Sub Form_Load()
Dim x As Integer
'Populate the array
For x = 0 To 9
  myArray(x) = x
Next x
End Sub
```

FIGURE 10.4

Accessing the
elements of a
single dimension
array.

I use another For loop to print the contents of each element in the array to a Picture Box control:

```
Private Sub cmdPrint_Click()
Dim x As Integer
'Print array elements
For x = 0 To 9
  Picture1.Print "Element " & myArray(x)
Next x
End Sub
```

The last two procedures handle program termination.

```
Private Sub cmdQuit_Click()
End
End Sub
Private Sub Form_QueryUnload(Cancel As Integer, UnloadMode As Integer)
cmdQuit_Click
End Sub
```

Multidimensional Arrays

Sometimes data cannot be accurately depicted and stored in a single dimension array. Suppose you want to store the x and y coordinates of a map or grid or the rows and columns of a record from a file. You can implement these and many other examples through the use of a two-dimensional array. Also known as multi-subscripted arrays, multidimensional arrays are not limited to just two dimensions. Although it is not uncommon to have three- and even four-dimensional arrays, this section concentrates on two-dimensional arrays only.

As depicted in Figure 10.5, it is easiest to visualize a two-dimensional array with rows and columns.

Like their singular counterpart, multidimensional arrays share similar scope to variables, and share a common name. They have like data types, and they are referenced through element numbers (or indices). The following statement creates a two-dimensional array with four rows and four columns:

```
Dim myArray(3, 3) As String
```

This gives the array a total of 16 elements. As shown in the next segment, you can also explicitly declare upper and lower bounds with two-dimensional arrays:

```
Dim myArray(1 To 4, 1 To 4) As String
```

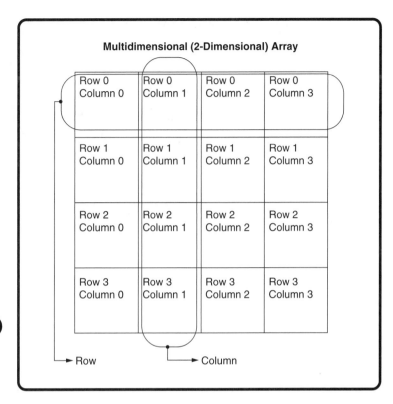

FIGURE 10.5

A two-dimensional
array with rows
and columns.

Both array declarations yield the same number of elements, 16. Looping constructs also play an important role in multidimensional arrays. For instance, to access a given element in a two-dimensional array, you need two loops, one inner and one outer. To see how this works, take a look at the following program depicted in Figure 10.6, which demonstrates a two-dimensional array.

FIGURE 10.6

Working with
multidimensional
arrays.

Here I declare a two-dimensional array of string data types. Total elements in this array are 16:

```
Option Explicit
Dim myArray(3, 3) As String '16 elements
```

To assign a string value to all elements in my two-dimensional array, I use an outer loop to get the row number and an inner loop to access the column. Notice that the inner loop iterates through all columns before moving on to the next row:

```
Private Sub Form_Load()
Dim liOuterLoop As Integer
Dim liInnerLoop As Integer

'Populate the array
For liOuterLoop = 0 To 3
  For liInnerLoop = 0 To 3
    myArray(liOuterLoop, liInnerLoop) = "Row " & liOuterLoop & ", _
Column " & liInnerLoop
  Next liInnerLoop
Next liOuterLoop
End Sub
```

Using similar looping techniques, I print the contents of each element to a Picture Box control:

```
Private Sub cmdPrint_Click()
Dim liOuterLoop As Integer
Dim liInnerLoop As Integer

'Print array elements
For liOuterLoop = 0 To 3
  For liInnerLoop = 0 To 3
    Picture1.Print myArray(liOuterLoop, liInnerLoop)
  Next liInnerLoop
Next liOuterLoop
End Sub
```

The last two procedures handle the unloading of the program.

```
Private Sub cmdQuit_Click()
End
```

```
End Sub

Private Sub Form_QueryUnload(Cancel As Integer, UnloadMode As Integer)
cmdQuit_Click
End Sub
```

How many inner loops do you think it would take to assign values to each element in a three-dimensional loop? What do you think this array would look like? I'll give you a hint: Visualize a Rubik's Cube, and you get a three-dimensional array. What about a four-dimensional loop? Can you visualize what that array would like? You can probably see that it becomes difficult to visualize or describe multidimensional arrays after a third dimension.

Dynamic Arrays

Fixed-sized arrays are perfect when you know the number of elements to work with. But what about the times you're unsure about the number of elements needed for an array? Should you take your best guess? Maybe the answer is just to create a huge array that would always be able to accommodate data. Well, I think you already know that neither of these options is the correct way to solve this problem.

Visual Basic, however, solves this problem for us through the use of dynamic arrays. Dynamic arrays are similar to their cousins in that they share a similar name, like data, and elements to access specific memory locations. What makes dynamic arrays unique is their ability to be resized. Essentially, they can increase and decrease at any time during program execution.

To declare a dynamic array, simply leave the bounds out of the parentheses:

```
Dim dynamicArray()
```

Once you declare the array, you can add elements dynamically through the ReDim keyword. The ReDim keyword allocates the number of elements to a dynamic array. Note that the ReDim keyword is actually an executable statement and therefore must be used in a procedure:

```
ReDim dynamicArray(4)
```

Like static-array declarations, the ReDim statement can use variable names for upper and lower bounds. In addition, you can set explicit bounds in a ReDim statement:

```
ReDim dynamicArray(1 To 5, x To y)
```

Note that every time a ReDim statement is executed, any previous data stored in the array's elements is lost.

If you want to preserve the contents of a dynamic array while increasing its size, use the Preserve keyword with ReDim. For example, you create a two-dimensional array as follows:

```
ReDim dynamicArray(5, 5)
```

Later, you need to increase the size of the array, but you do not want to lose its contents. You could you the Preserve keyword to dynamically increase the array's size and maintain its values:

```
ReDim Preserve dynamicArray(5, 10)
```

The Preserve keyword can only be used to increase an array's upper bound of its last dimension.

Control Arrays

As you have seen, arrays can have many data types. In addition to customary data types, Visual Basic supports the concept of control arrays. You can think of this array type as an array of objects, or in this case, an array of controls.

Control arrays support all types of Visual Basic controls. For instance, you could have an array of Labels, Command Buttons, Option Buttons, Text Boxes, Picture Boxes, or Images, to name just a few.

Why would you want an array of controls? Well, in short, you might want an array of controls for the same reason you would want any other array, such as creating and maintaining less code or combining like data (in this case, like controls). Beyond programming esthetics, control arrays offer the benefit of shared procedures and events.

To create a control array in Visual Basic during design time, simply add a control to your Form. Next, copy the control using either menu options or keyboard shortcuts, and paste the copy in memory to the same Form. A dialog box should appear asking whether you want to create a control array. After you select Yes in the dialog box, the new control is added and your control array is created. After which, you can continue to add controls to the array by pasting until you have the desired amount.

When a control becomes part of a control array, its name remains that of the control array, with an element or index indicating its specific identity (as shown in Figure 10.7).

TRAP Set all necessary control properties before making a control array. Otherwise, you will have to set control properties for each control in the array.

Double-clicking on any control in the array produces the same event. These shared events pass an index as an argument that you can use to identify each control in the array:

```
Private Sub Command1_Click(Index As Integer)
Command1(1).Caption = "Index 1"
End Sub
```

Beyond design time, Visual Basic offers a more dynamic approach to control arrays in runtime. During runtime, you can dynamically add controls and remove controls from a control array. You add and remove these dynamic controls using the Load and Unload statements:

```
Load ObjectName(Index)
```

If you want to load a control into a control array, you first must create the array in design time.

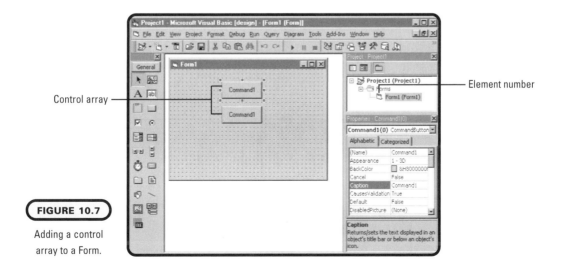

Control array

Element number

FIGURE 10.7

Adding a control
array to a Form.

TRAP Visual Basic generates an error if you try to load an index already in use.

When you unload controls from a control array, the index must be a valid index; otherwise, Visual Basic generates an error:

```
Unload ObjectName(Index)
```

It is also worthy to note that you cannot unload any controls from an array that were created in design time.

Okay, let me show you how these control arrays come together to build a small program as seen in Figure 10.8.

When the user clicks the Add Command Button, I first check whether the variable fiMaxElementId is not greater than 6. In other words, I do not want any more than 7 controls added. If I'm under the limit, I add another Label to the array using the Load statement. After that, I use the Top property to properly position the new Label directly underneath the previous Label:

```
Option Explicit
Dim fiMaxElementId As Integer

Private Sub cmdAdd_Click()
If fiMaxElementId = 0 Then
  fiMaxElementId = 1
End If
If fiMaxElementId > 6 Then
  Exit Sub
End If
```

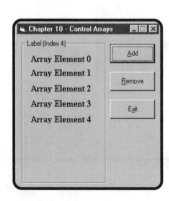

Demonstrating dynamic control arrays during runtime.

```
fiMaxElementId = fiMaxElementId + 1
Load lblLabel(fiMaxElementId)
lblLabel(fiMaxElementId).Top = lblLabel(fiMaxElementId - 1).Top + 400
lblLabel(fiMaxElementId).Caption = "Array Element " & fiMaxElementId
lblLabel(fiMaxElementId).Visible = True


End Sub
```

When the Remove button is clicked, I use the Unload statement to unload the current control created in runtime:

```
Private Sub cmdRemove_Click()
If fiMaxElementId <= 1 Then
  Exit Sub
End If
Unload lblLabel(fiMaxElementId)
fiMaxElementId = fiMaxElementId - 1
End Sub
```

When any of the Labels are clicked, they share the same click event as shown below. Using this shared event and the incoming index, I update the Frame's Caption property accordingly:

```
Private Sub lblLabel_Click(Index As Integer)
Frame1.Caption = "Label (Index " & Index & ")"
End Sub
```

The remaining part of the code closes the control array program.

```
Private Sub cmdExit_Click()
End
End Sub


Private Sub Form_QueryUnload(Cancel As Integer, UnloadMode As Integer)
cmdExit_Click
End Sub
```

The PictureClip Control

Now that you have an understanding of arrays, I can move on to an interesting control that uses an array-like concept to store images. The PictureClip control uses a grid-like system to store icons or bitmaps in one picture. Its specific benefit involves resources and efficiency.

To add the PictureClip control to your project, simply find the Components dialog box on the Project menu or right-click the Tools bar. Inside the Components window, find Microsoft PictureClip Control 6.0 as seen in Figure 10.9.

Once you add the PictureClip control from the Components window, you can add it to your Form as you do any other control. Figure 10.10 depicts a PictureClip control added to the Toolbox and one Form.

Beyond the benefits of efficiency, the PictureClip is also popularly used for animation. You might remember learning how to animate simple graphics earlier in this book. If you tried to create animation through image swapping, you may also

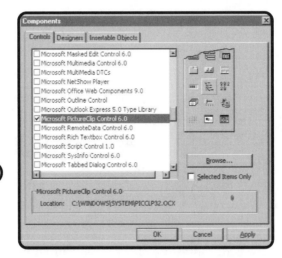

FIGURE 10.9

Finding the PictureClip control in the Components window.

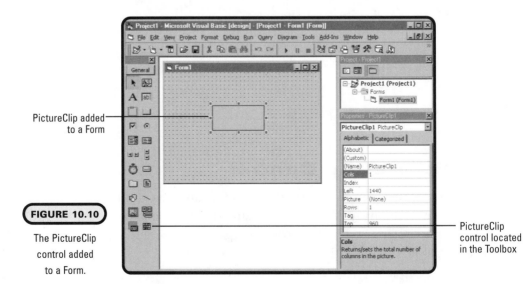

PictureClip added to a Form

FIGURE 10.10

The PictureClip control added to a Form.

PictureClip control located in the Toolbox

remember a sometimes choppy effect with the animation. Well, using the PictureClip control provides you a more seamless, and therefore better, animation.

The first step in creating animation with the PictureClip control is finding a bitmap image that contains a sequence of movements. You can try to create these bitmaps yourself, but if you're graphically challenged, as I am, you are probably better off finding an artist who can do the work for you.

You might find that searching the Internet can provide you with a number of downloadable pictures and animation stills. In fact, the CD accompanying this book has a number of character animation stills and other graphics provided by our friends at http://www.vbexplorer.com and created by professional artist Hermann Hillmann.

Once you find the right picture for your PictureClip control, you need to ensure that each subpicture is an equal part in the entire picture. In other words, the PictureClip needs to be a uniform grid of picture cells. Setting the Row and Column property of the PictureClip control starts this process. Once you define the columns and rows, the PictureClip creates a matrix of picture cells for you. Although a matrix is created, you are not guaranteed that each picture in a cell shares the same amount of real estate during a display.

To get a truly fluid animation, you need to ensure that each clipping region in the picture is the same. To accomplish this, you can either use programming techniques or simply modify the image. If you decide to use programming techniques, you need to work with the ClipX, ClipY, ClipHeight, and ClipWidth properties. Using these properties, you can access a specific region of the picture.

The basic process for displaying a picture cell uses the GraphicCell property of the PictureClip control. Using the GraphicCell property allows you to specify a certain region of the matrix and apply it to a Picture Box or Image control.

The following statement assigns the first picture cell of the Picture Clip control to the Picture property of a Picture Box:

```
myPicture.Picture = PictureClip1.GraphicCell(0)
```

The program depicted in Figure 10.11 uses a graphic that already contains uniform clipping regions.

After adding all necessary controls to my Form, I define my coordinate system of 8 columns and 8 rows, or 64 picture cells. Because my graphic already contains uniform clipping regions, it is not necessary for me to grab individual regions with ClipX and ClipY or ClipHeight and ClipWidth properties.

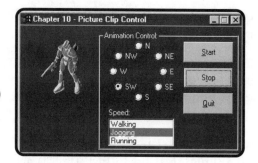

FIGURE 10.11

Using the
PictureClip control
to create animation.

Note that each cell range depicts a particular movement pattern, such as running in a westward direction, running to the south, and so forth:

```
Option Explicit
Dim fiCounter As Integer
Dim fiDirection As Integer
'***********************************************************
'Picture clip contains 8 columns and 8 rows
'(64 cells).
'Direction:
'4 = north, (cells: 32 - 39)
'5 = north east, (cells: 40 - 47)
'6 = east, (cells: 48 - 55)
'7 = south east, (cells: 56 - 63)
'0 = south, (cells: 0 - 7)
'1 = south west, (cells: 8 - 15)
'2 = west, (cells: 16 - 23)
'3 = north west, (cells: 24 - 31)
'***********************************************************
```

During Form load, I add a few items to a List Box, assign a default picture, and provide default animation criteria:

```
Private Sub Form_Load()
Dim x As Integer
lstSpeed.AddItem "Walking"
lstSpeed.AddItem "Jogging"
lstSpeed.AddItem "Running"
picAnimate.Picture = PictureClip1.GraphicCell(0)
lstSpeed.ListIndex = 0
optDirection.Item(0).Value = True
End Sub
```

When the user clicks the Start Command Button, I enable a Timer control after verifying an item in a List Box is selected:

```
Private Sub cmdStart_Click()
If lstSpeed.ListIndex = -1 Then
  Exit Sub
Else
  Timer1.Enabled = True
End If
End Sub
```

The Stop Command Button stops all animation by setting the Timer's Enabled property to false:

```
Private Sub cmdStop_Click()
Timer1.Enabled = False
End Sub
```

I use the List Box entries to determine the speed of the animation. I accomplish this by setting the Interval property of the Timer control:

```
Private Sub lstSpeed_Click()
Select Case lstSpeed.ListIndex
  Case 0
    Timer1.Interval = 250
  Case 1
    Timer1.Interval = 100
  Case 2
    Timer1.Interval = 50
End Select
End Sub
```

Using a multitude of Option Buttons (one for each direction), I assign the direction selected to a form-level variable and set the picture cell to the beginning picture as it relates to the selected direction:

```
Private Sub optDirection_Click(Index As Integer)
Select Case Index
  Case 0
    'North
    fiDirection = 0
    fiCounter = 32
```

```
    Case 1
       'Northeast
       fiDirection = 1
       fiCounter = 40
    Case 2
       'East
       fiDirection = 2
       fiCounter = 48
    Case 3
       'Southeast
       fiDirection = 3
       fiCounter = 56
    Case 4
       'South
       fiDirection = 4
        fiCounter = 0
    Case 5
       'Southwest
       fiDirection = 5
       fiCounter = 8
    Case 6
       'West
       fiDirection = 6
       fiCounter = 16
    Case 7
       'Northwest
       fiDirection = 7
       fiCounter = 24
End Select
End Sub
```

The Timer control's timer event performs the actual animation. Before animating, I determine the direction selected with a select case structure. After a direction is determined, I check for a valid number for that direction and assign a
picture cell to the Picture Box. Finally, I increment the form-level variable
fiCounter, which gets the next applicable picture cell:

```
Private Sub Timer1_Timer()
Select Case fiDirection
   Case 0
      'south
```

```
      If fiCounter > 7 Then fiCounter = 0
      picAnimate.Picture = PictureClip1.GraphicCell(fiCounter)
      fiCounter = fiCounter + 1
   Case 1
      'sw
      If fiCounter > 15 Then fiCounter = 8
      picAnimate.Picture = PictureClip1.GraphicCell(fiCounter)
      fiCounter = fiCounter + 1
   Case 2
      'west
      If fiCounter > 23 Then fiCounter = 16
      picAnimate.Picture = PictureClip1.GraphicCell(fiCounter)
      fiCounter = fiCounter + 1
   Case 3
      'nw
      If fiCounter > 31 Then fiCounter = 24
      picAnimate.Picture = PictureClip1.GraphicCell(fiCounter)
      fiCounter = fiCounter + 1
   Case 4
      'north
      If fiCounter > 39 Then fiCounter = 32
      picAnimate.Picture = PictureClip1.GraphicCell(fiCounter)
      fiCounter = fiCounter + 1
   Case 5
      'ne
      If fiCounter > 47 Then fiCounter = 40
      picAnimate.Picture = PictureClip1.GraphicCell(fiCounter)
      fiCounter = fiCounter + 1
   Case 6
      'east
      If fiCounter > 55 Then fiCounter = 48
      picAnimate.Picture = PictureClip1.GraphicCell(fiCounter)
      fiCounter = fiCounter + 1
   Case 7
      'sw
      If fiCounter > 63 Then fiCounter = 56
      picAnimate.Picture = PictureClip1.GraphicCell(fiCounter)
      fiCounter = fiCounter + 1
End Select
End Sub
```

The last part of the code closes the animation program.

```
Private Sub cmdQuit_Click()
End
End Sub


Private Sub Form_QueryUnload(Cancel As Integer, UnloadMode As Integer)
cmdQuit_Click
End Sub
```

Constructing the Video Poker Game

With all your newly acquired knowledge on arrays, you are now ready to tackle a larger program that uses many of the topics and technologies discussed in this chapter. Specifically, the video poker game uses arrays, control arrays, and a PictureClip control to build a blackjack game.

The Problem

Build a video poker game that implements some basic blackjack concepts (shown in Figure 10.13). The player will play against the house using the rules and guidelines shown in Figure 10.12.

The image used in the PictureClip control appears on the CD-ROM (deck.bmp).

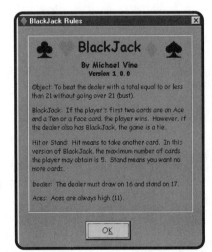

FIGURE 10.12

Rules and guidelines for blackjack.

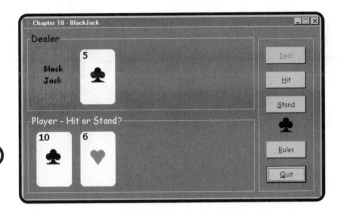

FIGURE 10.13

The blackjack
game.

Table 10.1 contains the controls and properties of the main Form for the black-jack game.

Table 10.2 contains the controls and properties of the rules Form for the black-jack game.

Note: Add your own Labels and Images to denote rules and provide graphical appeal.

A sample algorithm for the blackjack game:

1. Find or create a picture depicting a deck of standard poker cards suitable for use with the PictureClip control.
2. Open a new standard EXE project.
3. Add the PictureClip control to the project and the main Form.
4. Add the rest of the controls to the main Form.
5. Add another Form to the project for game rules.
6. Write code to initialize the deck. This should clear any scores or numbers from the player's and dealer's hands.
7. Write code to deal the first hand. This should specifically assign two random cards to the dealer and two random cards to the player.
8. Write code to calculate the player's and dealer's hands.
9. Write code to check for blackjack (21), tie games, busts (over 21), and the final outcome (who won?).
10. Write code to respond to the player asking for another card.
11. Write code to evaluate the dealer's hand. Specifically, the dealer should take another card if the hand is 16 or less (stay if 17 or greater).
12. Write code to show the rules Form.

TABLE 10.1 CONTROLS AND PROPERTIES OF THE MAIN FORM

Control	Property	Setting
frmMain	Caption	Chapter 10 – Black Jack
	Border Style	2 – Sizable
	MaxButton	False
pcDeck	Columns	13
	Rows	4
fraDealer	Caption	Dealer
fraPlayer	Caption	Player
Frame1	Caption	empty
cmdDeal	Caption	&Deal
cmdHit	Caption	&Hit
cmdStand	Caption	&Stand
cmdRules	Caption	&Rules
cmdQuit	Caption	&Quit
picCard(0)		
picCard(1)		
picCard(2)		
picCard(3)		
picCard(4)		
picCard(5)		
picCard(6)		
picCard(7)		
picCard(8)		

TABLE 10.2 CONTROLS AND PROPERTIES OF THE RULES FORM

Control	Property	Setting
frmRules	Caption	Black Jack Rules
	Border Style	1 – Fixed Single
Frame1	Caption	empty
cmdOK	Caption	O&K

The Implementation

Before writing any code, I define my PictureClip control by identifying how each suite relates to a particular picture cell:

```
Option Explicit
'**********************************************************************
'****************BLACKJACK VERSION 1.0.0***************
'****************By MICHAEL A. VINE**************************
'The deck.bmp picture clip contains 13 columns
'and 4 rows (52 cards or graphic cells).
'Graphic cells 0 to 12 are two of clubs to ace of clubs.
'Graphic cells 13 to 25 are two of diamonds to ace of diamonds.
'Graphic cells 26 to 38 are two of spades to ace of spades.
'Graphic cells 39 to 51 are two of hearts to ace of hearts.
'**********************************************************************
```

I declare two arrays for the blackjack game, one to hold the dealer's hand and one to hold the player's. Notice that I have three elements in the dealer's array and five in the player's. This basically says that the dealer will get three cards at maximum and the player five:

```
Dim fiDealersHand(2) As Integer '3 elements
Dim fiPlayersHand(4) As Integer '5 elements
```

The form load event executes the Randomize statement, calls a function to randomize the deck, and sets a few properties:

```
Dim fsWhoseTurnIsIt As String
Dim fiPlayersCardCount As Integer
Dim fiDealersCardCount As Integer
Dim fbStand As Boolean


Private Sub Form_Load()
picCard(0).Picture = picCard(8).Picture
Randomize
InitializeDeck
cmdHit.Enabled = False
cmdStand.Enabled = False
fsWhoseTurnIsIt = "dealer"
End Sub
```

The InitializeDeck procedure performs some housecleaning for me. Specifically, it sets the Visible property for all pictures to false, assigns the number 99 to each element in the player's and dealer's array, and initializes some form-level variables:

```
Public Sub InitializeDeck()
Dim liNumCards As Integer
Dim x As Integer

picCard(0).Picture = picCard(8).Picture
liNumCards = (picCard.Count - 1)
For x = 0 To liNumCards
  picCard.Item(x).Visible = False
Next x


For x = 0 To 2
  fiDealersHand(x) = 99 'No card assigned
Next x


For x = 0 To 4
  fiPlayersHand(x) = 99 'No card assigned
Next x
fiPlayersCardCount = 0
fiDealersCardCount = 0
End Sub
```

I use the concept of initializing player and dealer array elements to 99 throughout this program to tell whether a card has been dealt.

Notice that the code for Command Button Deal is minimal. It simply calls a function to initialize the deck and deal the first hand:

```
Private Sub cmdDeal_Click()
InitializeDeck
fbStand = False
DealFirstHand
End Sub
```

The process of dealing the first card is pretty straightforward. Notice that I only need to generate a random number between 0 and 51 and assign it to the corresponding picture cell of the dealer's first card:

```
Public Sub DealFirstHand()
Dim liCurrentCard As Integer
Dim lbCardAlreadyDealt As Boolean
```

```
'**************************Deal the first hand*************************
lbCardAlreadyDealt = True
'Assign dealer's first card
liCurrentCard = Int((51 * Rnd))
picCard.Item(0).Visible = True
fiDealersHand(0) = liCurrentCard 'Assign current card to dealer's hand
```

Dealing subsequent cards, however, is another story. As you can see in the following code, I need to perform some checking before assigning the next card. Specifically, I enter a loop until an available card is found. Within the loop, I generate a random number and check it against the first card dealt. You might notice that I'm checking only against the dealer's hand because I haven't dealt any cards to the player yet:

```
'Assign dealer's second card
Do Until lbCardAlreadyDealt = False
   liCurrentCard = Int((51 * Rnd))
   If fiDealersHand(0) <> liCurrentCard Then
      fiDealersHand(1) = liCurrentCard
        'Assign current card to dealer's hand
      picCard.Item(1).Picture = pcDeck.GraphicCell(liCurrentCard)
      picCard.Item(1).Visible = True
      lbCardAlreadyDealt = False
   End If
Loop
```

The process for dealing the remaining cards is pretty much the same. However, when I deal the player's cards, I must check the random number generated against not only the player's hand but also the dealer's:

```
lbCardAlreadyDealt = True

'Assign player's first card
Do Until lbCardAlreadyDealt = False
   liCurrentCard = Int((51 * Rnd))
   If (liCurrentCard <> fiDealersHand(0)) And _
   (liCurrentCard <> fiDealersHand(1)) Then
      fiPlayersHand(0) = liCurrentCard
        'Assign current card to player's hand
      picCard.Item(3).Visible = True
      picCard.Item(3).Picture = pcDeck.GraphicCell(liCurrentCard)
      lbCardAlreadyDealt = False
   End If
```

```
   Loop

   lbCardAlreadyDealt = True

   'Assign player's second card
   Do Until lbCardAlreadyDealt = False
      liCurrentCard = Int((51 * Rnd))
      If liCurrentCard <> fiPlayersHand(0) Then
         If (liCurrentCard <> fiDealersHand(0)) And _
         (liCurrentCard <> fiDealersHand(1)) Then
            fiPlayersHand(1) = liCurrentCard
             'Assign current card to player's hand
            picCard.Item(4).Visible = True
            picCard.Item(4).Picture = pcDeck.GraphicCell(liCurrentCard)
            lbCardAlreadyDealt = False
         End If
      End If
   Loop

   cmdDeal.Enabled = False
   cmdHit.Enabled = True
   cmdStand.Enabled = True
   fiPlayersCardCount = ScoreHand(fiPlayersHand, "players")
   fiDealersCardCount = ScoreHand(fiDealersHand, "dealers")
   If BlackJack = False Then
      fraPlayer.ForeColor = vbYellow
      fraPlayer.Caption = "Player - Hit or Stand?"
      fraDealer.ForeColor = vbBlack
      fraDealer.Caption = "Dealer"
   End If
   '**********************************************************************
End Sub

Private Sub cmdHit_Click()
Dim liCurrentCard As Integer
Dim lbCardAlreadyDealt As Boolean
Dim lbGoForIt As Boolean
Dim x As Integer
Dim innerLoop As Integer
Dim lbMax As Boolean
```

If the player elects to take another card (hit), I must check a number of criteria before dealing the card. First, I check that the array element is empty (99), and then I enter various loops where random numbers are checked against both the player's and dealer's hands:

```
'*********************Deal the next available card ********************
lbMax = True
lbCardAlreadyDealt = True
lbGoForIt = True
For x = 0 To 4
  If fiPlayersHand(x) = 99 Then
    Do Until lbCardAlreadyDealt = False
      liCurrentCard = Int((51 * Rnd))
      'Check the dealer's hand
      For innerLoop = 0 To 2
        If fiDealersHand(innerLoop) = liCurrentCard Then
          'lbCardAlreadyDealt = True
          lbGoForIt = False
        End If
      Next innerLoop
      'Check the player's existing hand
      For innerLoop = 0 To 4
        If fiPlayersHand(innerLoop) = liCurrentCard Then
          'lbCardAlreadyDealt = True
          lbGoForIt = False
        End If
      Next innerLoop
      If lbGoForIt = True Then
        lbCardAlreadyDealt = False
      Else
        lbGoForIt = True
      End If
      If lbCardAlreadyDealt = False Then
        fiPlayersHand(x) = liCurrentCard
        'Assign current card to player's hand
        picCard.Item(x + 3).Picture = _
        pcDeck.GraphicCell(liCurrentCard)
        picCard.Item(x + 3).Visible = True
        Exit For
      Else
        'Card is already in use; get another random card
```

```
                liCurrentCard = Int((51 * Rnd))
            End If
        Loop
    End If
Next x
```

After an available card is found, I check to see whether the player has received the maximum number of cards allowed. If not, the player can continue to receive cards until she has a total of five or until she has busted (gone over 21).

If the player has received her maximum number of cards, I disable various controls and end the round by setting another Boolean variable (fbStand) to true and calling the procedure DealerDrawStand:

```
For x = 0 To 4
  If fiPlayersHand(x) = 99 Then
    lbMax = False
  End If
Next x


If lbMax = True Then
  cmdHit.Enabled = False
  cmdStand.Enabled = False
  fbStand = True
  cmdDeal.Enabled = True
  DealerDrawStand
  fiPlayersCardCount = ScoreHand(fiPlayersHand, "players")
  fiDealersCardCount = ScoreHand(fiDealersHand, "dealers")
  BlackJack
Else
  fiPlayersCardCount = ScoreHand(fiPlayersHand, "players")
  fiDealersCardCount = ScoreHand(fiDealersHand, "dealers")
  BlackJack
End If
'****************************************************************
End Sub
```

Notice that I'm assigning the result of a function to some form-level variables. The form-level variables tell me later who wins the hand. The important or at least interesting thing here is that I'm passing two parameters to the function; one in particular is an array. Did you catch that?

To send an array (all elements) to a function, simply state the array name without parentheses or element number. You will see in a moment how to deal with the array once the function receives it.

As you will see shortly, setting the form-level variable fbStand to true essentially ends the game (providing the game is not already over through a blackjack or bust):

```
Private Sub cmdStand_Click()
fbStand = True
DealerDrawStand
BlackJack
End Sub
```

The BlackJack function is pretty straightforward; it simply checks a number of possible scenarios for blackjack, ties, and a number of other winning or game-ending situations:

```
Public Function BlackJack() As Boolean
BlackJack = False
```

Each condition uses one or two form-level variables containing the dealer's and player's current hands. When a condition is found to be true, I set a number of control properties and display the game's results through caption properties of frame controls:

```
If fiPlayersCardCount > 21 Then
   'Player Busts - Dealer Wins
   picCard.Item(0).Picture = pcDeck.GraphicCell(fiDealersHand(0))
   cmdStand.Enabled = False
   cmdHit.Enabled = False
   cmdDeal.Enabled = True
   fraPlayer.ForeColor = vbBlack
   fraPlayer.Caption = "Player"
   fraDealer.ForeColor = vbYellow
   fraDealer.Caption = "Dealer Wins!"
   BlackJack = True
   Exit Function
End If


If fiDealersCardCount > 21 Then
   'Dealer Busts - Player Wins
   picCard.Item(0).Picture = pcDeck.GraphicCell(fiDealersHand(0))
```

```
        cmdStand.Enabled = False
        cmdHit.Enabled = False
        cmdDeal.Enabled = True
        fraPlayer.ForeColor = vbYellow
        fraPlayer.Caption = "You Win!"
        fraDealer.ForeColor = vbBlack
        fraDealer.Caption = "Dealer"
        BlackJack = True
        Exit Function
    End If


    If fiPlayersCardCount = 21 And fiDealersCardCount = 21 Then
        'Tie game
        picCard.Item(0).Picture = pcDeck.GraphicCell(fiDealersHand(0))
        cmdStand.Enabled = False
        cmdHit.Enabled = False
        cmdDeal.Enabled = True
        fraPlayer.ForeColor = vbYellow
        fraPlayer.Caption = "Tie Game"
        fraDealer.ForeColor = vbYellow
        fraDealer.Caption = "Time Game"
        BlackJack = True
        Exit Function
    End If


    If fiPlayersCardCount = 21 Then
        'Blackjack - player wins
        picCard.Item(0).Picture = pcDeck.GraphicCell(fiDealersHand(0))
        cmdStand.Enabled = False
        cmdHit.Enabled = False
        cmdDeal.Enabled = True
        fraPlayer.ForeColor = vbYellow
        fraPlayer.Caption = "You Win!"
        fraDealer.ForeColor = vbBlack
        fraDealer.Caption = "Dealer"
        BlackJack = True
        Exit Function
    End If


    If fiDealersCardCount = 21 Then
```

```vb
  'Blackjack - dealer wins
  picCard.Item(0).Picture = pcDeck.GraphicCell(fiDealersHand(0))
  cmdStand.Enabled = False
  cmdHit.Enabled = False
  fraPlayer.ForeColor = vbBlack
  fraPlayer.Caption = "Player"
  fraDealer.ForeColor = vbYellow
  fraDealer.Caption = "Dealer Wins!"
  cmdDeal.Enabled = True
  BlackJack = True
  Exit Function
End If


If fiDealersCardCount = fiPlayersCardCount And fbStand = True Then
  'Tie game
  picCard.Item(0).Picture = pcDeck.GraphicCell(fiDealersHand(0))
  cmdStand.Enabled = False
  cmdHit.Enabled = False
  cmdDeal.Enabled = True
  fraPlayer.ForeColor = vbYellow
  fraPlayer.Caption = "Tie Game"
  fraDealer.ForeColor = vbYellow
  fraDealer.Caption = "Tie Game"
  BlackJack = False
  Exit Function
End If


If fiDealersCardCount > fiPlayersCardCount And fbStand = True Then
  'Dealer wins
  picCard.Item(0).Picture = pcDeck.GraphicCell(fiDealersHand(0))
  cmdStand.Enabled = False
  cmdHit.Enabled = False
  cmdDeal.Enabled = True
  fraPlayer.ForeColor = vbBlack
  fraPlayer.Caption = "Player"
  fraDealer.ForeColor = vbYellow
  fraDealer.Caption = "Dealer Wins!"
  BlackJack = False
  Exit Function
End If
```

```
If fiDealersCardCount < fiPlayersCardCount And fbStand = True Then
   'Player wins
   picCard.Item(0).Picture = pcDeck.GraphicCell(fiDealersHand(0))
   cmdStand.Enabled = False
   cmdHit.Enabled = False
   cmdDeal.Enabled = True
   fraPlayer.ForeColor = vbYellow
   fraPlayer.Caption = "You Win!"
   fraDealer.ForeColor = vbBlack
   fraDealer.Caption = "Dealer"
   BlackJack = False
   Exit Function
End If

End Function
```

The ScoreHand function is another procedure called throughout the life of my blackjack game. It takes two parameters, one containing an array of integers (a poker hand) and a string telling the function whose hand is being scored:

```
Public Function ScoreHand(currentHand() As Integer, _
whoseHand As String) As Integer
```

Notice that the parameter currentHand is actually an integer array that contains no element number. This is how the array mentioned earlier is received in the function:

```
Dim cardCount As Integer
Dim x As Integer
cardCount = 0
```

Depending on whose hand is being scored (although the calculations are the same), I use the select case's unique ability to check a list of criteria or conditions.

For example, I know that picture cells 0, 13, 26, and 39 contain the number two cards. If that condition is met, I simply add two points to the player's hand:

```
If whoseHand = "players" Then
   For x = 0 To 4
     If currentHand(x) <> 99 Then
       Select Case currentHand(x)
         Case 0, 13, 26, 39 'Twos
           cardCount = cardCount + 2
         Case 1, 14, 27, 40 'Threes
           cardCount = cardCount + 3
```

```
         Case 2, 15, 28, 41 'Fours
            cardCount = cardCount + 4
         Case 3, 16, 29, 42 'Fives
            cardCount = cardCount + 5
         Case 4, 17, 30, 43 'Sixes
            cardCount = cardCount + 6
         Case 5, 18, 31, 44 'Sevens
            cardCount = cardCount + 7
         Case 6, 19, 32, 45 'Eights
            cardCount = cardCount + 8
         Case 7, 20, 33, 46 'Nines
            cardCount = cardCount + 9
         Case 8 To 11, 21 To 24, 34 To 37, 47 To 50 'Tens and face cards
            cardCount = cardCount + 10
         Case 12, 25, 38, 51 'Aces
            cardCount = cardCount + 11
      End Select
   End If
 Next x
Else
 For x = 0 To 2
   If currentHand(x) <> 99 Then
      Select Case currentHand(x)
         Case 0, 13, 26, 39 'Twos
            cardCount = cardCount + 2
         Case 1, 14, 27, 40 'Threes
            cardCount = cardCount + 3
         Case 2, 15, 28, 41 'Fours
            cardCount = cardCount + 4
         Case 3, 16, 29, 42 'Fives
            cardCount = cardCount + 5
         Case 4, 17, 30, 43 'Sixes
            cardCount = cardCount + 6
         Case 5, 18, 31, 44 'Sevens
            cardCount = cardCount + 7
         Case 6, 19, 32, 45 'Eights
            cardCount = cardCount + 8
         Case 7, 20, 33, 46 'Nines
            cardCount = cardCount + 9
         Case 8 To 11, 21 To 24, 34 To 37, 47 To 50 'Tens and face cards
            cardCount = cardCount + 10
```

```
        Case 12, 25, 38, 51 'Aces
            cardCount = cardCount + 11
      End Select
    End If
  Next x
End If
ScoreHand = cardCount
End Function


Public Sub DealerDrawStand()
Dim liCurrentCard As Integer
Dim lbCardAlreadyDealt As Boolean
Dim lbGoForIt As Boolean
Dim innerLoop As Integer
```

The DealerDrawStand procedure contains the logic to determine whether the dealer should take another card. It's actually quite simple; the dealer either stands at 17 and greater or takes another card at 16 and less. If it is determined that the dealer will take another card, similar logic as shown earlier is used to loop until an available card is found.

```
'********************Deal the next available card *******************
If fiPlayersCardCount < 21 And fiDealersCardCount <= 16 Then
  lbCardAlreadyDealt = True
  lbGoForIt = True
  Do Until lbCardAlreadyDealt = False
    liCurrentCard = Int((51 * Rnd))
    'Check the dealer's hand
    For innerLoop = 0 To 2
      If fiDealersHand(innerLoop) = liCurrentCard Then
        lbGoForIt = False
      End If
    Next innerLoop
    'Check the player's existing hand
    For innerLoop = 0 To 4
      If fiPlayersHand(innerLoop) = liCurrentCard Then
        lbGoForIt = False
      End If
    Next innerLoop
    If lbGoForIt = True Then
      lbCardAlreadyDealt = False
```

```
      Else
         lbGoForIt = True
      End If
      If lbCardAlreadyDealt = False Then
         fiDealersHand(2) = liCurrentCard
          'Assign current card to player's hand
         picCard.Item(2).Picture = pcDeck.GraphicCell(liCurrentCard)
         picCard.Item(2).Visible = True
         Exit Do
      Else
          'Card is already in use; get another random card
         liCurrentCard = Int((51 * Rnd))
      End If
   Loop
   fiDealersCardCount = ScoreHand(fiDealersHand, "dealers")
End If
'***********************************************************************
End Sub


Private Sub cmdRules_Click()
frmRules.Show
End Sub


Private Sub cmdQuit_Click()
Dim liResponse As Integer
liResponse = MsgBox("Quit Black Jack?", vbYesNo, "Confirm")
If liResponse = vbYes Then
   End
End If
End Sub


Private Sub Form_QueryUnload(Cancel As Integer, UnloadMode As Integer)
cmdQuit_Click
End Sub
```

Summary

This chapter covered a lot of ground with arrays, their components, and Visual Basic's implementations. Specifically, you learned how to build and use single and multidimensional arrays. You learned some new tricks for specifying upper and lower bounds while watching out for those nasty off-by-one errors. You also saw some new controls such as the PictureClip and how it uses an array-like structure for managing picture cells.

I hope this chapter has shown you how important and helpful arrays and their spawn can be. If you found this to be an intriguing and exciting chapter, you are definitely on the right track toward a blissful career in computer science. If not, then don't feel bad; you're among the masses of beginning programmers who at some time or another questioned whether they really wanted to learn something like arrays.

My advice to you is sit back, relax, and think how far you have come from the first chapter. As a component of computer science, programming is not easy, although nothing worth getting ever is.

Congratulations on making it this far, and I look forward to showing you specific techniques on drag-and-drop technology in the next chapter.

CHALLENGES

1. Create your own animated character with the PictureClip control and a bitmap picture containing animation stills (such as the ones found on the CD).

2. Using an array of Picture Boxes, build a memory game. The user should be able to click on a Picture Box where an image is then shown. The image should stay up long enough for the user to click on another available Picture Box. If there is a match, then both pictures are shown and they become unavailable. The process continues until the user completes the memory game, time runs out, or he gives up. For more information on memory games, simply search the Internet with your favorite search engine for the keyword "game" or "memory game."

3. Modify the video poker game to allow for the concept of doubling down. Consult any blackjack literature for understanding the rules of doubling down.

4. Modify the video poker game to allow the user and dealer to use ace cards as low (1) and high (11) cards.

5. Modify the video poker game to allow the dealer to draw more than one card if required.

6. Create your own card game based on poker games or other popular card games.

Drag and Drop

This chapter is dedicated to a popular concept and graphical programming technique called drag and drop. You will learn not only the concepts for dragging and dropping, but also how the concepts are implemented through Visual Basic techniques and events. This chapter covers the following topics:

- Drag and drop technology

- Drag and drop properties

- Drag and drop events

- Constructing the puzzle game

Project: The Puzzle Game

The puzzle game will tax many of your newly learned skills to implement a challenging and fun-filled digital puzzle. Although the puzzle game uses many previously learned skills, its main objective is to demonstrate the capabilities of drag and drop technology. After this chapter, you will be able to build not only the puzzle game, shown in Figure 11.1, but also other intriguing games and programs using Visual Basic's drag and drop techniques.

Drag and Drop Technology

Drag and drop technology became feasible with the advent of graphical user interfaces (GUI) and various pointing and clicking devices, such as the mouse. Prior to pointing devices and graphical interfaces, there was no need to click something or drag something. If you wanted data, you simply typed a command or statement into a prompt. Nothing to click, nothing to drag, nothing to drop: Hey, it was the Stone Age—what can I say?

So when humans first discovered fire, I mean graphical interfaces, it was only natural to drag and drop graphical depictions of files and folders around the interface to perform various functions. The drag and drop capabilities greatly reduced time in performing daily and routine system tasks such as moving, copying, and deleting files. These tasks could still be performed through command-line syntax but took longer to perform and required detailed knowledge of operating-system-specific syntax and schema.

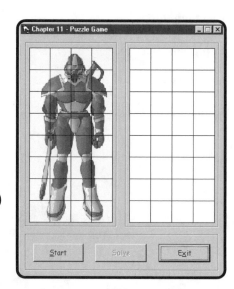

FIGURE 11.1

Demonstrating drag and drop technology with the puzzle game.

> ## IN THE REAL WORLD
>
> When working with GUI-based computer systems, it is only natural to think of such big companies as Microsoft, Apple, IBM, Netscape, and many more. But where did all this innovative technology such as the mouse, GUIs, Internet and network standards, and object-based programming come from?
>
> Surprisingly, the innovative company behind the genius is Xerox. Specifically, Xerox PARC (Palo Alto Research Center) developed the first commercial mouse, graphical user interface, WYSIWYG (what you see is what you get) editor, object-based programming, Ethernet, network and Internet standards, and many, many more first innovations.
>
> Located in Palo Alto, California, Xerox PARC is still active in many facets of new innovative technology development. For more information on PARC's innovative genius, go to http://www.parc.xerox.com/parc-go.html.

Graphical interfaces (in which drag and drop technology plays a key role) made using operating systems an easier task to learn and master for the general user population. Although using drag and drop technology was easy and intuitive for users, programming drag and drop was another story.

With Rapid Application Development (RAD) in mind, Microsoft provided a programmer-friendly drag and drop solution with Visual Basic events. As you will soon see, mastering drag and drop development is no longer as difficult as you might think.

Drag and Drop Properties

In drag and drop terminology, there are generally two objects of consideration, *source* and *target*, where the source is the object being dragged and the target is the desired drop location.

> ### Definition
>
> The *source* is the object being dragged. The *target* is the destination.

To learn drag and drop programming, simply add a few Image controls or Picture Boxes to your Form. Next, identify what objects will be source objects and set their DragMode property to 1 – Automatic and their DragIcon property to a similar or related picture.

For example, you can mimic the controls, properties, and form layout depicted in Figure 11.2.

FIGURE 11.2

Demonstrating
source and target
objects for drag
and drop
operations.

Table 11.1 depicts the controls and properties of the weather forecast program.

TABLE 11.1   CONTROLS AND PROPERTIES FOR THE WEATHER FORECAST PROGRAM

Control	Property	Setting
frmMain	Caption	Chapter 11 – Drag and Drop
	Border Style	1 – Fixed Single
Frame1	Caption	Drag a forecast from here:
ImgForecast(0)	Picture	Rain.ico
	DragMode	1 – Automatic
	DragIcon	Rain.ico
ImgForecast(1)	Picture	Sun.ico
	DragMode	1 – Automatic
	DragIcon	Sun.ico
ImgForecast(2)	Picture	Cloud.ico
	DragMode	1 – Automatic
	DragIcon	Cloud.ico
ImgForecast(3)	Picture	Snow.ico
	DragMode	1 – Automatic
	DragIcon	Snow.ico
Frame2	Caption	Drop the forecast here:
picDropBox	Appearance	0 – Flat
	BorderStyle	0 – None
	Picture	Empty
lblForeCast	Caption	Today's Forecast
cmdExit	Caption	E&xit

Drag and Drop Events

The DragDrop event occurs when a control has been successfully dragged and dropped over an object. This specifically occurs when an object is dragged over another object and the mouse button is released. The syntax for the event follows:

```
Private Sub Picture1_DragDrop(Source As Control, X As Single,_
  Y As Single)


End Sub
```

The source argument is the control being dragged; the x and y arguments refer to the current coordinates of the mouse pointer.

The DragOver event occurs when a drag and drop operation is in progress. It is useful for changing the mouse pointer (through the MousePointer property) to various icons when an object is being dragged:

```
Private Sub Picture1_DragOver(Source As Control, X As Single, _
Y As Single, State As Integer)


End Sub
```

Like the DragDrop event, DragOver has a source and x and y arguments. The DragOver event, however, has an additional argument called State. The State argument refers to the state of the control being dragged. The three states are

   0 – Enter

   1 – Leave

   2 – Over

You can use the DragOver event to initiate changes other than a difference in mouse pointer. For example, you might want to highlight the target object to signify that you are over a desired area or a restricted area. You might also want to change the caption properties of various controls to achieve similar results.

The Weather Forecast Example

As shown in Figure 11.2, the weather forecast program demonstrates drag and drop technology. A user can simply drag a weather icon such as rain, clouds, snow, or sunshine to a Picture Box. Once the drag and drop operation is complete, the Caption property of a Label control is updated to reflect the current weather status.

You can reference the properties and methods of the source through dot notation. For example, if I want to disable the incoming source, I can use its Enabled property as I do with any other object or control:

```
Source.Enabled = False
```

In the DragDrop event in the following code, I use the incoming source to decide what I want the Label's Caption property to say. Also, notice how I used the dot notation and a Select Case structure to access the index of the incoming source. If you recall from Table 11.1, the images are actually based in a control array:

```
Option Explicit

Private Sub picDropBox_DragDrop(Source As Control, X As Single, _
Y As Single)
On Error GoTo ErrorHandler
picDropBox.Picture = Source.Picture
Select Case Source.Index
   Case 0
     'Rain
     lblForecast.Caption = "Today's forecast calls for rain."
   Case 1
     'Sun
     lblForecast.Caption = "Today's forecast calls for sunshine."
   Case 2
     'Cloudy
     lblForecast.Caption = "Today's forecast calls for cloudy weather."
   Case 3
     'Snow
     lblForecast.Caption = "Today's forecast calls for snow."
End Select
Exit Sub

ErrorHandler:
  Exit Sub
End Sub

Private Sub cmdExit_Click()
End
End Sub
```

```
Private Sub Form_QueryUnload(Cancel As Integer, UnloadMode As Integer)
cmdExit_Click
End Sub
```

Constructing the Puzzle Game

I must admit that the puzzle game is one of my favorite games in this book. It uses all of the drag and drop techniques you learned in this chapter to build a digital jigsaw puzzle. After this section, you should have a clear understanding of how to build drag and drop capabilities into your own fun and easy-to-use puzzle games.

The image used in the puzzle game was created by professional artist Hermann Hillmann and provided by http://www.vbexplorer.com.

The Problem

Build a digital jigsaw program as seen in Figure 11.3. The program should allow a user to separate an image into random pieces. After that, the user should be able to drag the random pieces from one picture canvas and drop them into another to build the constructed picture.

In addition to dragging and dropping random pieces from the source picture canvas to the target picture canvas, the user should also be able to drag a puzzle piece from a picture cell in the target canvas to another cell in the target canvas.

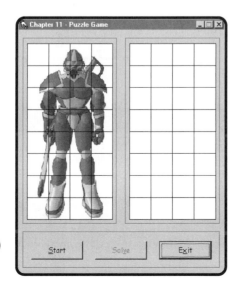

FIGURE 11.3

The puzzle game.

TABLE 11.2 CONTROLS AND PROPERTIES FOR THE PUZZLE GAME

Control	Property	Setting
frmMain	Caption	Chapter 11 – The Puzzle Game
	Border Style	2 – Sizable
	MaxButton	False
Frame1	Caption	Empty
Picture1(0 – 31)	Appearance	0 – Flat
	BorderStyle	1 – Fixed Single
	DragMode	1 – Automatic
	Picture	None
Frame2	Caption	None
Picture2(0 – 31)	Appearance	0 – Flat
	BorderStyle	1 – Fixed Single
	DragMode	1 – Automatic
	Picture	None
Frame3	Caption	None
cmdStart	Caption	&Start
cmdSolve	Caption	Sol&ve
cmdExit	Caption	E&xit
PictureClip1	Cols	4
	Rows	8
	Picture	Bitmap

The game should also provide the user with an option to see the puzzle solved.

Note that the puzzle game uses two separate control arrays made up of Picture boxes (32 in each array) to create two separate picture canvases.

A sample algorithm for the jigsaw puzzle program:

1. Identify an image suitable for use in a jigsaw puzzle.
2. Open a new standard EXE project.
3. Add all necessary controls to the Form, including both control arrays and the PictureClip control.

4. Using an array, the picture clip cell numbers, and the control array of Picture Boxes, write code to scramble the puzzle.

5. Write code to respond to DragDrop and DragOver events.

6. Write code to solve the puzzle.

The Implementation

The puzzle array holds integer values representing a corresponding picture cell number. Its main purpose is to ensure that duplicate images from the Picture-Clip control are not assigned to Picture Boxes during the scrambling process:

```
Option Explicit
'*********************************************
'**   Puzzle Game by Michael Vine   **
'*********************************************
Dim puzzle(31) As Integer '32 elements
```

Notice that I use the randomize statement in the form load event, which will generate random numbers for me later. Also in the form load event, I call a subprocedure I wrote called solve:

```
Private Sub Form_Load()
cmdSolve.Enabled = False
Randomize
Solve
End Sub
```

The solve procedure does two things for me. First, when called in form load, it shows the solved version of the puzzle to the user before she tries to solve it. (This is generally a good thing.) Second, I can reuse the solve subprocedure when the user gives up on solving the puzzle and wants the computer to do it for her.

In the click event of the Start Command Button, I simply set some control properties and call another subprocedure I wrote called initialize puzzle. As you will see in a moment, the initialize puzzle procedure actually scrambles the puzzle:

```
Private Sub cmdStart_Click()
cmdStart.Enabled = False
cmdSolve.Enabled = True
Initialize_Puzzle
End Sub
```

The first thing I do in this procedure is initialize array components with various types of data or settings. For example, I initialize the integer puzzle array elements to 99. I do this so I can compare the puzzle's elements later in the procedure. Also, I initialize the control array objects with various back colors. I use these back colors later to determine where the source (the argument in a Drag-Drop event) is coming from. To reset one of the picture canvases (control array), I use the LoadPicture method to clear any pictures from sight:

```
Public Sub Initialize_Puzzle()
Dim X As Integer
Dim innerLoop As Integer
Dim liRandomIndex As Integer
Dim lbUsed As Boolean
Dim lbFoundDup As Boolean

'Initialize puzzle components
For X = 0 To 31
   puzzle(X) = 99
Next X
For X = 0 To 31
   Picture1(X).Enabled = True
Next X
For X = 0 To 31
   Picture1(X).BackColor = vbBlue
Next X
For X = 0 To 31
   Picture2(X).Enabled = True
Next X
For X = 0 To 31
  Set Picture2(X).Picture = LoadPicture
Next X
For X = 0 To 31
   Picture2(X).BackColor = vbWhite
Next X
```

The remainder of this procedure's code may appear to be a little unnerving at first, but don't worry; it is not as bad as it looks. I first create a For loop structure that will iterate 32 times (one time for each control in the control array). Next, I enter another loop, this time a Do Until loop, which iterates until an available picture is found. This works by first creating a random number and then searching through all puzzle array elements with another For loop to see whether it has already been assigned. If it has been assigned, then I loop back to the beginning of the Do Until loop where I create another random number and continue the process until an available number is found:

```
'Assign a random picture cell to each picture
For X = 0 To 31
   'Ensure a picture does not receive a duplicate picture cell
   lbUsed = True
   Do Until lbUsed = False
      liRandomIndex = Int(32*Rnd)
      lbFoundDup = False
      For innerLoop = 0 To 31
         If puzzle(innerLoop) = liRandomIndex Then
            lbFoundDup = True
         End If
      Next innerLoop
      If lbFoundDup = False Then
         Picture1(X).Picture = PictureClip1.GraphicCell(liRandomIndex)
         puzzle(X) = liRandomIndex
         lbUsed = False
         Exit Do
      End If
   Loop
Next X
End Sub
```

When an available number is found, it is assigned to the corresponding puzzle array element and the corresponding control array object as a picture in a graphic cell.

In the DragOver event, I set the mouse pointer to 12. This number tells Visual Basic to set the mouse pointer to a no-drop icon:

```
Private Sub Picture1_DragOver(Index As Integer, Source As Control, _
X As Single, Y As Single, State As Integer)
Source.MousePointer = 12
End Sub
```

In addition to using numbers to set mouse pointers, you can also use Visual Basic constants as shown in Table 11.3.

TABLE 11.3	MOUSE POINTER SETTINGS	
Number	**Constant**	**Description**
0	vbDefault	Shape determined by the object
1	vbArrow	Arrow pointer
2	vbCrossHair	Cross-hair
3	vbIBeam	I-beam
4	vbIconPointer	Small square within a square
5	vbSizePointer	Four pointed arrow (north, south, east, and west)
6	vbSizeNESW	Double arrow pointing northeast and southwest
7	vbSizeNS	Double arrow pointing north and south
8	vbSizeNWSE	Double arrow pointing northwest and southeast
9	vbSizeWE	Double arrow pointing west and east
10	vbUpArrow	Up arrow
11	vbHourglass	Hourglass
12	vbNoDrop	No drop
13	vbArrowHourglass	Arrow and hourglass
14	vbArrowQuestion	Arrow and question
15	vbSizeAll	Size all
99	vbCustom	Custom icon (determined by the MouseIcon property)

The DragDrop event in the next code segment belongs to the picture control array that the user will use to construct the completed picture. I first determine where the image is coming from (the source argument); after that, I either exit the event or update the target control. Notice that I have to perform multiple conditions to determine what control array the source is coming from. This is because the user can drag and drop images from either control array:

```
Private Sub Picture2_DragDrop(Index As Integer, Source As Control, _
X As Single, Y As Single)
If Source.BackColor = vbBlack Or Source.BackColor = vbBlue Then
   If Picture2(Index).BackColor = vbBlack Then
      Exit Sub
   ElseIf Picture2(Index).BackColor = vbWhite Then
      Picture2(Index).Picture = Source.Picture
```

```
    Picture2(Index).BackColor = vbBlack
    Set Source.Picture = LoadPicture
    Source.BackColor = vbWhite
    Exit Sub
  End If
End If
If TypeOf Source Is PictureBox And Source.BackColor = vbBlue Then
  Picture2(Index).Picture = Source.Picture
  Set Source.Picture = LoadPicture
  Picture2(Index).BackColor = vbBlack
End If


End Sub


Private Sub Picture2_DragOver(Index As Integer, Source As Control, _
X As Single, Y As Single, State As Integer)
```

If the user is dragging an image over the target picture array, I change the mouse pointer to the default:

```
Source.MousePointer = 0
End Sub
Private Sub cmdSolve_Click()
Solve
End Sub
```

The solve procedure is pretty straightforward because I assign each graphic cell of the Picture Clip control to a respective Picture Box in the control array:

```
Public Sub Solve()
Dim X As Integer


cmdSolve.Enabled = False
For X = 0 To 31
  Picture1(X).Picture = PictureClip1.GraphicCell(X)
Next X
For X = 0 To 31
  Picture1(X).Enabled = False
Next X
For X = 0 To 31
 Picture2(X).Enabled = False
Next X
```

```
cmdStart.Enabled = True

End Sub


Private Sub cmdExit_Click()
End
End Sub


Private Sub Form_QueryUnload(Cancel As Integer, UnloadMode As Integer)
cmdExit_Click
End Sub
```

Summary

This chapter covered some basic history behind the development and uses of drag and drop technology. In addition, you learned firsthand how easy it is to create intuitive and fun programs with Visual Basic's drag and drop events. You learned specifically how to use DragDrop and DragOver events to control sources and targets.

In the next chapter, you will learn how to bundle and deploy your programs and games into a setup package using Microsoft's setup and deployment wizards.

CHALLENGES

1. Modify the puzzle game to use an image of your choice.

2. Enhance the puzzle game to allow a user to select from multiple images.

3. Enhance the puzzle game to offer a timer. The object of the game is to finish the puzzle in the time allotted. The timer should display a digital clock counting down the time remaining.

4. Design and develop the card game Solitaire. For information on how to play Solitaire, see Microsoft's Solitaire game from the Start menu under Programs, Accessories, Games, Solitaire.

Setup and Deployment

This chapter covers the concepts and application of program setup and deployment. You will learn how to incorporate your Visual Basic programs and games into setup routines that can be distributed and installed from CD-ROM, floppy disks, and local and network folders.

Specifically, this chapter covers the following topics:

- Package and Deployment Wizard

- Understanding distribution files

- Package process

- Deployment process

- Testing your setup program

- Uninstalling your Visual Basic program

The Package and Deployment Wizard

You may have noticed that your executable (EXE) files do not run on PCs other than your own. Visual Basic programs require various files other than your program's executable to successfully run on another PC (assuming the PC does not have Visual Basic installed).

Microsoft provides you with a solution to distributing your program in the form of the Package and Deployment Wizard. As shown in Figure 12.1, the Package and Deployment Wizard creates setup routines that provide viable package and deployment solutions for most programs or games you will create.

There are two main ways to access the Package and Deployment Wizard:

- Run it from within Visual Basic as an add-in.
- Run it standalone.

Running as an Add-In

Running the Package and Deployment Wizard as an add-in means that you launch its interface through an open Visual Basic project. To do so, you work the Add-In Manager, which adds functionality to the Visual Basic environment. In

---

IN THE REAL WORLD

The science of distributing and running applications, programs, or games is sometimes a highly debatable and controversial subject. The lines are generally drawn between two sides: those who believe in platform-dependent solutions and those who believe in platform-independent solutions.

Microsoft generally lends itself and its developers to creating and distributing platform-dependent programs built with languages such as Visual Basic. This means that a Visual Basic program compiled and packaged on a Microsoft Windows platform is intended and only guaranteed to run on a compatible Microsoft Windows platform.

Platform-independent languages such as Java are not tied directly to any one hardware or software system and therefore can work with all types of operating systems. The downside to such platform-independent languages is that they offer little to no interaction with the operating system. This is surely a safety mechanism for end users but is sometimes a limiting developing environment for programmers who want to tap into operating-system-specific functionality.

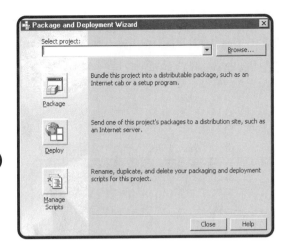

FIGURE 12.1

The Package and
Deployment Wizard
helps you create
distribution media.

other words, the Add-In Manager makes components such as the Package and
Deployment Wizard available within the project environment that might not
normally be accessible. Follow these steps:

1. Within a Visual Basic project, make sure all project components have been
   saved and that the project has been compiled into an executable file. To
   compile your project, simply open the File menu and click the Make x.exe
   item (where x is the name of your project).

2. From the Add-Ins menu item, select Add-In Manager (see Figure 12.2).

The Add-In
Manager

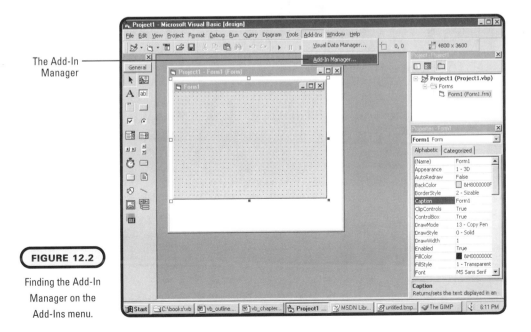

FIGURE 12.2

Finding the Add-In
Manager on the
Add-Ins menu.

3. As shown in Figure 12.3, select the Package and Deployment Wizard and the Load/Unloaded behavior check box from the Add-In Manager, and click OK.

You can now choose the Package and Deployment Wizard from the Add-Ins menu item (see Figure 12.4).

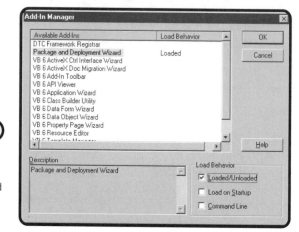

FIGURE 12.3

Selecting the Package and Deployment Wizard from the Add-In Manager.

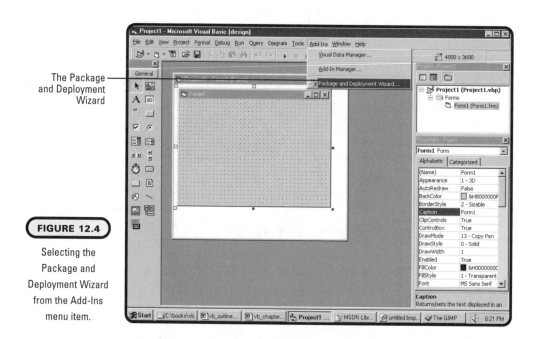

The Package and Deployment Wizard

FIGURE 12.4

Selecting the Package and Deployment Wizard from the Add-Ins menu item.

Running Standalone

To run the Package and Deployment Wizard in standalone mode, make sure your project has been saved and compiled. Exit the project and launch the Package and Deployment Wizard from Start, Programs, Microsoft Visual Studio 6.0, Microsoft Visual Studio 6.0 Tools (providing Visual Basic was installed as part of Visual Studio 6.0).

Understanding Distribution Files

Understanding Visual Basic's distribution files is the first step in creating a sound and successful setup package. Microsoft divides these distribution files into three categories:

- Runtime files
- Setup files
- Application files

Runtime Files

Required by all Visual Basic applications, runtime files are needed by your program to successfully run after installation. Known as *bootstrap files*, runtime files end with the DLL (Dynamic Link Library) extension. These runtime files let a compiled Visual Basic program run on a PC where Visual Basic is not installed:

> **Definition**
>
> *Bootstrap files* are runtime files required by all Visual Basic applications.

    Msvbvm60.dll

    Stdole2.tlb

    Oleaut32.dll

    Olepro32.dll

    Comcat.dll

    Asyncfilt.dll

    Ctl3d32.dll

Setup Files

Setup files install your Visual Basic program onto a user's PC. They consist of various files for running the setup package, configuring the setup package, and uninstalling your program from the user's machine.

Whether you are creating a setup package that will be distributed via CD-ROM, network drives, or floppy disk, the setup routine uses the files in Table 12.1.

Application Files

Application files are directly related to your Visual Basic program. They usually include your program's specific executable file, data files used for random or sequential file access, initialization files (INI files), and any other component files used by your project. Other such component files can include controls you have added to your project, such as the PictureClip or Multimedia control.

Fortunately, the Package and Deployment Wizard does a pretty good job at determining all the application files needed by a Visual Basic program.

TRAP Sometimes, the Package and Deployment Wizard is unable to identify all the application files needed for your program to successfully run.

Such files might include initialization files (INI files) and data files such as random and sequential access files. If you do not see all your application files listed during the packaging process, the Package and Deployment Wizard will let you manually specify them for packaging.

TABLE 12.1 SETUP FILES

Filename	Description
setup.exe	Program used during installation but prior to installing your program
setup1.exe	Program used specifically for installing your program
setup.lst	Text file used to configure the installation process
vb6stkit.dll	Dynamic link library used by the setup1.exe program
st6unst.exe	Program used to uninstall your Visual Basic application from a user's machine

Package Process

The packaging process involves identifying all the files necessary for deploying and installing your Visual Basic program. Distribution files are built into a cab (cabinet) file that expands during installation to distribute program files.

Although it is possible to create Internet packages, this chapter and section concentrate on creating standard packages that can be distributed on CD-ROM, floppy disk, or network drives.

The following steps apply for all standard packages:

1. Launch the Package and Deployment Wizard either in standalone mode or as an add-in. If launching the Package and Deployment Wizard in stand-alone mode, use the Browse button to find your Visual Basic project. Click the Package button (see Figure 12.5).

     HINT If you have forgotten to compile your project, the Package and Deployment Wizard can compile it for you at this time.

2. As shown in Figure 12.6, select Standard Setup Package and click Next.

3. The Package Folder screen, shown in Figure 12.7, prompts you to select a location where your setup package will be assembled. Find or create a destination folder on your local PC or network drive, and click Next.

4. As depicted in Figure 12.8, the Included Files screen shows you what files will be included in your setup package. (These are your distribution files.)

    This is when you include additional files needed by your program that were not identified by the Package and Deployment Wizard. After you are certain all distribution files have been identified, click Next.

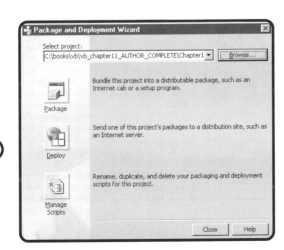

FIGURE 12.5

Identifying your project using the Package and Deployment Wizard.

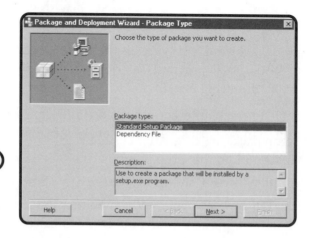

FIGURE 12.6

Selecting the standard setup package.

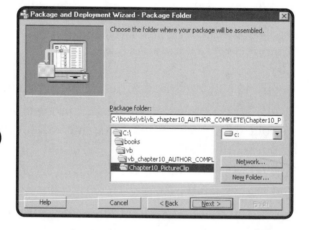

FIGURE 12.7

Choosing a destination folder for your setup package.

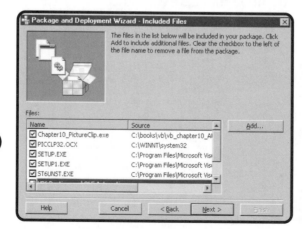

FIGURE 12.8

Identifying distribution files during the package process.

5. Shown in Figure 12.9, the Cab Options screen allows you to create single or multiple cab files.

   If you are going to be distributing your program via floppy disk, select the Multiple cab file option and click Next. Otherwise, select the Single cab option and click Next.

6. The Installation Title screen, shown in Figure 12.10, allows you to customize your setup package's title. After customizing your program's title, click Next. When running the setup program, the user sees this title.

7. The Start Menu Items screen, shown in Figure 12.11, allows you to create and customize a program group and item for your Visual Basic program. This program group and item are what the user sees after clicking the Start button and Program group. Click Next to continue.

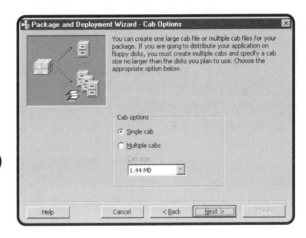

FIGURE 12.9

Selecting single or multiple cab file options.

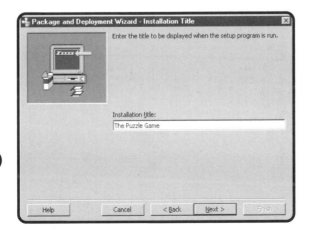

FIGURE 12.10

Customizing the setup program's title.

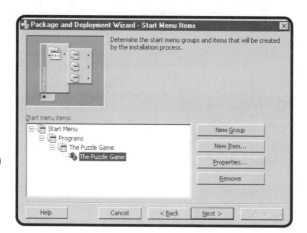

FIGURE 12.11

Customizing the program group and program icon.

8. You can change the destination path of some distribution files through the Install Locations screen (see Figure 12.12). This option is useful if your users will launch your program from a location other than their local drives. For most programs, however, the default install paths are recommended.

   After determining installation paths, click Next.

9. As shown in Figure 12.13, you can label one or more distribution files as shared. This prevents your uninstall program from removing the shared file unless there is no other program using it. For example, you might have multiple programs on a user's machine that also use a component in your program. In this case, it would be appropriate to flag this file as shared so that it would not be deleted when the program is uninstalled.

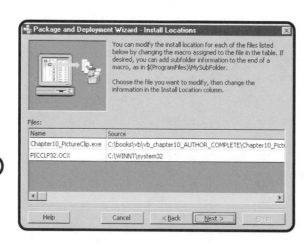

FIGURE 12.12

Changing the installation path of distribution files.

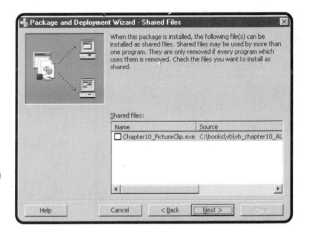

FIGURE 12.13

Determining
shared files.

Otherwise, the removal of this file during an uninstall might cause other programs to stop working. Click Next to continue.

10. The last step in configuring your setup package is naming your script, as shown in Figure 12.14. This allows you to reuse the script to build other setup packages using similar configurations.

After the packaging process is finished, Visual Basic displays a packaging report, as shown in Figure 12.15.

The packaging report displays information about your cab file and support directory. The support directory is created by default and contains all distribution files for rebuilding your cab file. Note that the support directory and its contents

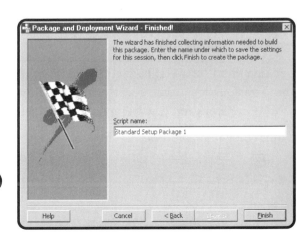

FIGURE 12.14

Naming your script
for future use.

FIGURE 12.15

The packaging report prepared after the packaging process.

are not required to install your program, nor are they required for distributing your setup package.

In the event that your cab file is deleted, you can use files in your support directory to re-create it. Specifically, you need your DDF file (which contains information about your Visual Basic project) and the makecab.exe file. The makecab.exe file is generally located in the Microsoft Visual Studio\VB98\Wizards\PDWizard directory.

The easiest way to rebuild a cab file is to go to a DOS prompt (Start menu/Programs/Command prompt) and change directory to where the makecab.exe file is located. From the command prompt, type the following statement:

```
makecab /f path\ddf_filename.ddf
```

path is the drive and directory location of your DDF file, and ddf_filename.ddf is the filename of your DDF file.

Deployment Process

The Package and Deployment Wizard allows you to deploy your prepackaged Visual Basic program to various locations. Locations can include media such as CD-ROM, local directories, network folders, floppy disks, and even the Internet.

This section focuses on deployment methods as they relate to the standard setup package:

1. Launch the Package and Deployment Wizard and select Deploy (see Figure 12.16).

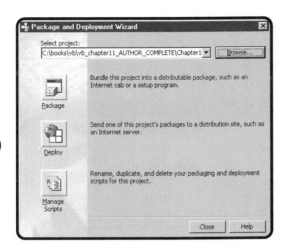

FIGURE 12.16

Selecting the
Deploy option from
the Package and
Deployment
Wizard.

2. Next, select the package you want to deploy (as shown in Figure 12.17) and click Next.

3. For network or local folders, select the folder deployment method as shown in Figure 12.18 and click Next.

4. After selecting folder deployment, choose an existing directory or create your own and click Next (see Figure 12.19).

5. Next, select a name for your deployment package that can be reused in the future and click Finish (see Figure 12.20).

Similar to the packaging process, a report is generated at the end of deployment (see Figure 12.21).

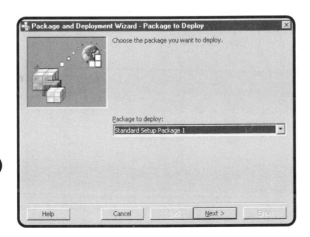

FIGURE 12.17

Selecting the
package for
deployment.

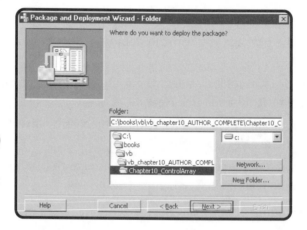

FIGURE 12.18

Folder deployment
for network and
local directories.

FIGURE 12.19

Choosing an
existing deployment
directory or
creating your own.

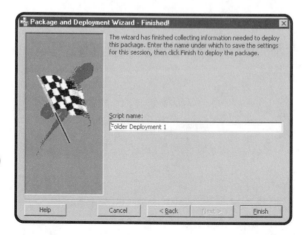

FIGURE 12.20

Entering a
deployment
package name.

FIGURE 12.21

The deployment
report.

After the deployment process is finished, you can distribute your program to users (provided you deployed to removable media such as CD or floppy disk) or have them access the setup package from local or network folders.

Testing Your Setup Program

Once you reach the package and deployment phase, you might think testing and debugging is over. On the contrary: Good programmers ensure their software packages install and run correctly from a new installation.

Your best bet for testing the packaging and deployment process is to install your program on a PC that does not contain an installation of Visual Basic or your program.

From a clean PC (one that does not contain an installation of Visual Basic or your program), click the Start menu and select Run.

From the Run dialog window (shown in Figure 12.22), type the following statement:

```
Drive:\Setup
```

Drive is the drive and directory containing your setup package.

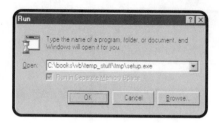

FIGURE 12.22

Running your setup
program.

Note that you can accomplish the same task by double-clicking your setup executable in Windows Explorer.

TRAP It is advisable to save and close any open programs on the PC prior to running
the setup program.

The setup routine guides you through a few installation options before completing program installation. Depending on the PC's configuration, it might be necessary to restart the machine before the installation can continue. In this event,
let the setup program restart the machine. (Save and close any open programs
first.) If the PC requires a reboot, re-launch the setup routine so that it can continue with the program installation.

TRAP There may be times when the setup program prompts you to overwrite newer
files with older files contained in the setup program. It is advisable to not overwrite newer files with older ones because this might prevent other programs
from working correctly.

Again, choose *not* to overwrite any newer files with older versions.

After the setup routine is finished, launch your program from the Programs
menu group and test all program functionality.

Uninstalling Your Visual Basic Program

Sometimes, you or your users might need to uninstall your program. Remember
from the section "Setup Files" earlier in this chapter that Visual Basic deploys
st6unst.exe for uninstalling a program.

You run the st6unst.exe file in conjunction with the Add/Remove Programs
option in the Control Panel (see Figure 12.23).

FIGURE 12.23

Uninstalling your
Visual Basic
program.

After you locate your program in the Add/Remove Programs window, highlight it
and click Add/Remove as seen in Figure 12.24.

Remember that you should not remove any shared files during program removal.
If shared files are found, Windows alerts you first.

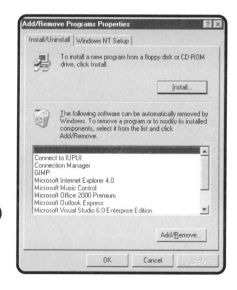

FIGURE 12.24

The Add/Remove
Programs dialog
box.

Summary

This chapter covered the process of building setup and deployment routines. You learned how to use Visual Basic's Package and Deployment Wizard to create a setup package for your program and how to deploy it to various mediums such as CD-ROM, floppy disk, networks, and local folders.

You went beyond creating setup packages and deployment to learn how to test your setup routine and uninstall your program when the need arises.

Common ASCII Codes

The ASCII codes in Table A.1 represent the most common character sets supported by Microsoft operating systems.

TABLE A.1 COMMON ASCII CODES

Code	Character	Code	Character
32	Space	33	!
34	"	35	#
36	$	37	%
38	&	39	'
40	(	41	)
42	*	43	+
44	,	45	-
46	.	47	/
48	0	49	1
50	2	51	3
52	4	53	5
54	6	55	7
56	8	57	9
58	:	59	;
60	<	61	=
62	>	63	?
64	@	65	A
66	B	67	C
68	D	69	E
70	F	71	G
72	H	73	I
74	J	75	K
76	L	77	M
78	N	79	O

TABLE A.1   COMMON ASCII CODES

Code	Character	Code	Character
80	P	81	Q
82	R	83	S
84	T	85	U
86	V	87	W
88	X	89	Y
90	Z	91	[
92	\	93	]
94	^	95	_
96	`	97	a
98	b	99	c
100	d	101	e
102	f	103	g
104	h	105	i
106	j	107	k
108	l	109	m
110	n	111	o
112	p	113	q
114	r	115	s
116	t	117	u
118	v	119	w
120	x	121	y
122	z	123	{
124			125	}
126	~	127	Del (delete key)

APPENDIX

What's on the CD

The CD that accompanies this book contains sample Visual Basic games, a freeware character pack, and a number of recommended Web links. The CD also has all the sample code and sample files that I used throughout the book.

Running the CD with Windows 95/98/2000/NT

I wanted to make the CD user-friendly and consume less of your disk space, so no installation is required to view the CD. This means that the only files transferred to your hard disk are the ones you choose to copy or install. You can run the CD on any operating system that can view graphical HTML pages; however, not all the programs can be installed on all operating systems.

If autoplay is turned on, the HTML interface automatically loads into your default browser.

If autoplay is turned off, access the CD by following these steps:

1. Insert the CD into the CD-ROM drive and close the tray.
2. Go to My Computer or Windows Explorer and double-click the CD-ROM drive.
3. Find and open the start_here.html file. (This works with most HTML browsers.)

 The first window you see contains the Prima License Agreement. Take a moment to read the agreement, and if you agree, click the I Agree button to accept the license and proceed to the user interface. If you do not agree to the terms of the license, click the I Disagree button. The CD will not load.

Running the CD with Macintosh OS 7.0 or Later

I wanted to make the CD user-friendly and consume less of your disk space, so no installation is required to view the CD. This means that the only files transferred to your hard disk are the ones you choose to copy or install. You can run the CD on any operating system that can view graphical HTML pages; however, not all the programs can be installed on all operating systems.

Access the CD by following these steps:

1. Insert the CD into the CD-ROM drive and close the tray.
2. Double-click the icon that represents your CD-ROM.
3. Find and open the start_here.html file. (This works with most HTML browsers.)

The first window you see contains the Prima License Agreement. Take a moment to read the agreement, and if you agree, click the I Agree button to accept the license and proceed to the user interface. If you do not agree to the terms of the license, click the I Disagree button. The CD will not load.

The Prima User Interface

The opening screen of the Prima user interface contains navigation buttons and a content area. The navigation buttons appear on the left side of the browser window. Navigate through the Prima user interface by clicking on a button. Each page loads and the content displays to the right.

For example, if you want to view the source code, click on the button labeled Source Code. The new page that loads includes links to all the available source-code files on the CD. Each chapter's files are compressed for easy distribution. You can uncompress the files using any unzip program. You can download WinZip from http://www.winzip.com/. Alternatively, if you want to view the uncompressed files you can navigate to the /Source Code folder on the CD. Each chapter has a separate folder.

It is not necessary to use the Prima user interface to access the contents of the CD-ROM. If you feel more comfortable using a file system, you can explore the CD through your operating-system interface. You should find the file structure logical and descriptive.

To resize the window, position the mouse over any edge or corner, click and hold the mouse, drag the edge or corner to a new position, and release the mouse when the size is acceptable.

To close and exit the user interface, select File, Exit.

Index

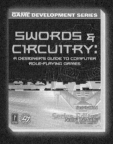

PRIMA TECH's *fast&easy* series

Fast Facts, Easy Access

Offering extraordinary value at a bargain price, the *fast & easy* series is dedicated to one idea: To help readers accomplish tasks as quickly and easily as possible. The unique visual teaching method combines concise tutorials and hundreds of screen shots to dramatically increase learning speed and retention of the material. With PRIMA TECH's *fast & easy* series, you simply look and learn.

PRIMA TECH
A Division of Prima Publishing
www.prima-tech.com

Call now to order
(800)632-8676 ext. 4444

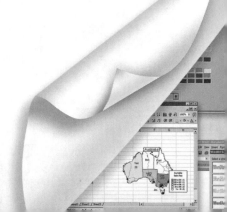

ARE YOU READY FOR A CHANGE?

FOR A CHANGE.

Some publishers create books they think you want. We create books we know you want. That's because when computer users talk, we listen. Isn't it time for a change? PRIMA TECH.